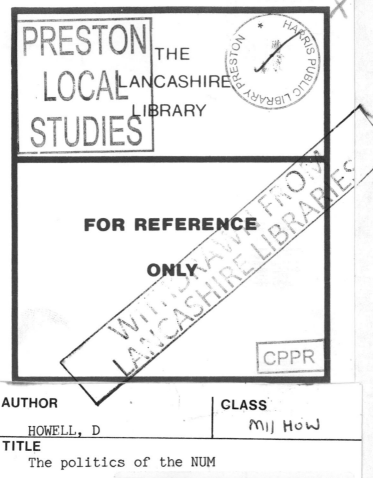

The politics of the NUM

A Lancashire view

David Howell

Manchester University Press

Manchester and New York

Distributed exclusively in the USA and Canada by St Martin's Press

Published by Manchester University Press
Oxford Road, Manchester M13 9PL, UK
and Room 400, 175 Fifth Avenue,
New York, NY 10010, USA

Distributed exclusively in the USA and Canada
by St. Martin's Press, Inc.,
175 Fifth Avenue, New York, NY 10010, USA

British Library cataloguing in publication data
Howell, David
    The politics of the NUM.
    1. Great Britain. Coal industries. Trade Unions.
    National Union of Mineworkers. Political aspects
    I. Title
    331.88'122334'0941

Library of Congress cataloging in publication data
Howell, David, 1945–
    The politics of the NUM / David Howell.
        p.   cm.
    Bibliography: p.   04220237 ᛮ
    Includes index.
    ISBN 0-7190-3022-6. — ISBN 0-7190-3023-4 (pbk.)
    1. National Union of Mineworkers. 2. Trade-unions—Great Britain—
Political activity. I. Title.
HD6668.M6152N354   1989
322'.2'0941—dc19

ISBN 0 7190 3022 6 *hardback*
     0 7190 3023 4 *paperback*

Disk conversion and typesetting by Megaron, Cardiff, Wales
Printed in Great Britain by
Billings and Sons Ltd., Worcester

Contents

Preface

This book attempts an interpretation of the politics of the National
Union of Mineworkers. It does so by focusing on the politics of the
Union's North Western – colloquially Lancashire-Area. There are
good reasons for this choice other than geographical contiguity. For
several years Lancashire had an importance within the National
Union that belied its size. It was the initial power-base of Joe
Gormley, National President for more than a decade until his
retirement in 1982. Historically Lancashire's policies and
prejudices were those of the Right. Studies of the NUM's politics
have tended to look at the traditionally left-wing coalfields. An
adequate understanding requires a redressing of the balance.

Much of this study concentrates on the events of the last five
years and in particular on the year of the strike. But the analysis rests
on a fundamental claim that understanding those twelve months
requires a much longer historical perspective.

My debts during this book's preparation have been varied and
massive. Most crucially there are those that I owe to members of the
Lancashire NUM. They have given me whatever understanding I
have of the politics of their union. At the risk of being invidious
some individuals should be mentioned – Frank King of Parkside,
Area President; Steve Howells, Paul Hardman, Billy Kelly and
Ernie Short of Agecroft, Dennis Pennington, once of Bold; Bernard
Donaghy, Agent and ex-Area President. All have taken a continuing
interest in this project. They would disagree about much con-
cerning the politics of the NUM, but I hope they all feel that their
help has been worthwhile. Sid Vincent, the former Lancashire
General Secretary, gave me unreserved access to the Union records.
Roy Jackson and the staff at the Area Office have been unfailingly

courteous and helpful during my sojourns there.

I am grateful to Hywel Francis and to Gareth Rees for their initial suggestion that something should be written on the Lancashire miners. My discussions with them and other academics supportive of the miners' cause have been of great value. In particular I would mention Huw Beynon for his rich knowledge and infectious enthusiasm.

The late stages of writing were complicated by an academic exchange to the University of Queensland. Michelle Dicken typed the bulk of the draft and coped with the vagaries of the international postal system. The preparation was completed in Brisbane by Sue Harris and Carole Parker. Judith, Alan and Katie have lived with the Lancashire miners for a long time. All have helped in very different ways to make the task less onerous and more enjoyable.

This is in no sense an official history of the Lancashire NUM. The judgements and the misjudgements are my own.

David Howell
Manchester
October 1988

1

A most traditional Union

The winding gear has gone, but most of the surface buildings remain. Massive and brooding, they await the demolition gang. Some National Coal Board notices remain – most, prominently and ironically 'Coal Sales Office'. But the pit name has gone. Once it was displayed prominently, but this is 'Bold Colliery' no longer.

Away from the pit, across the slag heaps, stands the housing estate that locals call 'cement city'. Many who were once Bold miners live here, so not surprisingly, on the edge of the estate there remains Bold Miners' Club.

This happens to be St Helens but it could be many places in Britain's battered regions – the monuments to what were once jobs, the closing down of the future. The cannibalisation of dreams. As if the specific place matters. Three years before, Bold was the centre of the miners' strike in Lancashire, the pit where the action achieved early support in the coalfield, the Club from which campaigns were plotted and forays made to picket other pits and to solicit support across Britain and Europe. In the months of hope and of defiance, 'Bold NUM' proclaimed on badges and posters symbolised the commitment of activists across the Lancashire coalfield. Some found the unorthodoxy and the irreverence inspiring, conventional and troubled union officials could feel disturbed and threatened.

But these months must be recaptured across the debris of defeat. The marginalisation of such exceptional events occurs at so many different levels. The brute fact of closure means the physical destruction of a workplace, of what gave a meaning to resistance. Defeat can destroy the credibility of collective action, promoting passivity or the espousal of individualism.

Then there are the verdicts of the commentators now beginning to be consecrated as the accepted historical assessment. Faced with the enduring evidence of the miners' defeat, the polemics of yesterday's headline are transmuted into the 'scholarly' text in which comfortable prejudice is served with supportive footnoting. The exceptional events can be explained by the revolutionary and unrepresentative ambitions of the miners' national leaders. It was a last manifestation of a dying form of class politics, a 1980s equivalent of the Highland Clearances.[1]

There exists an alternative literature forged often in the communities that have endured the twelve months' stoppage and all that has happened since.[2] Its positives are significant; the jagged edge of experience is set against the urbane assessments of metropolitan commentators, the insistence on local particularities, the sense of specific communities indicts easy generalisations. Yet the vigorous alternative has its limitations. Often it is produced by people whose experience of the strike lay in the Women's Groups, in the Support Groups, in the making of links between villages and an endless variety of localities. The National Union of Mineworkers is present in such accounts only at Branch level. Local officials are characterised by the extent to which they were supportive of the activists' work. But the wider world of NUM politics barely exists, despite the fundamental fact that the Union initiated the action and eventually the Union terminated it. It is at this point that the alternative literature tends to become superficial. Union politics is something that happens somewhere else. This abdication surrenders the field to the 'new realists'. Their explanations may be crude but in the absence of rivals, they hold the field and frequently define the terms of debate.

This book attempts to remedy this neglect. It looks at the politics of the NUM through the experiences of one Area, Lancashire. The dominant culture of this predominantly right wing coalfield was the product of miners' experiences and Union factionalism over several decades. In 1984, like its contemporaries elsewhere, this coalfield was vital to the choices made and the options rejected.

At the beginning of *The Eighteenth Brumaire* Marx considers that perennial problem for historians of the relationship between creativity and constraint. One comment on the role of ideas may serve as a starting point – 'the traditions of all the dead generations weigh like a nightmare on the brain of the living'. The emphasis should be applied of course not just to the politics of mid-nineteenth century France; it offers one signpost for the understanding of British trade unions.

They are prisoners of their pasts, both real and mythical, in so many ways – the sanctity of their Rule Books; the weight given to precedent, the timeless quality of rhetoric; the nostalgia expressed in their banners; the yearly round of conferences, executive meetings and wage bargaining, perhaps most fundamentally, the distinctive yet often elusive ethos of each organisation, the legacy of past battles reflected in durable factional alignments. Nowhere is such a sense of the past more pervasive than in mining trade unionism. The Lodge banners demonstrate reverence to past leaders, Robert Smillie, Arthur Cook, Peter Lee, or to traditional principles of solidarity. The collective memory of mining communities encapsulates a litany that is so often sombre, perhaps expressed at the level of one community rather than national events – 'Featherstone' and 'Tonypandy'; sometimes the scope is all-inclusive – '1921' and '1926' require no elaboration.

One durable manifestation of these traditions can be found in the architecture of Miners' offices – Red Hills in Durham with its statues of the Durham Miners' early leaders. Barnsley with its pinnacle and its memorial to an early generation of Liberal officials. At Bolton, the Lancashire and Cheshire Miners opened their office relatively late in 1914, but when they did so, they provided another commentary on the character of Edwardian mining trade unionism. The style expresses, even in a poor coalfield, the optimism borne of expanding membership and increasing evidence of industrial effectiveness. Two years previously the Miners had embarked on their first national strike and had won from the Liberal Government a limited recognition of the minimum wage principle. The early years of the Bolton office saw the miners securing benefits, as under wartime pressures the Government took control of the industry. Increased wages and shorter hours fed the hope that there was more to come. The advances had been based on an achievement long sought by the M.F.G.B. – the introduction of a significant national element into wage determination. By the end of 1920, the membership of the Lancashire and Cheshire Miners stood at a peak of 90,000. Then came decontrol, the defeats of 1921 and 1926, wage cuts, short time working, unemployment. In Lancashire the confidence of 1914–21 never returned; when late in 1944 the MFGB gave way to the National Union of Mineworkers, Lancashire brought only 40, 000 members into the reorganised national body. The post-war demand for coal coupled with nationalisation stabilised employment in the Lancashire coalfield, but the pit closure programmes of the sixties hit the county severely. Between 1958 and 1971 forty-five collieries were closed; compensating developments were few. By the end of this process, the Union could only count 12,000 members despite the fact that in the 1960s it had absorbed smaller constituents of the NUM.

So much had changed, yet through the disputes, the inter-war depression, two wars, nationalisation, more closures, the routines of the Union continued. Every month the Lancashire Executive met in the downstairs Board Room in Bolton, surrounded by furnishings dating back to the building's opening; most months an Area Delegate Conference met in the upstairs Conference Hall. The full time officials sat on the platform. Delegations from each Branch sat often in their customary places in the body of the hall. Successive full-time officials might leave individual imprints on the Union, but the routine of meetings continued – the legacy a sequence of records dating back beyond 1914 to the early days of the Lancashire Federation and the MFGB. The procedures of the Union seemed to carry on regardless of external crisis – and then in 1984, this pattern suffered a fundamental disruption.

The events of one day offer a dramatic representation. At the end of April 1984, strike action for pit closures had lasted for several weeks. In Lancashire although there had been an early ballot against a strike, the coalfield had divided. Some miners became committed supporters of the strike, some said they would work until a national ballot and were escorted by police past pickets. Many seemed unsure; they had a respect for picket lines and a basic loyalty to their Union, but after all there had been a coalfield ballot and this could justify working in the absence of pickets, until a national ballot occurred. After a Special National Delegate Conference on 19 April, all hope of a national ballot died and Lancashire had to confront the fact of its own disunity. An Area Conference failed to reach a consensus between the union sections; instead delegates dispersed to hold Branch meetings in the hope that somehow a panacea would emerge. The delegates were to meet again on the last day of the month. They never met; when delegates came back to Bolton, they found the offices occupied by strikers. Banners decorated the building. The full-time officials and staff had left the premises. Outside on the pavement, a spokesman for the 'no strike without a ballot' section was dismissive: 'Are we going to give in to this rabble? This is not democracy.'³ The occupiers' response was advice to 'stuff your ballot up your arse'. ⁴

The routines of decades had collapsed – the regular pattern of meetings, pressure for public solidarity, the etiquette that characteristically canalised debates, the expectations that somehow a muddled compromise could prevent an open rupture. All had failed.

Any adequate understanding of the coal dispute of 1984–85 must incorporate an awareness of its unique features. Such perception can be marginalised, as one legacy of defeat proves to be the reestablishment of routine, not quite the same as the older one perhaps, but a patterning that obscures much of the episode's distinctiveness. An attempt to understand the dispute through the experience of the Lancashire Area necessitates an awareness of that Area's character. What were the traditions of all the dead generations?

The construction and style of Miners' offices was not only a statement of current achievement and future hopes; it was, above all perhaps a declaration of autonomy. There might be a Miners' Federation of Great Britain, but what mattered took place in the individual coalfields, where local conditions of production, marketing opportunities and problems, the strength and weaknesses of local management could best be appreciated. Beyond such practical considerations, there lay parochialism and a coalfield chauvinism that could be developed by District Officials keen to establish their credibility both locally and nationally – a battery of unavoidable considerations and emotional sentiments that could threaten any national strategy by the MFGB. Moreover, although the creation of the National Union of Mineworkers represented a cautious attempt to deal with this problem, the effective consequences were limited. Despite its title, despite nationalisation, behind the facade many long-standing sectional tendencies remained.

Any portrait of the ethos of a constituent union of the NUM is a difficult task. Each one is rather like a football team – a distinctive history and style, eccentricity, loyalties and enmities, often with an elusive character against which attempts at formulation appear inadequate and crude.

At its peak, the coalfield was geographically extensive. Its heartland lay in the flat countryside between Manchester and Liverpool, in the towns of Leigh, Wigan and St Helens and in satellite villages. Many miners worked on the western side of Salford, whilst the presence of Bradford Colliery in the heart of East Manchester demonstrated that in Lancashire, mining was an industry of city and town as well as of pit villages. But sometimes it was carried out in locations that contrasted sharply with the distant horizons of its heartland. Always in Lancashire the Pennines provide a brooding backcloth, and in the north-east of the County, coal was produced in the narrowing valleys around Accrington, Burnley and Bacup. Moreover, as the union proclaimed, it was the Lancashire and Cheshire Federation. Mining extended into north-east Cheshire, into districts long since gentrified where only the occasional slag-heap, pub name or miners' row offers the memory of a very different past. Even the construction of a coalfield Federation represented a triumph for the benefits of solidarity over localism. Indeed the cohesion of the individual pit was not always buttressed by the occupational homogeneity of an adjacent village. Many miners did not live in communities where mining was the near exclusive occupation. In 1911 the coalfield had 100,000 miners; more than 30,000 lived in Manchester, Oldham, Blackburn, Bolton, Burnley, St Helens and Wigan. Only in the last two towns did mining rank as the single largest source of employment. In St Helens it was rivalled by glass-making and even in Wigan cotton was significant. Elsewhere, of course, and especially in north-east Lancashire, cotton was very much king in those pre–1914 years, whilst in the Manchester and Salford conurbation mining was just one strand in a kaleidoscope of working-class occupations. The Lancashire Federation could never establish the hegemony over the region's trade unionism and politics that could be claimed by counterparts in Durham and South Wales.

Nevertheless Lancashire was present at the birth of the Miners Federation of Great Britain in 1889 and provided the new national organisation with its first Secretary, the reserved and zealous bureaucrat, Thomas Ashton. As an old coalfield, Lancashire already faced problems of profitability. Many of the better seams were worked out. Those remaining were subject to faulting.

Haulage distances from face to pit bottom were often long. The coalfield included some of the deepest – and thereby in terms of initial cost most expensive – workings in Britain. In the years before the First World War Lancashire suffered two major disasters – in August 1908, seventy-five deaths at the Maypole Colliery in Hindley and then in December 1910, 344 were killed at the Hulton No. 3 pit. The economic consequences of production problems were low wages, long hours and minimal fringe benefits. There was little evidence of the employer paternalism that characterised some sections of the East Midlands coalfields. Equally as a domestic producer, the Lancashire experience differed from that of the large exporting districts such as South Wales or the North Eastern coalfields. The Lancashire problem was that of competition with more advantaged districts within the home market, and not the economic roller coaster of the export trade. Predictably, Lancashire became an early exponent of MFGB policy on the eight hour day through legislation, minimum wage levels and a shift from district to national wage settlements. During the 1912 strike a journalist for a national Liberal newspaper highlighted the urgency of the minimum wage principle:

> In Lancashire the men will tell you it is a matter of life and death. For years the history of the Lancashire coal industry has been a history of miserable strikes following miserable strikes in weary and often futile repetition, of lock-outs and actions at law. The cumulative effect is an estrangement between masters and men such as exists nowhere else except in South Wales.[5]

In one respect, the coalfield's miners appeared precocious. In 1900, the Lancashire Miners sent delegates to the foundation conference of the Labour Representation Committee, and although affiliation was not immediate, Lancashire did join in May 1903, more than five and a half years before the MFGB as a whole. In the 1906 and 1908 ballots on MFGB affiliation to the Labour Party, as it had now become, Lancashire voted in favour by a majority of over two to one. This early enthusiasm for Independent Labour owed relatively little to the appeal of Socialism within the coalfield. Rather it indicated a significant trait within Lancastrian politics. In some other coalfields miners' representatives had been elected under the Liberal banner, a political position capable at least until the 1900s of casting the miners' industrial loyalty in political terms. But in Lancashire, this process was very difficult. The electorate of the coalfield divided significantly along religious and ethnic lines and attitudes towards Irish Home Rule could symbolise darker ethnic sentiments. Labour politics was presented as a pragmatic method of ensuring the union's political influence, not a Socialist alternative but almost an apolitical one. From 1906, the Lancashire Miners always had their sponsored Labour MPs. The character of this political attachment, its lack of Socialist content was revealed perhaps in one significant non-event. Despite the difficult post–1921 situation, the coalfield never became a centre for the left-wing developments that affected mining trade unionism in South Wales and parts of Scotland. Instead there dominated a cautious Labour politics much like that of County Durham.

This lack of political radicalisation did not mean that the Lancashire Miners were industrially passive in the battles of the 1920s. They had more to lose than most from the collapse of national wage bargaining. In June 1921, after two and a half months of the lock-out, Lancashire returned the highest percentage in rejection of the Government's and owners' terms. Two weeks later when the MFGB were clearly defeated, only Lancashire amongst the larger coalfields opposed a return to work.[6] But '1926', the growth of non-unionism and unemployment eroded such resistance. Throughout the rest of the inter-war period and subsequently, Lancashire stood on the right within the NUM. The Communist Party had some influence within the coalfield but the dominant outlook was the pragmatic machine type Labour politics that had produced the early move to political independence. It was characterised by such officials as the Secretary, Peter Pemberton, and the Agent, John McGurk, a consistent hammer of the left in Labour Party debates. But Lancashire could never really share the priorities of many Midlands coalfields where political caution was complemented by a degree of economic self-confidence. In its combination of a broadly right-wing political outlook with an awareness of economic pressures, once again Lancashire had features in common with the union of the north-eastern coalfields.

Where Lancashire differed from the north-east was in its lack of representation among national officials. After Ashton retired from the Secretaryship in 1919, Lancashire provided neither National President nor General Secretary for more than half a century. South Wales, Yorkshire, Northumberland and Durham were the dominant elements. Lancashire was a declining coalfield numerically less important than it had been. Only in 1971 with the election of Joe Gormley as National President did Lancashire move back into the national spotlight. From then on, although a small area, Lancashire would become significant within the National Union. The elusive tradition mattered not least as it was refracted through the style and tactics of the President.

The durability of Area tradition left its mark on and was guaranteed by the structure of the NUM. When the MFGB leadership had considered the possibility of a National Union in 1943, they had ruled out a comprehensive rationalisation: 'In view of all the difficulties involved, difficulties which at this stage it is considered are insurmountable, any possibility of the complete dissolution of the present district organisations has been ruled out.'[7] The same realism was articulated by a long-standing supporter of the ideal of One Miners Union – the South Wales President, Arthur Horner:

> If I have a complaint against this scheme it is such an emasculated scheme . . . we have to take into account not only the general interests of the men which would drive me to one all-out Mineworkers' Union involving the liquidation of the District Unions. But we have to be realists and take into account the vested interests of the Districts . . .[8]

A National Union could not be constructed on a blank sheet of paper. The Rule Book of the National Union as passed by a Special Conference in August 1944 clearly institutionalised the cautious approach.[9] Labels changed. The constituent unions of the old Federation became Areas of the National Union; their officials became Area Officials of the NUM, but retained much of their power. The Areas collected money and retained a sizeable pro-portion. Such a resource facilitated the continuation of the diverse sentiments which went along with divergent procedures and a range of industrial and political policies.

This potentially divisive structure held together well for many years. The National Union was dominated by a solid right wing majority based on a coalition of Areas – Northumberland, Durham, Yorkshire, Nottinghamshire, Lancashire, plus some smaller con-stituents. Opposed to them, there was a left wing minority centred on Scotland and South Wales with support from the small Kent coalfield and, less consistently from Derbyshire. The Right controlled the National Presidency – in succession Will Lawther, Ernest Jones and Sidney Ford. It had the formidable backing of Sam Watson, the

Durham leader, intellectually sharp, and until his retirement in
1963, the NUM representative on the Labour Party's National
Executive. Most fundamentally the Right controlled the Union's
National Conference, and its NEC. Certainly the Left twice won
contests for the General Secretaryship on both occasions with South
Wales Communists, Arthur Horner in 1946 and Will Paynter in 1959.
Yet both operated within the constraints laid down by the political
balance within the Union.[10]

The relative weakness of the Left was in part a product of the ease
with which the emotions of the Cold War shaped the Union's
factionalism. Communists largely from Scotland and South Wales
tended to dominate the NUM Left. Often talented individuals, they
could be made the objects of familiar denunciations whenever a
majority for the Right seemed problematic. Such strategies drew
upon a widely shared interpretation of the miners' post-war
experience. The coal owners had gone, thanks to a Labour
Government, and here was a continuing justification for the NUM's
loyal support for Labour's leadership on *any* issue. Throughout the
thirteen years of opposition, often characterised by bitter factionalism within the Party, the NUM never deserted the Party Leadership.
Despite significant continuities in the miners' experience, straddling
the creation of the National Coal Board, the official Union position
was always to present the NCB as an ally in what was a new era. For
a decade such a perception could be fortified by the buoyant
demand for coal. As closures began to escalate in the late fifties, the
orthodox line could be preserved by arguing that another Labour
Government would solve all the problems.

For several years, effective debate within the NUM was limited
and the content of decisions was predictable. Many Areas were
right-wing fiefdoms presided over by Area officials who saw no
need to revise their views and who were impatient of criticism.
Lancashire in the fifties fitted neatly into this pattern. Certainly
there was some Communist presence centred around one of the full-
time Agents, Jimmy Hammond. He had been elected in 1942, a year
of relative Communist strength in trade unions. Subsequently he
had been Area President for three terms and in each of his
Presidential Addresses, he showed no reluctance about demonstrating his political loyalties. But this tendency was clearly a
minority one. The dominant stand was that of the loyalist Right
personified by the Lancashire Secretary, Edwin Hall: 'Teddy was a

so called moderate. He ruled this Area with an iron hand. Some fifty Branches in this Area at that time. Ted could ring thirty-five up and say, 'this is the way we're going', and those Branches would follow. They had no mind of their own'. Hall had an eye for potential officials. Sid Vincent, later to occupy Hall's job, recalled that it was the old martinet who helped him think through the route from Branch level to full-time Official: 'he advised me how to go about it'.[11] After Hall had retired, Hammond looked back to his rule through a comparison that was heavily critical of the past: 'The Lancashire Area is less repressed today than in its whole history . . . It is a good start when the Officials can work together in decent spirit without looking over their shoulders to watch that there is no misrepresentation or suspicion.'[12] Such an epitaph for an era was particularly striking, given that Hammond had been a candidate in the election for Hall's successor and had become embroiled in a bitter dispute with another candidate – the eventual victor, Joe Gormley.

The recriminations surrounding this contest in the Autumn of 1960 cast a revealing light on the politics of the Lancashire NUM and the outcome, the victory by Gormley, would leave its legacy down to the events of 1984. According to both Gormley and Vincent, Edwin Hall tried to fix his own successor Arthur Bubbins, an outsider from Accrington whom Hall could have perhaps manipulated. Gormley had some reason to consider himself a more credible candidate. Although not an Area Official, but President of the Bold Branch, he was already a Lancashire representative on the Union's National Executive. Apparently he persuaded Hall that the latter's advocacy of Bubbins would have politically disastrous consequences: 'If you think your man can win . . . I'm afraid you're mistaken . . . It can only result in Jimmy Hammond walking away with the election . . .'[13] So Hall switched his support. After weaker candidates had been eliminated and their second preferences counted, Gormley was elected on the eighth count with 13,188 votes to Hammond's 8,014. Then the real arguments began.[14] The validity of some Branch returns was queried at an Area Conference, and on a card vote, the relevant minute was referred back to the Lancashire Executive. An internal enquiry produced a marginally amended result, but Hammond and his supporters continued to allege that at some Branches, the vote was greater than the number reporting for work on the election day.[15] Thus at Bold, Gormley's home pit, the number entitled to vote was 1,585; this was little more than the recorded poll of 1,536. From these, Gormley had received 1,278 first preference votes and Hammond only 62. Although the Executive maintained that the result should stand, Gormley resigned the Secretaryship at a Special Area Conference.[16] The prospect of a second contest did not end the acrimony. At a subsequent Conference a Hammond supporter claimed that 'everyone in this Conference knew the ballot had been rigged and rigged in a shameful manner.'[17] From a different standpoint, another delegate refuted Hammond's allegation of a 114 per cent poll at his Branch, but his comments hardly exorcised all suspicions: 'the votes might have been overdone in some instances. It might have been at Plank Lane or it might not . . . .'[18]

The recriminations ended with the NEC instructing that a new ballot 'be held forthwith'.[19] The allegations were never investigated. Instead, early in 1961 six candidates fought for the Secretaryship with, on the fifth count, a result similar to the previously disputed outcome – Gormley 10,585, Hammond 7,351.

This result had significance both for the Lancashire Area and for the National Union. The defeat of Hammond was perhaps a decisive setback to the Left's hopes of controlling Lancashire. Hammond remained as an Agent until 1968 but Gormley was always firmly in charge. 1968 also marked the almost total disappearance of the Lancashire Left. The closure of the large Mosley Common Colliery meant the disappearance of a Branch traditionally aligned with the Left. Its Branch Secretary, the Communist Mick Weaver, had been a forceful critic of the Bolton establishment and by its size the pit's Branch could act as a focus for others unhappy with the Area Leadership. From that moment few advocates of a left position could be found in the Area's institutions. For several years the Branch Secretary at Bold, Jimmy Dowd, stood virtually alone;[20] after his retirement, the role of critic was taken by John Hensby of Cronton.

The Left's virtual disappearance was in contrast to the burgeoning strength of Gormley, not just in Lancashire but also nationally. Although moving straight from the pit to the major full-time post in the Area, he rapidly dominated Lancashire, became a regular contributor to debates at national level, and from 1963 succeeded Sam Watson in the important position as Miners' nominee to the Labour Party's National Executive. Soon he seemed the coming man on the Union's Right, but it was a Right facing a crisis of authority. Pit closures had been a problem since the late fifties as the market for coal contracted, but from 1965 the industry's crisis meant a political dilemma for the Right. Once more there was a Labour Government, but closures did not diminish. They increased. Here was a formative experience for many who would be active until and through the 1984 strike.

Notes

1 For an influential example of this genre see Martin Adeney and John Lloyd, *The Miners' Strike of 1984–85: Loss Without Limit* (Routledge, London, 1985).

2 See for example, The people of Thurcroft, *Thurcroft: A Village and the Miners' Strike. An Oral History* (Spokesman, Nottingham, 1986); Raphael Samuel, Barbara Bloomfield and Guy Boanes (eds), *The Enemy Within: Pit Villages and the Miners' Strike of 1984–85* (Routledge, London, 1986); Vicky Seddon (ed.) *The Cutting Edge: Women and the Pit Strikes* (Lawrence and Wishart, London, 1986); Norma Dolby, *Norma Dolby's Diary: An Account of the Great Miners' Strike* (Verso, London, 1987).

3 *Manchester Evening News (MEN)*, 30 April 1984.

4 *Morning Star (MS)*, 1 May 1984.

5 Cited in R. Challinor, *The Lancashire and Cheshire Miners* (Frank Graham, Newcastle, 1972), p. 235.

6 The figures are summarised in Robin Page Arnot, *The Miners: Years of Struggle* (Allen and Unwin, London, 1953). The Lancashire vote to continue the resistance in mid-June 1921 was 64,084 to 7,417 compared with the national figures of 434, 614 to 180, 724 (p. 327) or 89.63 per cent cf the national figure of 70.67 per cent (p. 328). Apart from Lancashire, only four small coalfields opposed the final settlement two weeks later (pp. 330–1).

7 Report to the Miners' Federation of Great Britain Executive Committee, June 1943, cited in R. Page Arnot, *The Miners In Crisis and War* (Allen and Unwin, London, 1961), p. 406.

8 Cited in *ibid*. p.411.

9 See Miners' Federation of Great Britain Report of Special Conference on Reorganisation of the Federation (Nottingham, 1944).

10 For reflections on their positions, see Arthur Horner, *Incorrigible Rebel* (MacGibbon and Kee, London, 1960), chs 8–11, and Will Paynter, *My Generation* (Allen and Unwin, London, 1972). Analysis of this period in coalfields with very different political leaderships can be found in Andrew Taylor, *The Politics of the Yorkshire Miners* (Croom Helm, London, 1984), chs 1 and 5, and Hywel Francis and David Smith, *The Fed: A History of the South Wales Miners in the Twentieth Century* (Lawrence and Wishart, London, 1980), ch. 12. Note also Martin Harrison, *Trade Unions and the Labour Party* (Allen and Unwin, London, 1960), pp. 137–42

and Lewis Minkin, The Labour Party Conference (Allen and Unwin, London, 1978), pp. 169–70.

11 Sid Vincent, interview with Kim Howells, 1980. *South Wales Miners' Library.*

12 See Jim Hammond, Presidential Address, NUM (North Western Area) Annual Conference, 1963.

13 Joe Gormley, *Battered Cherub* (Hamish Hamilton, London, 1982), p. 49. His account is at pp. 48–51. This presentation is similar to that by Vincent on the South Wales Miners' Library tape.

14 The dispute can be traced in the records of the NUM (Lancashire Area) from October 1960 to January 1961. The first major argument was at the Area Conference, 15 October 1960.

15 See Hammond's comment at Lancashire's Area NEC, 24 October 1960.

16 See his statement at Special Area Conference, 29 October 1960.

17 Mosley Common Delegate at Area Conference, 12 November 1960.

18 Plank Lane Delegate, *ibid*.

19 See Area NEC, 24 November 1960. Letter from Paynter was dated 17 November.

20 As noted in Vic Allen, *The Militancy of British Miners* (The Moor Press, Shipley, 1981), p. 320.

2

New strategies for old: Gormley and the Left

The sixties was the decade when the miners' world turned upside down. The advent of the Labour Government in 1964 did not stem the flood of pit closures; indeed the administration's zealous pursuit of industrial modernisation meant that the cutting of 'uneconomic' capacity was pursued with little regard for either long-term energy needs or social costs. Delegates to the 1965 NUM National Conference heard the Minister of Power, Fred Lee, a Member for a constituency containing many Lancashire miners, employing arguments not dissimilar from those advanced by Ian MacGregor almost two decades later. The industry should be relieved of 'the deadweight of many collieries which do not cover even their running expenses'. For the miners who remained the future would be rosy: 'we shall have a more concentrated and mechanised industry employing fewer men, but capable of providing them with a good rising standard of life . . .'[1]

Unfortunately for many of Fred Lee's constituents and for many others in the Lancashire coalfield, their pits counted as part of the 'deadweight'. Between 1960 and 1964 twenty Lancashire pits had closed; between 1965 and 1970 thirteen more did so. In the earlier period the coalfield lost over eight and a half thousand mining jobs and in the later one over eleven and a half thousand. In many ways, Lancashire's bleakest year was 1968 with six closures and nearly 5,800 jobs gone including the coalfield's show piece at Mosley Common. This last closure included the abandonment of substantial reserves after years of sometimes acrimonious debate about the pit's viability. For the first time under nationalisation, Lancashire's miners experienced compulsory redundancies. By the time Labour lost office in June 1970, the number of Lancashire pits had fallen to

eleven; within another year it was down to nine. Against this
massive cutback, there were few compensating developments. An
effectively new pit came into operation at Agecroft on the fringes of
Salford, whilst production began at Parkside Colliery in Newton-
le-Willows.

The Area Union showed little willingness to fight this onslaught.
Many of the coalfield's pits were high-cost producers: some were
clearly approaching exhaustion. By 1964 Hammond, once again
Lancashire President, was taking a relatively fatalistic attitude
towards closures:

> Whatever we have attempted, and however much we have investigated,
> we have only succeeded in one or two cases, in keeping pits going that
> the Board has specified for closure. This has been the case also in the
> other coalfields where closures have been on a similar or greater scale. It
> has made little difference whether the leadership was 'left' or 'right'.[2]

This was certainly true – left-wing Scotland and South Wales;
right-wing Durham and Lancashire; the seemingly inexorable logic
of profitability transcended political differences. Hammond's
response was to oppose any fight against closures on principle: 'we
need to stop continually shouting about each and every pit whatever
the circumstances. We only raise false hopes, and create unnecessary
disillusion in the Trade Union. Often the propaganda is raised even
when it is known that nothing can be done, and the wildest
allegations made without the least foundations.' Clearly a leading
spokesman for the Left in Lancashire was far from claiming that
pits should be operated until exhaustion; equally he seemed
doubtful about any strategy other than that of selective lobbying for
good cases.

In one crucial respect Lancashire differed from other declining
coalfields such as South Wales and Durham. The regional depend-
ence on coal had never been so exclusive. In the sixties, other
industrial employment was buoyant in Lancashire and, as Gormley
acknowledged, men were often ready to take their redundancy
money because jobs outside the industry were available and
attractive. But for those who remained, these years were ones of
demoralisation, a corrosive legacy for those who sought to rebuild
an effective union.

The response developed in Lancashire was for constructive
dialogue with the NCB in order to improve performance at pits with
a credible future. This was the way forward presented by Gormley

to the 1965 National Conference already perturbed by the Wilson Government's energy policy: 'Mosley Common was well known, but we demanded an investigation into the damned pit, and we found out why it was uneconomical. Everybody was walking about with a chip on their shoulder from the Manager downwards. As soon as we got the chips removed, the pit started bouncing and it's now one of the best units.'[3] It did not bounce for long. In April 1967, the Lancashire Executive heard that the Board wished to close Mosley Common as it had lost £6 million since 1960. Once again it was decided to go in for a policy of co-operation in which agreements should be kept and absenteeism cut.[4] Gormley claimed that in the harsh economic climate Lancashire had to be competitive, and at the moment the coalfield was losing 11s a ton. Much of this could be debited to Mosley Common. As the situation became more desperate at the pit, Gormley clarified his strategy: 'any one talking about militant action was a sure way of shutting Lancashire . . . It was no use people coming to the rostrum quoting platitudes, that would never save the industry, it would only be as a result of our whole determination to get on the backs of management and our own men to keep the machines running.'[5] But by the end of the year, the co-operative strategy had failed; Mosley Common would close. Gormley in restrospect, would claim that this episode demonstrated the 'sterility of "militant" tactics': 'I'll never forgive the people responsible. The NUM leadership there. Ah yes, the so-called militants, the fighters for this, that and the other. Well they fought all right, but all they succeeded in doing was to close a bloody good pit.'[6] Against this there endured a belief amongst some Lancashire activists that the closure represented the failure of co-operation and that the Area leadership had not been too concerned about the demise of a traditionally militant branch.[7]. But by 1968, such resentment did not affect the making of policy within the Lancashire Area. Gormley and his supporters were very firmly in control and he was achieving increasing influence in a National Union where many right wing figures found difficulty in responding to Labour Government policies.

The problem was epitomised at the very top of the Union in the policies of the National President, Sidney Ford. His loyalty to the Wilson Government knew few qualifications. By 1967 as closures mounted inexorably, he expressed concern about Government policy, but within such limits as to negate its impact:

> The Government has found it necessary to take steps which have made heavy demands upon the loyalty of its supporters; as candid friends we are entitled to criticise, but I make a distinction between legitimate criticism and malicious attacks designed not to help the Government but to destroy it. There is no question of betrayal simply because unpleasant decisions have to be made.[8]

In no way did the National President query either the role of the Labour Government or the fundamental economic arguments; neither did Area Officials from ultra-loyal coalfields such as Northumberland and Durham.

Such incapacity to respond to the crisis inevitably provoked criticism, so much so that by March 1968, the NEC discussed the possibility of some form of industrial action as a protest. Although this tactic was rejected in the NEC, a Special National Delegate Conference found several speakers prepared to advocate such a course. Paynter's introduction to the debate was characteristically judicious,[9] but the debate witnessed one significant development. Most contributors spoke in their areas traditional terms – South Wales for some form of industrial action; Northumberland completely opposed. But from the Yorkshire coalfield there came contrasting voices. One representative of right wing orthodoxy insisted that a strike 'would absolutely ruin this Union and our industry because . . . we are economically as weak as ever we have been in history.'[10] Against this, there were radical claims from Yorkshire. The time-honoured strategy had failed: at the end of the road we are in the same position now as we were eight years ago, faced with an absolute absence of any steps being taken to prevent the destruction of our industry.[11]

A colleague backed strike action with the simple argument 'there is no other choice'.[12] As yet such views were in a minority in Yorkshire, but they were harbingers of a fundamental shift in the politics of that Area that would eventually upset the traditional political balance within the National Union. As yet, the Old Guard could hold the line – and within this majority, Lancashire played its part. The Gormley line of constructive dialogue dominated discussions; one Branch speaker referred to strike action as 'just suicide'.[13] An ultra-loyalist sponsored MP suggested 'you often do more good by stealth' and talk of a one day strike was 'completely silly'.[14]

Gormley's increasing prominence within the National Union brought him into the thick of the controversy over pit closures in his role as a member of the Labour Party National Executive. During the run-up to the 1964 Election, he had argued the case for loyalty within his union and to Party policy;[15] afterwards his role was frequently that of a loyal supporter of the Government against its Party critics. But the state of his own industry clearly raised pressure for this perspective. The 1967 Party Conference had passed an NUM resolution calling not just for an 'overall energy plan' but also for Government underwriting of social costs until the transitional period ended. This went beyond Government policy, and NEC attempts to make progress on the issue achieved nothing. Although Gormley spoke to the 1968 NUM Conference of his bitterness over the fate of the resolution, other sources have suggested that his intervention in the Labour Party had a ritualistic quality.[16] The lack of progress helped to produce a breach in the pattern of NUM loyalty at the 1968 Party Conference. The proceedings had had a dramatic beginning with protesting miners entering the conference hall during the opening Address from the Chair; subsequently a section of the Party NEC's Report dealing with fuel policy was referred back on the initiative of the NUM delegation. This was so, despite wording calculated to avoid such opposition, and despite appeals from Gormley to avoid such a public rift. The opposition was clearly indicative of the deep resentment in the coalfields over closures, but once again the Conference decision had no practical significance for the industry.

By 1968 Gormley could claim to be the most credible contender for national office on the NUM Right. He was tough and resourceful; he was clearly opposed to the Left, but in a way that seemed preferable to the discreet administrative style of Ford, or the crude anti-Communism and Labour loyalism of some Yorkshire and North Eastern officials.[17] He showed some signs of having thought through some response to the closures and the problems posed by the Labour Government. Moreover, when Will Paynter retired at the end of 1968, Gormley was at the plausible age of fifty one.

He became the sole nominee of the Right within the Union, and found himself opposed by a single opponent, Lawrence Daly, General Secretary of the Scottish Area. Until 1956, the latter had been a member of the Communist Party; leaving in the political crisis of that year, he did not immediately join the Labour Party. Indeed he played the leading role in forming the Fife Socialist League, the one significant organisational product of the New Left debates that flowed from that momentous year. He was elected to the Fife County Council as a League candidate and on the same ticket obtained 4,886 votes in West Fife in the General Election of 1959; but by 1962 the League's isolation and stagnation led him to join the Labour Party. Daly was a working-class intellectual with a distinctive political past, but in a fundamental fashion he demonstrated a significant political development on the NUM Left. It was increasingly difficult for opponents effectively to attack the Left with the old anti-Communist slogans, since its base had broadened to include several who had left or never been Communist Party members.[18]

The frozen factionalism of the Cold War was starting to melt. Daly was nevertheless seen widely as the outsider. His experience of full-time Union posts was less than Gormley's. The Scot had worked on the face until 1963, he had then been elected a Fife Agent, followed by election to the Scottish Secretaryship two years later. Only in 1966 had he joined the NEC. Yet there were auguries which favoured him, most significantly his nomination by Yorkshire – a bastion of the Right.

Gormley retrospectively saw himself as 'the odds-on certainty . . . I seemed to have everything going for me',[19] but Daly spoke frequently in other coalfields and produced a pamphlet, *The Miners and the Nation*, published by the Scottish Area. This argued that the shift in fuel policy – so vital for both miners and the nation – required a more militant attitude. It was a response to the failures of the existing leadership; the result – Daly 115,531 votes, Gormley 105,501 – suggested perhaps some desire to leave behind the years of passivity. Gormley blamed his close association with the Labour Party at a time when the Wilson Government's unpopularity had reached unparalleled depths. But Sid Vincent, the Lancashire Agent, drew another moral. He commented that the Gormley campaign had lacked organisational strength: 'In the Area there appeared a succession of documents promoting Lawrence Daly. We went into battle half-heartedly. We couldn't spend any money. People in this Area were watching very keenly.'[20] Next time would be different – but before then the passivity that had characterised Union reactions to Board and Government would be dramatically challenged.

Significantly the challenges came, not over closures which had caused so much unhappiness for more than a decade, but firstly over surface workers' hours and subsequently over wages. In real terms, miners' wages had slumped badly reflecting the decreasing demand for coal and miners, and also the legacy of the NUM's failure to play the market during earlier years of coal shortage. In 1948, average miners' wages had stood at 29 per cent above average earnings in manufacturing; by 1960 the gap had narrowed to 7.4 per cent and by 1970 stood at 3.1 per cent less – a weekly reminder of the devalued position of the miner, and another indictment of the years of cautious policies.

Moreover, changing conditions of production had helped to reform the method of payment. In 1955 less than 10 per cent of production was power loaded; a decade and a half later the proportion was over 92 per cent. In Lancashire the proportion rose from 4.5 per cent in 1953 to 44.5 per cent in 1960 and 92 per cent in 1966. This changing work environment went along with changes in the wage structure. In 1955 a national daywage structure was formulated for almost all other than faceworkers. The extent of differentials for the same tasks between Areas meant that implementation proved difficult. Even at the face, Area Power Loading Agreements began to emerge, albeit with different systems of payments. In this context, Lancashire was an exception. There was no Area agreement; instead power loading payments were settled by pit and even by seam. In 1965 and into the early months of 1966, opinion on the NUM National Executive gradually moved in favour of a daywage for face workers, without any incentive element. Apart from the principled case for equity, those in low wage coalfields could hope that such a strategy could bring their wage up to the level of the best paid. The NCB saw no relevance in payment by results in the context of near-universal mechanisation. A daywage system might aid deployment between faces; it allowed more control over wage costs and could end the perennial local disputes over piece rates.

When a Special National Conference was held on the proposed scheme in April 1966, Hammond welcomed the scheme for the effect that it would have on the consciousness of miners. The existing system strengthened acquisitive individualism:

> It brings out the worst instincts in men and even the ones who are receiving the £7 a shift because they, themselves, instead of developing a more socialistic conscience begin to talk and argue like Tories . . . There is nothing brings their mentality more in keeping with socialist progress than when they are all in common on a similar foundation.

The dream was all very well, but Hammond admitted there were practical difficulties: 'we shall have a struggle in our Area, we shall have to meet all those pieceworkers who want to continue, especially those who think they will be on good faces in the years that lie ahead'.[21] When a Lancashire Conference met, the Delegates faced a recommendation to accept the scheme, but they voted widespread opposition. Gormley claimed that the preceding Branch meetings had been filled with highly-paid pieceworkers. On a show of hands the scheme was approved narrowly, but on a card-vote the opposition of the large collieries ensured rejection by 320 to 80.[22] Nevertheless, across all Areas of the NUM the scheme was ratified by a relatively small majority.

One basis for Lancashire's opposition was perhaps the relatively-advantaged position of the coalfield's pieceworkers under the old system. Average earnings per shift on Lancashire power loading faces stood in October 1965 at 84s 3d, third only to Kent and Nottinghamshire and equal with North Derbyshire. Such a level compared sharply with 71s 6d a shift in South Wales and no more than 66s a shift in Durham.[23] The Lancashire payment levels negotiated at pit level could be presented as one more item in Gormley's constructive way forward: 'There would be no need to even them up if you were all doing your jobs in your Area as we are doing it in the North Western Area.'[24] This image of the tough effective negotiator was one developed by Gormley in his years as National President; its origins lay in the piecework system of Lancashire 'I have always had damn good wages for myself, damn good wages for the teams I lead, damn good wages for the Lancashire lads and damn good contracts, and we had damn good wages since I became President.'[25] With memories of the relatively advantaged position of Lancashire faceworkers until 1966, it was hardly surprising that the Area remained unhappy about the absence of any incentive element – a concern that a decade later would be highly relevant in the politics of the National Union.

But such divisions lay in the future. The immediate legacy of the National Power Loading Agreement was to help create a widespread wage-based militancy. 1971 was the target date for the equalising upwards of wage rates. The protracted process would in itself guarantee resentment in traditionally better paid Areas, but even this slow move towards equality was initially hindered by the Wilson Government's incomes policy. More fundamentally, miners' wages fell increasingly behind those in other industrial sectors; the fears of further closures and the belief in industrial weakness combined to inhibit any militant response.

In October 1969, the spell was broken – and in a fashion that anticipated some of the controversies of 1984. The occasion was not wages, but a perennial demand that the minority of surface workers whose basic week was over forty hours should have this reduced. The beneficiaries would be some of the weakest sections in the industry – ill-paid, often working in appalling conditions, frequently former underground men no longer fit for their old jobs. Traditionally they had taken a peripheral role in a union often dominated by faceworkers and craftsmen, but now they became the focus for a mobilisation that ended the miners' passivity.

The issue had been raised at the 1969 National Conference in terms that suggested that in some quarters patience was wearing thin. The stock response from a Durham official – 'we have failed because we have not got the bargaining power we had in the past'[26] – was just one more repetition of an already redundant apology. By early October, the Left in Yorkshire were pressing for industrial action to force the Board to act. The NEC reacted inconclusively on the issue and two days later there were dramatic events at the Yorkshire Area Council. After the Area President had been voted out of the Chair, a strike motion was passed by eighty-five votes to three. On Monday 13 October every Yorkshire pit but one was stopped; the next day, the stoppage was complete. Now the strike was spread into the adjoining coalfields – North Derbyshire and Notts – by the Doncaster Panel's flying pickets. Gradually, the traditionally left wing coalfields joined in. There was a series of local responses in Scotland, whilst in South Wales the demand was initially for a national strike through a Special National Conference. But within a week twenty four South Wales pits, 16,000 members, were on strike.[27]

The spread of the strike was in the face of serious obstacles. The Coal Board characterisation of it as economically disastrous was predictable. But within the NUM the strike proved divisive. The new General Secretary, Lawrence Daly was concerned at the gap between the strikers' tactics and the National Rule Book, and there was strong resistance to the strike on the part of Area and Branch officials.

The Yorkshire pickets came only slowly across the Pennines. As late as the day shift on 21 October, Lancashire, along with Durham,

Northumberland, North Wales and Cumberland, was unaffected by the strike. Then, pickets arrived at Agecroft, then the largest pit in the coalfield. Faceworkers on the afternoon shift refused to go underground after appeals from a twenty strong picket. One claimed, 'We intend to bring the Lancs coalfield to a standstill'; but Agecroft represented an isolated success. When some pickets moved along the East Lancs Road to Astley Green their appeals met with no response from a workforce facing the threat of closure.

Next day, the discussions shifted from pit gates into the Area's formal structure. Gormley had made a hurried return from a Spanish holiday having missed a NEC meeting which had considered not only the surface hours question, but also the state of negotiations on the 1969 wage claim. On the latter question, the Coal Board had produced a generally acceptable response to the Union's admittedly modest claim, but had insisted that both issues had to be considered as elements in a single package. Accordingly the NEC had decided to call a Special Conference to recommend acceptance of the deal prior to an individual ballot vote – a constitutionally impeccable procedure which the NEC's majority hoped would remove the attraction and the legitimacy of the strike movement.

The Lancashire Executive had responded to this lead by recommending acceptance of the Coal Board's offer and by instructing members not to join the unofficial strike.[28] But four days later the pickets were in Lancashire and the next day a Special Area Conference met with Gormley, now back in the coalfield. Arguments were presented which would prove durable amongst the coalfield's full-time and Branch officials. Gormley's opening remarks emphasised his strategy for maintaining what was left of the coalfield; the minutes record his statement that: 'whatever happened in other coalfields, unofficial action was not going to happen here, because we were fighting to make sure that Lancashire continued as a coal-producing county irrespective of what some other people thought, people whom, it would seem, did not want to keep the mining industry on its feet.' Admittedly there was concern if men felt that they should be joining a strike and not working but 'they were doing the right thing and were working within the rules of the Union'.[29] These arguments were elaborated more colourfully by Sid Vincent at that time one of the Lancashire Agents: 'These men [are] not interested in the Lancashire Area or any other area, they

were interested in crippling the industry and were just anarchists.'[30]
An Executive member added a touch of anti-Yorkshire sentiment:
'Yorkshire never protested when the Lancashire pits were being
closed down due to them sending coal from Yorkshire into
Lancashire.'[31]

Alongside this parochialism, there went support for Gormley's
emphasis on the Rule book. A Craftsmen's delegate evoked a
contrast that would become familiar in 1984: 'We should have a
ballot and let us see what all the workers say, let's have everyone's
point of view, not just those few who seem to be gifted with shouting
the loudest.'[32] Similarly, a Delegate from Sutton Manor colliery in
St Helens articulated another theme that would resonate through
the arguments of 1984: 'If they [are] going to have a strike, let it be
done democratically by a ballot vote. It [is] no good, some in and
some out.'[33] The debate did include some of the arguments that had
fuelled strike action elsewhere. One speaker saw the strike tactic as
justified by its results, saying that 'the Yorkshire miners had
achieved more in one week than the NEC had done in fifteen years . . .
and it was about time the National Officials were made to get on
with their jobs. Everything was always pushed back, even at local
level, they got the same threat – the pit was in jeopardy, it would
close etc.'[34] But other delegates spoke against this assessment.
Strike action would not defend the coalfield, for 'the Area had come
a long way and we ought not to throw it on one side by irresponsible
strikes'.[35]

This perspective was developed by Gormley in his concluding
remarks. He emphasised a self-consciously 'realistic' approach to
negotiations. Since his election as Area General Secretary, the
coalfield had experienced a major reduction in the number of
disputes. Instead he attended the meetings and argued his case with
the Board, and had 'made more progress on behalf of our members
on such things as concessionary coal than had been achieved by the
so-called militant attitudes of previous years.' Contrary to the
claims of some delegates he felt that the strike had been counter-
productive: 'It had only resulted in a hardness of the Board's
attitude.'[36] The result of the Conference was an overwhelming vote
of twenty-three to two to accept the Board's offer. As they left the
Bolton offices, delegates and Executive members met Yorkshire
pickets who claimed they would be back next day in busloads to
speak directly to the members.

However within a few days, the stoppage had ended when some leaders of the Yorkshire strike obtained an assurance from the TUC General Secretary, Victor Feather, that he would attempt to secure an independent enquiry on the surface hours question. The coalfields might be back at work, but when the National Delegate Conference met on 30 October the exchanges showed that relations within the Union would not continue in their traditional style. Daly, the successful candidate of the Left, less than a year before, defended NEC decisions as a valid estimate of what was obtainable;[37] delegates from coalfields involved in the strike attacked the yoking together of the wages and hours questions. When loyalists emphasised the need to stick to the Rule Book, a South Wales delegate gave a sharp response: 'There is bound to come a time when the men will say "To hell with the constitution, if it does not give us what we demand for 22 years" This is what has happened.'[38]

Gormley's contribution was characteristic, claiming that Union officials had been effective and that he, at least, knew his members' priorities. There was little of the unreasoned onslaught on 'militancy' that characterised many on the NUM Right. On the strike itself he made a distinction that would reappear in the Lancashire controversies of 1984: 'I don't condemn people for being on strike – but what I will condemn is when they go into other areas to picket, and instead of peacefully picketing trying to manhandle people . . . who do not agree with them.'[39] Yet the initial outcome of the Conference showed an unprecedented loss of control by the NUM Right as delegates rejected the package deal by 168 votes to 165. But this was followed by a show of hands favouring a national individual ballot by sixty to forty-four. Now the outcome was guaranteed as wages and surface hours were combined on the ballot paper. A relatively significant wage increase affected all voters: the failure on surface hours was directly relevant for a tiny minority. Thus the package was accepted by 193,985 votes to 41,322. Of the minority almost 24,500 came from just two areas, Yorkshire and South Wales. In Lancashire the vote to accept was over 8.5 to one.

Superficially the 1969 strikes ended in a failure, but beneath the arithmetic of the ballot, taboos had been broken. Despite the numbing weight of the years of decline, despite the reservation of some left-wing officials, despite the lack of organisation, it had happened. For a generation of activists particularly in Yorkshire, 1969 was a formative experience.

The pressure on the Union's right wing was leaving its mark. The 1970 National Conference found Ford absent through illness, and his deputy the National Vice-President Sid Schofield, attacked the minority out to undermine the credibility of full-time officials and prepared to 'incite' unconstitutional action. This time the Left carried its campaign on to the floor of the National Conference with a focus on the wages question. A composite resolution on wages was moved by a 31-year-old Yorkshire delegate, as yet little known outside his own coalfield. Arthur Scargill expressed the mood of those who had led the previous year's strike – the resolution must be adopted and then pursued effectively. Failure

> will release an anger that will make last October look like a Sunday school picnic. No longer will our membership accept that a small increase is better than none. They are fed up with being asked not to rock the boat. They have been told to remain passive and what has it got us? Half the coalmining industry has been obliterated . . .[40]

The resolution with its specific targets – £30 NPLA Grade A; £22 underground minimum and £20 surfaceman was passed with NEC support. But there remained the crucial question mark over the zeal with which the NEC majority would implement it. A South Wales resolution contained slightly lower targets but incorporated a demand for strike action should the Coal Board fall short of the Union's demands. In contrast this was opposed by the NEC and by speakers from right-wing coalfields, but it was passed narrowly.

The debate and the consequential wage bargaining occurred in the new political environment resulting from the election of the Heath Government. The new administration sought to limit public-sector pay rises to 12 per cent compared with the NUM's 33 per cent demand. Predictably the Board's response fell below the levels specified in either the Yorkshire or the South Wales resolution and the NEC decided on a strike ballot. Under the existing Rule Book, the hurdle was a tough one, a two-thirds majority. The outlooks of Area officials varied. Some campaigned vigorously for the stipulated policy; others perhaps saw the holding of a strike ballot as sensational enough in itself to marginally improve the Board's offer. Perhaps there were those who hoped that it might restore 'normality' to the Union with militant strategies checked by the votes of a usually passive majority.

The result was a stark demonstration of the divergent industrial and political traditions in the Areas. Overall the vote was 143,466 to 115,052 in favour of a strike – at 55.5 per cent well below the constitutional requirement. But five Areas – South Wales 83 per cent, Scotland 78 per cent, Cumberland 75 per cent, the Scottish Enginemen 70 per cent and Kent 67 per cent had passed the two-thirds hurdle. Yorks at 60 per cent came next – the shift to the 'left had made progress there, but did not rest yet on a majority equivalent to those in the traditional left coalfields. Several Areas produced majorities under 60 per cent. Amongst them were two traditionally cautious Areas whose delegates had opposed the South Wales resolution that had produced the ballot – Durham had polled 53 per cent for a stoppage, and in Lancashire the margin was even tighter 4,901 to 4,647.

This result was followed by strikes in some of the left wing coalfields, but often in a less coherent fashion than the previous year.[41] In Yorkshire action was less solid, and whilst Area leaders in Scotland and South Wales responded to activist pressures, there was little co-ordination. Some came out as others returned to work. But 1970 saw new pressures on officials in traditionally right-wing coalfields. When the Board slightly improved its offer, the Durham Executive recommended acceptance on 5 November, but within four days two Durham pits had voted to strike.

In Lancashire too, the Area leadership faced a less predictable prospect; there had been a slim majority for a strike and Vincent claimed the members were 'very bitter and determined'. By 5 November, face chargemen at Bickershaw were banning overtime, and by the time the Lancashire Executive met four days later, the ban had spread to six more pits including the large collieries at Agecroft and Parkside. Bold Branch had suggested a one-day strike.

Executive members were lobbied by men from Bickershaw and responded by opposing unofficial action, but instituting an official overtime ban. It was the minimal response, as Gormley acknowledged: 'it was felt that unofficial strike action would have been inevitable unless the Executive took action'.[42] Gormley's own attitude to the Left's campaign became clear on the day that the Lancashire ban began, 11 November. Along with officials from other right-wing Areas, he produced a statement deploring the 'unconstitutional methods now being employed by certain Groups in the NUM'. Some individual officials could be less diplomatic.

Albert Martin of Nottinghamshire had already referred to 'substituting mob rule for the rule of law and the ballot box'. When the NEC met on 13 November the tensions were expressed in heated clashes outside the national offices as right-wing officials faced demonstrations from Scotland and South Wales. Gormley claimed that he had been hit and that Martin had been kicked.[43] His anger was expressed not just to left-wing NEC members at the time, but at a subsequent meeting of the Lancashire Executive. The Area's officials had taken the unconstitutional step of lifting the overtime ban and now asked for retrospective ratification by the Executive. Their specific justification was that the NEC had decided to hold a second ballot on the Board's latest offer.

Gormley expanded the argument, moving the focus away from the unfulfilled wage demands to the government of the Union. Now the decision was 'whether this Union [is] going to be governed by the democratically elected leaders or whether they [are] going to be governed by decisions made as a result of intimidation by mob rule . . . the issues [are] quite different to what they were last week.' The Executive were divided over the officials' action but backed their ending of the ban by seven votes to four.[44]

Although strike action was declining, the Lancashire leadership faced difficulties in getting a return to normal working. In several Branches, the Officials' action produced resentment. At Bickershaw a meeting showed an overwhelming majority for maintaining the ban. The Sutton Manor Branch Secretary informed a Special Delegate Conference that the officials initiative had produced 'utter chaos'. At Bold craftsmen terminated the ban, but many of the pit's NUM Branch stopped work and returned only when the craftsmen agreed to reimpose the ban. A Delegate Conference voted for normal working by twenty-one to one and the next day the ban ended at Bickershaw, Parkside and Sutton Manor. But at Agecroft and Bold – an unlikely pairing in the light of 1984 – the ban remained for another week.

As Gormley acknowledged, when strike action elsewhere was declining 'the whole object of any decision which had been made was to keep the Lancashire pits from striking'.[45] But the events of November 1970 showed how discontent over wages was affecting even a traditionally cautious coalfield. Right-wing officials faced increasing difficulties in managing their organisations. They had to ride with and hope to canalise the tide of wage based militancy.

Gormley had acknowledged these pressures earlier that year when,
at the Lancashire Annual Conference, he had distanced himself
from the existing national leadership. 'I think it is time we got off
our knees. We have been acquiescing too long . . . we can no longer
continue this role, this passive role we have had . . . I think we have
done a disservice to the Union and ourselves . . .' He declared a
priority at odds with one of his objections to the 1969 strikes 'If
acceptance of a high wage policy means pit closures, it means pit
closures. We may have to pay the consequences. As long as we know
that and back it up to the hilt, let's go for the high wages'.[46] Here was
a signposting of the strategy pursued by him as National President.

The opportunity soon arrived. In March 1971, Sir Sidney Ford
announced his retirement on grounds of ill-health. The Left's
nominee was Michael McGahey, President of the Scottish Area and
a member of the Communist Party. Some auguries seemed to favour
him. Compared with the time when Daly had won the contest for
the General Secretaryship, the Left seemed to have strengthened its
position. The strikes of 1969 and 1970 had placed the old Right on
the defensive. A sizeable section of the NUM now seemed ready to
stop bowing to the seemingly 'inevitable' and to give industrial
action a try. But unlike Daly, McGahey was a Communist, an
attachment that could be used to influence prejudices in some
coalfields and he was vulnerable to the argument that one coalfield
should not provide both national full-time officials. Moreover,
Gormley had carefully distanced himself from the negative style of
many on the Right and this time the Lancashire Area organised an
uninhibited election campaign.[47]

Little more than two weeks after Ford's announcement, Lancashire had not only nominated their Secretary, a Delegate Conference
had agreed to give 'full physical and financial support'.[48] In mid
April the Lancashire Executive considered how to put this commitment into effect. They agreed to publish an official campaign
document with perhaps a follow-up. They also decided to campaign
in other coalfields 'it was agreed that the Secretary, along with the
President, draw up a list of the numbers of cars and canvassers we
would need from each Branch to undertake this campaign.'[49]
Vincent drew up the first campaign document 'Amazingly Joe
didn't agree with it. He said there were some things that weren't
factual . . . I said "Aye Joe, listen. You've not got to be like this. If
you tell a white lie or two to achieve your ambition" . . .'[50]

The Lancashire campaign provoked a critical response from the McGahey camp on the grounds that it involved canvassing and thereby breached Union rules. The National Executive's Organisation Sub-Committee had laid down that candidates might provide a 250 word biographical statement for distribution as a poster. Any suggestion that this should be the only publicity was arguably negated by a letter from National Office on election practice. In 1968, a comparable document had explicitly forbidden the issuing of leaflets or other publicity; the 1971 version did not include this prohibition. The Gormley camp interpreted this as a licence for unrestricted campaigning.[51]

Early in May, the Lancashire Executive refuted 'allegations of unscrupulous tactics' and argued that there had been strict compliance with the rules.[52] This interpretation was underwritten at the May NEC Meeting. In response to Scottish protests, the acting President, Sid Schofield, a Gormley supporter ruled that Lancashire had acted properly. The NEC decided to recognise the existing situation: 'this election should be a free for all as far as publicity is concerned'.[53] Here was the green light for the Lancashire Executive to produce another document.

The ballot was scheduled for the week beginning Monday 24 May. That Sunday, 'an army of cars left the Area', all expenses paid by the Union. The campaigners were armed with the new pamphlet written by Vincent but published under Gormley's name. They went across the coalfields, including the McGahey strong-holds – South Wales, Yorkshire and even Scotland. In each coalfield the Lancashire contingent had a team captain to co-ordinate action. Links were made with local sympathisers and the pamphlet was distributed. When hostile Branch officials intervened, the Lancashire men replied that they were just ordinary members keen to argue Gormley's case.

Vincent served as Yorkshire team captain, ensconced in a hotel receiving reports about sympathetic and hostile encounters. One altercation foreshadowed future arguments. The Lancashire canvassers met forceful opposition at Woolley Colliery, Arthur Scargill's home pit. They were thrown off the premises. Late at night, Vincent returned with some colleagues, tipped the baths attendant £5 and Gormley pamphlets were placed in all the lockers.[54]

McGahey's campaign never developed the same penetration and in Lancashire any attempt to mobilise support for Gormley's opponent met with little tolerance. One Branch official entered Bickershaw Colliery yard with McGahey literature. He and two supporters were asked to leave. They continued to distribute leaflets outside the pit gates. 'The weather was very bad . . . some . . . members wanted to know why this Branch Secretary had been turned off the premises. This had the effect that some . . . started distributing McGahey leaflets.'[55] Apart from getting wet, 'the luckless official became the object of a complaint to the Lancashire Executive. The response cast a searchlight on the style of the Area's politics in the Age of Gormley. It referred to a scurrilous attack and campaign, and in particular rejected allegations that Gormley had too much power: 'This Union is not a one-man band and the business and affairs of the Union are conducted by the Executive Committee and the Officials and any decisions made by them are ratified by Conference . . . any attack on an individual is an attack on the whole administration of the Union'.[56] This was supplemented by the threat of action against Branch officials who repeatedly flouted a conference decision. The controversy duly died but, not before Vincent had suggested that members' activities should be governed by more than the Area Rule Book, stating that 'It was an unwritten rule that no Branch official enter another pit yard dealing with subject matter which could cause trouble'.[57] How this could be reconciled with the Lancastrians' campaign tactics, he did not elaborate!

Such tactics proved successful. Gormley won decisively by 117,663 votes to 92,883 and there was further criticism from left-wing Areas. But the Area's leader had become a National Official. Perhaps more than ever, despite its diminished membership, Lancashire stood as a significant element on the NUM Right.

Notes

1   NUM Annual Conference 1965, p. 187.
2   NUM (North Western Area) 1964. Presidential Address to Annual Conference.
3   NUM Annual Conference 1965, p. 236.
4   NWA Special Executive, 27 April 1967.
5   NWA Conference, 16 September 1967.
6   Gormley, *Battered Cherub*, p. 57.
7   When Paynter was questioned in Lancashire about the NEC's attitude to Mosley Common, his response seemed similar to Gormley's retrospective indictment: 'the best answer to that question was – why didn't

Mosley Common take a more effective step to save Mosley Common?'
NWA Weekend School, 31 March 1968.

8   NUM Annual Conference 1967, Presidential Address, p. 38.
9   NUM Special Delegate Conference, 15 March 1968, pp. 16–18.
10   *Ibid.* p. 27 (Tommy Burks).
11   *Ibid.* p. 23 (Jock Kane).
12   *Ibid.* p. 37 (Mick Welsh). See also Tommy Mullany at p. 31.
13   NWA Conference, 18 November 1967 (J. Gorden of Bold).
14   *Ibid.* Michael McGuire, the MP for Ince.
15   E.g. NUM Annual Conference 1963, p. 272.
16   See NUM Annual Conference 1968, p. 230; for the suggestion that
Gormley's opposition had its limits see Minkin, *The Labour Party
Conference*, p. 305.
17   Thus at the 1968 NUM Conference he was prepared on behalf of
Lancashire to support the South Wales resolution on Vietnam separating
himself from the Durham speaker. See pp. 177–8 of the Conference report
and p. 179 for the surprise of the South Wales mover, Emlyn Williams.
18   For Daly's political career see William Thompson 'The New Left in
Scotland' in Ian MacDougall (ed.), *Essays in Scottish Labour History* (John
Donald, Edinburgh,), pp. 207–24: E.P. Thompson, 'A Special Case' in his
Writing by Candlelight (Merlin, London, 1980), pp. 65–76.
19   Gormley, *ibid.* p. 72.
20   Vincent tape.
21   NUM Special Delegate Conference, 15 April 1966, pp. 42–3.
22   NWA Annual Conference, 12 May 1966; for Gormley's claim that
Branch Meetings had been packed, see p. 24.
23   See Minutes of JNC Union Side, 24 March 1966.
24   NUM Special Delegate Conference, 30 October 1969, p. 34.
25   NWA Annual Conference, May 1981.
26   NUM Annual Conference 1969, p. 137 (Kit Robinson).
27   For the events see Taylor, *The Politics of the Yorkshire Miners*, pp.
191–4 and Allen, *The Militancy of British Miners,* ch. 12.
28   NWA Executive, 17 October 1969. For the impact of the pickets see
MEN, 21 and 22 October 1969.
29   NWA Special Area Conference, 22 October 1969.
30   *Ibid.*
31   *Ibid.*
32   *Ibid.* (St Helens Craftsmen Delegate).
33   *Ibid.* Lord Robens in his *Ten Year Stint* (Cassell, London, 1972), p.
23 claims that fear about the pit's future led to a hostile reception for the
pickets at Sutton Manor.
34   NWA Special Conference, 22 October 1969. Significantly the
Delegate was from Parkside, a newly opened pit.
35   *Ibid.* (Hapton Valley Delegate).
36   *Ibid.*
37   NUM Special Conference, 30 October 1969, pp. 3–8.
38   *Ibid.* p. 26 (C. True).
39   *Ibid.* p. 33.

40 NUM Annual Conference 1970, p. 138.

41 See Taylor, *The Politics of the Yorkshire Miners*, pp. 197–201; Allen, *The Militancy of British Miners*, pp. 161–3. For the dispute in Lancashire see *MEN* beginning 6 November 1970 until resumption of normal working at the end of the month.

42 NWA Executive, 9 November 1970.

43 See Gormley, *ibid.* pp. 75–6.

44 NWA Executive, 16 November 1970. The seven to four vote is given in the Minutes of the Area Special Conference, 21 November 1970.

45 NWA Special Conference, 21 November 1970.

46 NWA Special Conference, May 1970.

47 See Vincent tape for an account of how the Gormley campaign was run.

48 NWA Conference, 20 March 1971.

49 NWA Executive, 16 April 1971.

50 Vincent tape.

51 As Gormley expressed it in his autobiography on p. 77, 'the rules are pretty flexible'.

52 NWA Executive, 5 May 1971.

53 NEC, 13 May 1971.

54 Vincent tape.

55 NWA Executive, 1 June, and Conference, 19 June 1971.

56 NWA Executive, 1 June 1971.

57 NWA Conference, 19 June 1971.

3

The containment of radicalism

As Gormley left Bolton for Euston Road, the Lancashire coalfield suffered the last of this devastating series of closures. Now it would remain in a relatively stable state for more than a decade.

Three pits survived in and around St Helens – Bold, modernised in the 1950s with new surface buildings and extended shafts, Sutton Manor, reorganised in the fifties and sixties but equipped with a largely pre 1914 pit top, and Cronton like its neighbours, always at risk from geological difficulties. To the East, Parkside Colliery, Newton-le-Willows, contrasted with the overall contraction of the coalfield. Developed at a cost of £13 million, its construction had been contemporary with the early years of the industry's decline. Production began in 1966; by 1971 it provided employment for around 1,700 miners, a reception pit for some men made redundant by shut downs elsewhere.

In 1971 Golborne, Bickershaw and Parsonage were separate collieries, in a line stretching west to east from Golborne village to the centre of Leigh. Beginning in 1973, they were transformed into a complex with the development of underground roadways permitting all coal to be wound at Bickershaw. The rationalisation continued; from the start of 1983, Parsonage eased to be a separate administrative unit. The creation of the Complex included, predictably, a decline in employment. In the decade from 1973, the number working in these pits fell from 3,300 to 2,100.

Agecroft Colliery on the outskirts of Salford was another product of fifties optimism. An old pit on the same site had ceased production in 1932, but the proving of large reserves led to the construction of a new pit, opening in 1960. A decade later its employment level was equivalent to Parkside, but during the seventies and early eighties, reorganisation produced a decline in employment. In 1973 almost 1,700 worked at Agecroft, a decade later the figure was under 900.

If the modern shafts and pit top of Agecroft were now the outpost of the Lancashire coalfield to the east, several miles to the north the small Hapton Valley pit survived as the last producer in the Burnley coalfield. Agecroft was a memorial to a brave new world for coal that never happened; Hapton Valley in its isolation recalled an age that had passed, a world where traditional customs survived and managers were well advised not to query too much. But it was a world also whose existence was threatened by geological problems.

The Area Union structure included eighteen Branches. Nine of them covered the surviving pits. Two more organised those employed at the workshops at Kirkless and Walkden, and one organised those employed in licensed mines. The remainder were the legacy of two mergers. In 1963, the Lancashire and Cheshire Area had absorbed a small organisation with a long name, the Lancashire, Cheshire and North Wales Colliery Enginemen's, Boilermen's and Brakesmen's Federation. This brought the winders into the main organisation, not just in Lancashire, but also in the small North Wales coalfield. These new members were organised in two Branches, one for each coalfield, although over time some winders joined the pit Branches at their workplaces. A more substantial amalgamation occurred as from July 1968. After much touting of the possibility, the Craftsmen's organisation, the Lancashire and Cheshire Colliery Tradesmen and Kindred Workers were absorbed. As a result separate Craftsmen's Branches

Table 3.1   Membership of Craftmen's Branches as at 31 December 1974

Craft Branch	Members covered
Ashton and Haydock (245 members)	Surface craftsmen at Parkside surface and Underground craftsmen at Golborne.
Leigh (266 members)	Surface craftsmen at Plank Lane surface and Underground craftsmen at Parsonage.
Clifton and Pendlebury (102 members)	Surface craftsmen at Agecroft.
St Helens (454 members)	Both categories at Bold, Cronton and Sutton Manor.

were established for the new membership, typically covering more than one pit. In fact, the guidelines were uneven and not always honoured.

There was no separate craft organisation at Hapton Valley. The Area organisation thus combined geographical and functional units in a distinctive fashion. Elsewhere craftsmen retained their separate organisations, as in Durham, Northumberland and Scotland, or were absorbed in to the pit Branches. The Lancashire structure institutionalised sectional differences and raised the prospect that controversial action could be eroded by a lack of cohesion between Branches covering the same pit.

Beyond the formal structure the political style of the Lancashire Area underwent no significant change after Gormley's departure. He was succeeded by Sid Vincent, who shared many of the same political priorities and offered a less abrasive variant of the same style. As with his predecessor, he cultivated the image of a 'bloody straight-talking Lancastrian'. Within his Area meetings, he developed considerable flair in dealing with potential critics. As one political opponent has reflected, 'He could handle them – just like a fisherman, he'd give them something to bite on and then land them one by one.'[1] He would have made a good Parliamentary Whip exuding *bonhomie*, but with a keen eye for each man's vulnerability. At one level he was a character, always ready to stand the lads a round in the interests of unity. But beneath the amiability there was a willingness to organise. He claimed to keep in close contact with the Branches, attending meetings to head off trouble but making sure that enough of his own 'commonsense' people were there. With such preparation, a prominent critic could be isolated at his own Branch – 'he never got out of his kennel'. In retrospect Vincent contrasted his approach with the more passive leadership of his Durham contemporaries, Kit Robinson and Alf Hesler; by their negligence they allowed a Left to develop.[2] Vincent succeeded to the Lancashire seat on the Union's National Executive where he acted as an organiser for the right-wing pro-Gormley faction. Initially he also took the NUM nomination for a seat on the Labour Party's National Executive. His position within the Party was captured in his criticism of Tony Benn's Chairmanship of the 1972 Conference: 'He played to the gallery . . . he proved himself to be a very poor Chairman indeed. Some of his remarks were, to say the least, very naive.'[3]

Vincent succeeded to Gormley's Party role for only two years beginning at the 1973 Party Conference. He was then replaced as the Miners' nominee by the South Wales President, Emlyn Williams. This shift for a nomination traditionally the preserve of the NUM Right, was an early indication that there was some movement within the Union's politics. But despite the challenge from the Left, the Right under Gormley's Presidency maintained a majority on the Union NEC and on most issues within the National Conference. Such control required concessions by a traditionally adroit President, but within this framework the Lancashire Area not only remained part of a majority within the institutions of the National Union, but saw its priorities and style articulated by the National President. Although of the Right, Gormley, the self-consciously blunt Lancastrian and former faceworker, provided a muscular contrast with his predecessor Sid Ford, a product not of the pit, but of the Union bureaucracy. Under the new style, the NUM rapidly found itself in the first national coal stoppage since 1926.

Lancashire played a significant part in the preparation for what, was for many, a leap into the unknown. When the 1971 National Conference met under Gormley's Presidency, he articulated a tough line on wages, and a wage resolution was carried setting targets for the forthcoming negotiations and instructing the NEC to consult members on industrial action if the Coal Board's response was unsatisfactory.[4] But there remained the hurdle that had frustrated such a mobilisation the previous year – the requirement for a two-thirds majority in any national strike ballot. A Lancashire resolution proposed the reduction of the majority to 55 per cent; backed by the NEC, it achieved the required two-thirds majority for a rule change against the opposition of some traditionally cautious Areas.[5] The significance of this amendment was soon apparent. An inadequate Coal Board response was followed by a National Delegate Conference, an immediate overtime ban (exposing the inadequacy of the basic wage, and cutting production), and the holding of a strike ballot. The result was 58.8 per cent for a stoppage; in Lancashire the pro-strike vote had increased compared with the previous year – the margin was now 4,882 (36.5 per cent) to 3,770.

The result of the 1972 strike can structure perceptions of the emotions with which miners entered the struggle. Increasingly abrasive management tactics during the overtime ban had strengthened the will to fight, but such determination need not have been based on optimism. The pessimistic legacy of the years of decline was hard to withstand; the Board's tactics tried to support any pessimism. The Lancashire Area fought the strike, like its counterparts elsewhere, as a united body. There was considerable criticism of the reluctance of COSA (the white-collar section of the National Union) to instruct local members to stop work, but this was no more than a distraction from the principal task of immobilising coal movements in the region.[6] Branches combined in groups to organise picketing of power stations, fuel depots and open-cast sites. Propaganda material was prepared for distribution to power station workers. By the beginning of February, major power stations were picketed continuously and Transport and General Workers Union drivers were respecting picket lines when instructed to make oil deliveries. But Lancashire officials did raise one spectre: 'The stations are now desperate and are making attractive offers to pirate firms and drivers. The station management are now warning the Police of delivery times and on five occasions since Thursday last 27 January, police have escorted pirate tankers in.'[7]

But against the shape of things to come in 1984, coal movements were nil, supplies in power stations' yards were dwindling, support from other relevant unions was solid. Coal was blacked completely in the region's docks, all ASLEF and over a hundred NUR Branches had been circulated and the response had been completely supportive. In the context of a Government ill-prepared for a struggle, the symbol of the mass picket at Saltley Gates was the enduring image of 1972, as the Wilberforce Report prefaced a NUM victory. After negotiations had ended, Vincent reported back to a Lancashire Conference, 'the general consensus of opinion is that this Union has made the biggest step forward in its history'[8] In a fundamental sense, the 'biggest step' concerned, not the financial benefits resulting from the strike, but that its solidarity and outcome – the panic introduction of power cuts and the Heath Government's very public capitulation – suggested that the years of passive acceptance were over. For miners with long memories or with a sense of history, 1972 was the effective answer, not just to the years of contraction, but to the disaster of 1926.

Within the Union, the Left could claim the credit. Its spokesmen had pushed for an assertive strategy for years; the victory could be held to vindicate them. Michael McGahey became highlighted as a classic figure of reactionary demonology whilst the Yorkshire employment of the flying pickets, now in an official cause, focused attention on the leadership there and especially on Arthur Scargill. But the credit would not flow simply to the Left. The victory had been won under Gormley's Presidency. Cautious Areas claimed that their dedication to the strike had not been bettered: the Lancashire self-characterisation was typical – 'they had been as solid and as militant if not more so, than any other Area in the country.'[9]

Most fundamentally, there was the temptation to draw easy conclusions about the victory, about the tactics used, about the solidarity of the Union, about the receptivity of other key unions towards the miners' case, about the lack of preparation and, in the event, lack of resolve by the State. Understandably, but misleadingly, the old pessimism could be replaced by a spirit of easy optimism about the power of the NUM.

In particular, the Left within the NUM felt this buoyancy. The aftermath of the miners' victory saw conflict over the Heath Government's trade union legislation, in which its requirements were flouted with impunity and effectiveness. The presence of the Left on the NEC was strengthened further as McGahey became National Vice-President, and the Left faction came within striking distance of a NEC majority by the end of 1973. Moreover, Yorkshire with Scargill as President and Owen Briscoe as Secretary was firmly in the Left camp, and the weather vane Derbyshire Area elected Peter Heathfield as its General Secretary. But against this progress the NUM Left had had one major setback. The Union's wage negotiations in the winter of 1972–73 had run into a Government incomes policy beginning with a ninety day freeze and then in the Spring of 1973, a limit of £1 per week plus 4 per cent. Eventually, at the end of March 1973, miners balloted on the latest Coal Board offer, and in effect, on whether they would strike against Government policy. The winter had ended, the prospect was clearly not as encouraging as fifteen months earlier, yet so sharply had the NUM's image changed that a pro-strike majority was widely anticipated. In fact, the result, 143,006 to 82,361 against striking sharply demonstrated that the miners' 1972 victory would not lead automatically to an attack on Government pay policy.

Once again the cycle of tabling a demand, negotiations and then . . . began. At the 1973 NUM Conference McGahey emphasised the need to develop industrial action along the lines of the 1971–72 dispute, and pressure from the Left for an overtime ban began to mount. In Lancashire the demand was easily deflected in favour of support for the NEC majority's slower pace. But late in October 1973, a Special National Delegate Conference agreed on an immediate overtime ban. As yet there was no clear prospect of when or indeed whether a strike ballot would be held. The situation had some parallels with the problems facing the NUM a decade later. Daly travelled to Bolton and clarified the situation at a Lancashire Conference: 'There will be a ballot. We have always consulted the membership by means of ballot vote but the timing of the ballot will be decided by your elected representatives . . .'[10] Already in the early weeks of the overtime ban the Government, now in Phase III of its incomes policy, had entered the ring. Alongside attempts to rejig the Board's offer within the limits of the policy, ministers spoke of the political motivation of some miners' leaders. Their objective was clearly to separate off the bulk of miners who were assumed to want a wage settlement from the 'unrepresentative' Left officials and activists who could be portrayed as exploiting a frustration over wages for political purposes. The Government's concern was deepened by the international oil crisis, as the Six Day War provided the occasion, if not the cause, for a massive increase in oil prices. The general air of crisis was intensified as the Government introduced a mass of measures to deal with the fuel situation. Football fans found their mid-week matches switched from floodlit evenings to afternoons; more seriously, from January 1974 British industry was placed on a three-day week.

A majority of the NUM leadership stuck doggedly to its overtime ban despite pressure from the Left for a ballot. Eventually, on 24 January 1974 the NEC agreed to move to a strike ballot. They did so having considered reports that coal stocks at power stations were showing little decline. The NEC's decision was by the narrowest of margins – thirteen votes to twelve. In this vote the Left was backed by just enough others to win the day. Vincent was one of those crucial members. He said subsequently that he felt the overtime ban had not been effective enough.[11]

In the days prior to the ballot, Government ministers attempted to highlight the alleged political dimensions within the NUM strategy. One flashpoint was provided by a McGahey speech where he had suggested that if troops were employed, miners should explain their action to them. Earlier, when meeting the Prime

Minister, he had emphasised that he wished to see an end to the Government; the means remained unclear, but the style of his comments contrasted with Gormley's at that same meeting, that 'the Union were not in this exercise to bring the Government down . . . [but] to try to get real wages for the industry'.[12]

Following reports of McGahey's comments about miners and troops, cautious sections of the Labour movement moved to distance themselves. Many Labour MPs, including several NUM-sponsored ones from Lancashire and other Areas, signed an Early Day Motion critical of McGahey. Within the Lancashire Executive the response was sharp.

> Some members of the Executive Committee introduced this subject which was met with spontaneous reaction from the whole of the Executive Committee in relation to Michael McGahey's damaging statements on TV and in the Press . . . a continuance of these statements would certainly lose public support and could well lose the support of the miners for strike action in the forthcoming ballot.[13]

Appropriate telegrams were sent to McGahey in Scotland and to the Euston Road office. How far this action was encouraged by Gormley is unclear, but certainly in 1974, the tensions between Left and Right factions were much greater than two years earlier. Such divergencies were little evident in the ballot result. Almost 81 per cent nationally backed a strike with the traditional Left Areas producing pro-strike results of more then 90 per cent. But the right-wing coalfields showed strong support for the dispute; in Lancashire just over 82 per cent backed a strike.

Along with this solidarity, there went a firm desire by many Area officials to retain control of the strike in a way that had eluded them in 1972. One sharp incentive to do this was the belief that Heath would call an election, an expectation realised two days after the ballot result was announced. Even before the result was known, the Lancashire Executive had decided that strike activities would be more centralised than in 1972. Committees based on the Bolton office would co-operate with the Branches for picketing and financial activities.[14] Once the election was announced, then some within the Union argued that large-scale picketing would only enhance the Government's prospects of a victory. Gormley failed to persuade the NEC to suspend the strike for the election period, but the same NEC decided to restrict pickets to a maximum of six.[15] When the issue was discussed at a Lancashire Conference, Vincent emphasised electoral prudence, stating that: 'The Union did not wish to damage the Labour Party by losing votes . . . picketing must be kept to a minimum and avoid confrontation.'[16] Such caution contrasted with evidence of rank and file enthusiasm. The Sutton Manor Branch Secretary reported that '350 members had volunteered for picketing'. In general, 'several delegates were of the opinion that pickets were being discouraged by the Union.'[17]

Full-time officials emphasised the need to accept NEC policy; effectively, this happened. This second strike had a very different character. It was overshadowed by the election and the narrow, and to many unexpected, defeat of the Heath Government. This, and the succeeding settlement of the Miners' claim through the Labour Government removing the constraints imposed by its predecessor, gave another dramatic dimension to the myth of an all-powerful NUM. The Government had not been merely humiliated as in 1972, it had been evicted. But such a judgement uncritically embraced by people of very different political persuasions ignored difficult questions.

The Government had gambled on a 'Who Governs Britain?' election and had lost narrowly, the victim more of a significant upsurge in the Liberal vote than of any shift to the Party associated with the NUM. In fact, Labour in February 1974 showed little recovery from its failure in 1970. The NUM owed much more to the complex interrelationship between the electoral system and what was (in votes, but not in seats) more of a three horse race than had been the case since 1929. The election outcome could draw a veil over any scepticism about the NUM's strategy. Suppose the Heath Government had won again, what would the Union have done? Could picketing have been stepped up? Would it have been effective or would the attempt have found a State more prepared than in 1972, and now fortified with the legitimacy of an electoral victory? Would such a predicament have weakened the resolve of other unions to support the NUM? The questions were never raised after 1974 because success seemed to provide a sufficient answer.

The politics of the National Union after the 1974 dispute centred around a largely successful holding operation by the Right against an increasingly self-confident Left. Gormley used his political ability to push policies that he favoured and to kill off those that he disliked. He was aided by a NEC structure that over-represented the smaller and often more right-wing Areas, and by his adroit use of the individual ballot to undercut conference decisions. Yet there were more fundamental factors that went beyond personality and the utilisation of union structures. For five years after the 1974 strike, the NUM had to work with a Labour Government concerned most of the time with limiting wage demands. Until the Autumn of 1978, this strategy had a decisive level of acceptance within the TUC. Those within the NUM who wished to accept wage restraint could draw on a fund of loyalty to the Labour Party and the wider trade union movement. Moreover, if loyalty proved an inadequate emotion, a severely practical point could follow. Could the NUM hope to pursue successfully a wage demand against the policy of the Labour Government and without support from other unions? Equally, the Left's credibility had been based significantly on a wage-centred militancy; naturally it was hoped that this would widen into a more radical outlook incorporating other industrial and political questions. In 1974, there was little evidence that this was happening beyond a narrow but influential group of activists. Even the Left's credibility on the wages question could be vulnerable if its campaigns were blunted by appeals to loyalty, to practicality, and by strategies that sought other means to achieve wage improvements.

Leading figures in the Lancashire NUM wished to give unequivocal loyalty to the Labour Government. When Labour achieved a slim overall majority in the second 1974 election, some Lancashire MPs addressed a Delegate Conference in Bolton. One contributor, the sponsored Member, Michael McGuire, demonstrated an unquestioning commitment: 'It is a question of keeping a still tongue and letting Wilson and the Labour Government get on with what is going to be a very difficult task indeed.'[18]

By the time of the NUM National Conference at the start of July 1975, the Government was facing a severe financial crisis. On the first day the pound fell five cents against the dollar. In such a context and given the images of 1972 and 1974, media attention focused fiercely on the miners' wage debate. Lancashire had tabled a resolution having as its objective £100 in a 'normal working week' for the highest-paid underground grade. But the proposed time-scale was all important: 'Whilst realising that the figure may not be attainable in one round of negotiations . . . it should become priority number one in the Miners' Charter.' In contrast, a Yorkshire resolution demanded £100 a week as an immediate objective – a position attacked by Gormley in his Presidential Address as unrealistic and damaging to the Labour Government. The latter resolution was modified in the Conference's Business Management Committee, and was then passed unanimously; but the wages debate demonstrated the degree of acrimony and mistrust within the Union.[19] Lawrence Cunliffe, a Lancashire Executive member, was scathing about the Yorkshire 'ultimatum'. He responded to suggestions from the Left that only they could be effective in wage bargaining: 'I am sick and tired of us moderates being told we are weak and incipient [*sic*] and anaemic in our attitudes to this . . . there have been some distortions and lies told . . . about the moderates.'[20] In moving the modified Yorkshire resolution Arthur Scargill insisted that the removal of 'demands' for 'seeks' did not mean the abandonment of the resolution as presenting a feasible target. Yet his acknowledgement that the NEC would negotiate and consider any offer was seized on by Gormley:

> I am pleased to see Arthur has clarified the position and said it is the NEC's job to interpret Resolutions. I know what I was told in the Business Committee and I know what I was told in the NEC and I keep these things in my mind for future reference.[21]

This 'clarification' was quickly employed.

Within days of this exchange the Government and the TUC General Council had reached agreement on a counter-inflationary policy centred around a flat-rate maximum increase of £6 a week. When the Miners' National Executive discussed this policy, its defenders attempted to legitimise the proposal by pointing to a resolution submitted by the Union to the previous year's TUC. This had given 'full support' to TUC/Labour Party attempts to resolve Britain's economic problems. Against this, critics of the £6 policy pointed to a resolution passed at the 1974 National Conference opposing any form of incomes policy, and also to the immediately preceding adoption of the Yorkshire resolution on wages.

The response of those supporting Government policy, most notably Gormley and Lawrence Daly emphasised constitutional interpretations and wider loyalties. The blank cheque provided by the 1974 TUC resolution was 'the official policy' of the Union, no appeal against this having been made to Annual Conference. Moreover, the recent Scargill-Gormley exchange was now utilised. The £100 wage demand had been accepted on the basis that it 'would not tie the hands' of the NEC. £100 a week for faceworkers was a Union objective, but not necessarily an immediate one. Moreover, the target could not be considered divorced from the current economic context of high inflation and a sliding pound. The NUM should be prepared to consider a wider 'national interest', at any rate under a Labour Government.[22]

Pressure from left-wing NEC members for a Special Conference was rejected: instead, in the 'interests of democracy', there would be an individual ballot. The Lancashire Executive predictably recommended support for the £6 policy, although at a subsequent Area Conference, it was clear that one or two Branches were unhappy at the wage ceiling.[23] The national ballot demonstrated the pull of loyalties when a policy was endorsed by the TUC and a Labour Government. 60.5 per cent backed the £6 strategy; the Lancashire proportion was just a fraction less than the overall balance. Yet such restraint inevitably produced dissatisfaction even in loyalist Lancashire. By the end of the year one Branch delegate sounded a significant note of disillusion: 'In the light of the present inflation the claim now seems stupid . . . the NUM members [have] been used to bring about the defeat of the Tory Government in February 1974 and the members [are] now being used to keep the Labour Government in power.'[24] The £6 policy ended in May 1976 and was replaced by the Labour Government's Stage II policy – 5 per cent with a ceiling of £4. The Lancashire Area's Annual Conference was about to begin as negotiations ended between Government and TUC. The platform produced a statement of support for the General Council's new position on incomes, coupled with a demand that the Government act quickly on unemployment and prices.[25]

Delegates were divided in their responses. One emphasised that NUM officials both at Area and National levels 'over the years had stated they would not accept any incomes policy no matter what shade of Government was in power. Conference was now being asked to bulldoze through a policy which they had not had a chance to discuss . . . it was an incomes policy.'[26] Another critic prophesied all too accurately the terminus of such accommodations: 'This type of policy would certainly bring down the Labour Government and it would not do the trade unions any good.'[27] But others saw no alternative to acceptance. One speaker with a divided delegation simply said he 'would not go against a Labour Government'.[28] Nine Branches were prepared to accept the policy, nine were not. On a card vote, the Stage II formula was rejected narrowly by 104 votes to 100.

The remainder of the conference saw a succession of speakers – Lawrence Daly, Len Murray and Tony Benn all arguing for the Government's and the TUC's policy. The National Secretary argued that a 'Go it alone' policy would isolate the Miners within the Labour Movement. But the power of persuasion mattered less than the factional balance within the NUM's National Executive. At its May meeting a majority agreed to a ballot on the policy, backed by a recommendation for acceptance.[29] The result showed that the doubts expressed at the Lancashire Conference were widely shared. The majority in favour of the recommendation fell to 53.4 per cent; in Lancashire it was 56 per cent. But this vote was employed not just to determine the Union's position at a special TUC called to discuss the policy. It was also used by Gormley at the NUM's 1976 Conference as a means of ruling out of order all wages resolutions. Inevitably there was a lengthy wrangle over the President's ruling. Despite the Lancashire Conference vote, Vincent called on another source to legitimise his position: 'I voted in favour of the Chairman's ruling and other NEC members did purely and simply because the ballot in their Areas more or less guided them that road.'[30] Consistently the conference split 145 to 128 in favour of the Chair on the relevant votes. The strategies used by the Left and Right also came up for debate when attempts were made unsuccessfully by right-wing Areas to extend the requirement of a national ballot to any proposal for an overtime ban. Despite the NEC's recommendation to accept, this failed to gain a majority, let alone the 66 per cent needed for a rule change. Nevertheless a COSA delegate anticipated some of the emotions of 1984: 'They would prefer to be their own judges and interpreters of democracy . . . free . . . of the political pressures through the comparative secrecy of the ballot vote.'[31] Similarly, when the Left successfully moved a resolution deploring the NEC's failure to prosecute recent wage demands, Gormley presented a view of NUM constitutional practice that raised fundamental issues.

> Since these Rules were written, we have all accepted the fact that the final policy making body of this Union are the individual members . . . [(they]) decide how we should tackle things irrespective of the decision of this Conference . . . over the years the ballot vote has superseded quite a lot of the decisions made at the Conference. I hope we will always have that flexibility.[32]

Quite what that flexibility could involve would become apparent in the next eighteen months.

For the moment, Vincent had to deal with Lancashire critics who objected to his vote for a ballot at the May NEC meeting. He denied that he had broken any mandate from the Area Conference, although it was unclear whether his case rested on constitutional principle or practicality: 'You don't mandate an Executive Committee Member . . . he cannot deal with . . . new circumstances.' The situation had altered, other unions had declared their support for the policy. Any wage struggle would involve conflict with the Coal Board, the Government and other unions. It would be a hopeless campaign. 'What barmy general takes his troops onto that battlefield to win a bloody battle that you cannot win?'

In 1972 and 1974 T&GW drivers had refused to cross NUM picket lines into power stations 'on this occasion, they would not be in support'. He also raised the spectre of pit closures and gave a clear view of his own strategy. 'I was asking the Board for favours . . . the Board had made noises behind the scenes. Purely and simply we were involved in a battle at Sutton Manor and Agecroft to keep the pits alive and the Board were watching me, watching to see whether I was irresponsible and that is what finally made up my mind.' Perhaps the greatest argument for Vincent was time. More than three months had passed since the contested vote; as the Area President suggested, 'There was no point in debating the whole matter again'.[33]

Procedural manipulation, appeals to loyalty, fears of going it alone – all were used with some effect to constrain the NUM Left. But the sizeable anti-vote in the Stage II ballot showed that there was significant resentment at wage restraint. If something were not done, then the dam constructed by the NUM Right might well collapse. This pressure led to the most bitterly contested issue of the Gormley era – the end of the National Power Loading Agreement and the introduction of Area Incentive Schemes. This meant the destruction of a powerful unifying factor in the prelude to and through the 1972 and 1974 strikes. More than ever before, it made the rules and conventions of the Union a question of bitterly partisan debate. In this episode, Lancashire played a significant role.

During the countdown to the 1974 strike, a Coal Board member, Wilfred Miron, drafted a report for the Chairman, Derek Ezra, on the growth of Left influence in the NUM and on possible methods of reversing this. He painted a picture of a Union NEC dominated increasingly by 'Marxists'. Eric Clarke, Peter Heathfield and Emlyn Williams, all members of the Labour Party, would work with the 'known' communists, McGahey, Bill McLean and Dai Francis. Scargill was highlighted as the figure most likely to replace Gormley. In seeking methods of rolling back their influence, Miron saw long-term salvation in the introduction of automation, cutting back on the number of mines and reducing the proportion of NUM members. But in the shorter term his assessment emphasised the regrettable tendency for other NUM officials to swim with the tide of wage militancy. Instead, the economic objectives of the membership should be met in a way that would isolate the Left. 'One step in this direction would be to revert to some form of local pit or district incentives based upon Agreements negotiable locally which would restore to some of the traditionally moderate leaders the authority and influence they have increasingly lacked since the NPLA and the Third Wage Structure . . .'[34] A slim basis for exploring such a strategy could be found in the Wilberforce recommendations that had heralded the NUM's 1972 victory. One proposal was for a productivity deal to be worked out and paid from 1 September 1972. When Lawrence Daly spoke that May at Lancashire's Annual Conference, he distanced himself from the interest expressed by Gormley and Vincent. His grounds were equity – a shield against the tyranny of geology, and safety – an incentive scheme gave an incentive to disregard health and safety regulations.[35]

When Gormley spoke to the Lancashire delegates, a year later, he acknowledged that the Union had decided for a national scheme, but then poured cold water on this. It would have little impact: 'there is a big feeling at National level from some quarters, that we should get it down to the Areas.'[36] Vincent articulated a similar response after the 1974 dispute. Although any scheme suggested would be national, 'the Area would certainly benefit from a local productivity agreement.'[37] Although some Lancashire Branches had previously opposed any Area scheme, there were many in the coalfield who looked back to the years before 1966 when Lancashire had been near the top of the league in piece-rate payments. This sentiment became clear at the Area's 1974 Conference when an unambiguous resolution was passed: 'That the NEC seriously consider that collieries be given the chance to

negotiate locally . . . knowing local conditions for a local productivity bonus . . .'[38] This was accompanied by a wages resolution which
could be seen as pointing in the same direction. The recent actions were
seen as 'costly but necessary' but hopefully there could be a system
of wage settlements 'with the object of trying to avoid regular
confrontations.'[39]

At last, in September 1974, the NEC considered a scheme for
productivity payments, national in its percentages but with a local
basis for determining norms. The Lancashire Area regarded these
proposals as inadequate and a stormy National Conference produced
more negotiations.[40] A revised scheme was considered by the NEC
on 30 October and a fourteen to twelve majority decided on a ballot
with a recommendation to reject. Vincent was in the minority, and
on his return to Lancashire his support for the scheme was endorsed
by the Area Executive. They felt that the new proposals moved a
substantial way towards their preferred Area basis for any productivity deal. They included a pit/face scheme for faceworkers,
team-based payments for development workers, and a national
scheme for everyone else.[41]

Vincent argued that he was justified in opposing the NEC
recommendation. Other NEC members did so, and anyway Lancashire reserved the right to make its own decisions. However, a
Delegate Conference refused to make a substantive judgement;
instead the scheme would go back to the Branches for discussion.[42]
When delegates met again, they threw out the schemes, but added
an important rider – they wished to continue productivity discussions
with the NCB.[43] This qualification proved more significant than the
subsequent ballot result. In Lancashire, the percentage against the
scheme was 61.5 per cent an almost exact parallel with the national
picture.

Yet Lancashire continued as a proponent of such a scheme.
Appropriate resolutions were submitted to the 1976 and 1977
National Conferences. On the first occasion, the NEC voted to
oppose, and the resolution was withdrawn. But in 1977, the
supporters of Area Incentives launched a formidable challenge. A
slightly more forthright South Derbyshire resolution was debated,
arguing that if the National Union could not reach agreement on an
Area Scheme then individual Areas could go it alone. Lancashire's
resolution was not debated; instead, a member of the delegation
seconded the South Derbyshire proposal.[44] Against them were

aligned the traditional left-wing Areas plus some others unhappy about the divisive impact of such proposals. This debate took place, however, after two years of wage restraint and supporters of Area incentives were optimistic. They were disappointed. Delegates voted by a narrow margin of 137 to 134 against the South Derbyshire resolution. Gormley, his own preference well known debunked the verdict – 'it was a pretty fair draw'.[45]

Pro-incentive officials tried to discredit the decision. The Cokemen's Area had proved decisive in the vote, and Vincent, reporting to Lancashire, suggested that their opposition was somehow improper: 'They were the only NUM Area . . . which was currently enjoying a £3 per week incentive arrangement . . . known as an efficiency bonus . . . They were not miners . . . they would not have been affected by incentive arrangements for the miners.'[46] Although Gormley had already ruled at the July NEC that the Conference vote had to be accepted, he must have welcomed the immediate response of several NEC members.[47] They claimed that they were under pressure to 'go it alone'. This sentiment was articulated in the Lancashire Executive less than a fortnight after the National Conference decision. Vincent advised against a direct approach to the Coal Board: 'Our approach should be to the NEC advising them of the gut reaction of the membership in this Area.'[48] Accordingly, the Lancashire Executive decided to write to the NEC demanding an individual ballot. When an Area Conference met the next day, Vincent supplemented this with a suggestion that Branches should write similar letters.

Predictably, when the National Executive met at the beginning of September it had to deal with letters from several Areas on the Incentive question. Gormley ruled out of order a suggestion for a ballot vote to set against the Annual Conference decision.[49] But Vincent offered a way forward. He recalled that since 1974, several members of the NEC had been involved in a Working Party on incentives. The full Executive had overwhelmingly accepted its findings in May 1977, and more relevantly, the same verdict had been reached by that year's National Conference. This had not been in any self-conscious sense. Rather it occurred 'when they accepted without any comment Page 38 of the NEC Report . . .'[50] This 'tacit consent' could legitimise further negotiations on an incentive scheme. Six weeks later, a majority of the NEC accepted basic proposals for incentive payments and agreed to put the proposals, not to a Special Delegate Conference, but to an individual ballot.[51]

Some of the arguments promoting such a scheme were discussed by a previous opponent, Lawrence Daly, when he spoke at a Lancashire Weekend School. He acknowledged the experiences that fuelled opposition: 'The piece work jungle under which I and my father worked . . . apart from the incentive to ignore the safety and health regulations, it also gave coal companies the opportunity to set one coalfield against the other, one colliery against the other and man against man.' But set against these sentiments, Daly advanced industrial and political considerations. The NUM had backed the TUC's position on incomes, but within this there was scope for self-financing productivity schemes. If the Union spurned this opportunity, then miners' wages would stagnate and the achievements of the early seventies would be eroded. Moreover, a ballot had committed the NUM to the TUC's twelve month rule for wage settlements. That meant no deal before 1 March 1978 whereas the recent conference resolution on wages called for £135 for facemen by 1 November 1977. Unless the Incentive option was pursued, the consequences could be industrial isolation and political disaster.

> We might well lead ourselves into confrontation, not only with the Labour Government, but with the rest of the trade union movement, and that personally I am not prepared to do. It might suit some of our good friends, the ideologists of the Labour Left, but more so it will suit Margaret Thatcher and Sir Keith Joseph . . . despite all the difficulties of the last two or three years, a Labour Government is worth keeping in power.[52]

Whatever the supporting political arguments, the National Executive decision to ballot members precipitated a bitter row. The Kent Area took the issue to court arguing that the proposal was unconstitutional. The Annual Conference had made its decision and no Special Delegate Conference had provided the necessary authorisation for a ballot. The judicial decision controversially rejected the Kent claim. Rather, it held that a secret ballot 'is the very essence of the democratic process'.[53]

The verdict only hardened the acrimony, with Area Officials opposed to incentives producing leaflets and advertising in the press. This strategy was inevitably controversial: it became even more so when 55.75 per cent voted against the scheme. Predictably, the core of opposition came from coalfields traditionally antipathetic to such schemes. With 83 per cent voting 'No' in both Scotland and South Wales, no-one could claim credibly that such Area Officials were out of step with their own members. But rejection was guaranteed because in some coalfields favourable to incentives a sizeable minority voted 'No' – almost 40 per cent or over 10,000 votes in Nottinghamshire and in the smaller Lancashire coalfield, 3,377 or over 45 per cent rejected the scheme. The Government's incomes strategy seemed less secure; within the NUM it was a time for recrimination and perhaps for reading Machiavelli.

The NEC met and considered the result on 10 November. Vincent claimed, 'It was the worst meeting of any description that I have ever attended.'[54] Gormley immediately set the tone. Although later he would rule that the ballot result should be accepted, his initial comments helped to subvert its legitimacy: 'It was the dirtiest campaign that [has] ever been carried out in this Organisation . . . a politically motivated organised campaign to get the incentive scheme rejected.' He alleged that anti-incentive officials had blocked the distribution of material from Head Office and that in some coalfields where officials opposed the scheme, there were already incentive schemes at some pits.

This onslaught was followed by some declarations of unilateral action. Ken Toon from South Derbyshire informed the NEC that his Area had already approached the Coal Board for an Area scheme. Nottinghamshire and the Midlands wished to follow suit. Discussion also focused on the Yorkshire campaign against the scheme. Daly felt that Yorkshire's resources could distort the procedures of the National Union. 'He thought this Union was a democratic organisation but . . . people were doing just what they wanted according to the amount of money an Area had and the campaign they could mount'. Vincent acknowledged the effectiveness of a Yorkshire press advert but insisted that: 'It was . . . fraudulent . . . grossly inaccurate . . . and had led thousands of our members to vote against the incentive scheme because they thought it was a factual document.' A move to accept the ballot result 'without any other reservations' was defeated by fourteen votes to eight with two abstentions. Instead, acceptance was coupled with criticism of those who had campaigned for a 'No' vote in opposition to a NEC recommendation. Vincent found no difficulty in endorsing these strictures although he had justified such dissent at the time of the 1974 incentives ballot. Moreover, the NEC decided to leave discussion of Areas' requests to go it alone until the next meeting, a delay which could only encourage those who wished to go ahead.

The Lancashire Executive seized the opportunity, voting ten to two to seek permission at National level for an Area scheme on the grounds that this was already Area policy. Subsequently an Area Conference witnessed a rearguard action by a few delegates and Executive members against the introduction of an Area scheme.[55] Vincent justified the constitutionality of the request by reference to Rule Thirty Six of the National Union. 'The Area Executive Committee . . . shall act for the Union in all matters of a purely Area character . . . no Area shall have power to complete any such negotiations and enter into an agreement thereon without the previous approval of or under power delegated to them by the National Executive Committee.[56]

This interpretation was highly tendentious. The Lancashire President, Bernard Donaghy, looking back on the tortuous negotiations argued that the purpose of Rule Thirty Six had been not to license Area agreements but rather the opposite: 'Everybody . . . knew full well that the intention of that rule was to limit and restrict the spread of Area agreements and eventually have national agreements to cover all our members.'[57] But, in the heat of battle, the dubious understanding could be used as a constitutional justification. Moreover, it appeared that the Rule Thirty Six tactic had been considered for some time. The Lancashire resolution submitted to that year's National Conference had referred specifically to Areas being permitted to negotiate local incentives 'subject to the provisions of Rule Thirty Six'.[58] Vincent now claimed that Gormley had told him, presumably in the summer, that such a resolution was unnecessary, since such a request would fit within the existing rules.[59] If so, then clearly some Officials were already considering the possibility of local schemes, should a national shift to Area-based incentives prove impossible.

Some Lancashire Conference Delegates did speak out for acceptance of the ballot result or for further exploration of the national scheme. But the weight of argument favoured an Area scheme. Some emphases foreshadowed later animosities and controversies. The St Helens Craftsmen Delegate took a cavalier attitude on the ballot. Alleged misrepresentation in the campaign provided a justification, for 'if rejection of the ballot had been moved, it would have been seconded and carried by the NEC and this would have given the National President a way out of their present dilemma'.[60] The Pendlebury spokesman presented a dichotomy that would reappear more than six years later: on the one side the ordinary miner, on the other, the politically motivated official. 'It was the men at the pit who had suffered, not Arthur Scargill, by the division in the Union.'[61]

In Lancashire, insecurity about the future could never be absent and Vincent bolstered his support for Area incentives by characterising them as a defence against pit closures. Production must be raised, otherwise the consequences could be grim: 'If the position [is] not rectified next year, the Board would start looking at grossly uneconomic pits . . . there [are] three pits in Lancashire which lost a lot of money last year and were expected to make heavy losses again this year . . .' Although the coalfield was only a small part of the industry, it could benefit from any improvement, since if we had an incentive scheme which would increase production and Lancashire was making a contribution . . . it would keep the wolf away from the door.'[62] This prudential argument was typical of Area strategy marked as it was by pragmatic responses to the years of decline. What was less clear was how far Officials such as Vincent really believed that stagnant productivity resulted from a lack of incentive. The Board's engineers believed that improvement should be pursued through increasing machine use and reliability. Arguably, the incentive strategy was much more of a political tactic to limit Left influence within the NUM – itself a persuasive argument for Vincent and several NEC colleagues.

Certainly the Lancashire Delegate Conference was persuaded, whether by considerations of productivity, job security, and higher wages at a time of restraint or traditional factional loyalties. The vote was decisive thirteen against three and at the December NEC meeting Vincent was in the fifteen to nine majority for Area schemes. In Lancashire the decision was acted on rapidly, but soon complaints were heard that the scheme was too demanding. Once the decision of principle had been made, the fine print began to be examined. Complaints were heard of 'norms and standard tasks that would make it difficult indeed to earn realistic bonuses.'[63] There was effectively an acknowledgement of past gullibility: 'The Management and the NCB generally were now painting a different picture than the utopia . . . they had presented a few weeks ago.'[64] But the issue was effectively settled and even the most resistant

Areas soon found themselves accepting that once some Areas had negotiated schemes, then standing aloof was not a viable option.

The devious route to a decision left a massive legacy of bitterness. Bernard Donaghy's belief that Rule Thirty Six had been misused led to his informing the Lancashire Executive that he was resigning the Presidency. He explained this in terms not normally associated with Lancastrian reactions to Gormley's regime. He said that: 'The National President . . . in his opinion had shown scant regard for the constitution of the Union by encouraging Areas to return to local agreements and in his opinion the National President had misused his power and debased the office he holds.'[65] This was a brief demonstration; early in 1978 Donaghy withdrew his resignation.

If there was criticism even in Lancashire, there was anger in Areas where incentives had been thoroughly opposed. These Areas had won at National Conference: perhaps to their own surprise they had triumphed in a national ballot. Such successes had counted for nothing. The Kent Area's unsuccessful legal action had produced judicial approval for the democratic credibility of an individual ballot; presumably any judge should be appalled by the subsequent flouting of the ballot verdict. So Yorkshire, South Wales and Kent returned to the courts in an attempt to prevent the NEC sanctioning Area schemes. Curiously the judge's verdict did not focus simply on whether the previous ballot decision ruled out such local initiatives. His observations went wider; the ballot lost its status as an ideal form of democratic procedure. 'The result of a ballot nationally conducted is not binding upon the National Executive Committee in using its power in between conferences. It may serve to persuade the Committee to take one action or another or to refrain from action, but it has no great force or significance.'[66] This episode had a seminal impact on the attitudes of the NUM activists. When the ballot issue was debated in the spring of 1984, it was easy to refer back to the autumn of 1977. Nottinghamshire and South Derbyshire, so insistent in 1984 on the sanctity of the ballot had flouted the earlier decision.

Such exchanges were symptomatic of a deeper problem. Although Gormley and his supporters were able to retain control of many key decisions, they were coming under increasing pressure. Normally the Right could just control the NEC but its domination over National Conference was not always so predictable. Moreover, the recourse to a national ballot favoured by Gormley might fail to produce the desired outcome when an issue such as incentives raised deep emotions about safety and cut throat competition. Moreover, it was not just a question of arithmetic. Several Left officials were forceful and articulate; they could sometimes persuade doubters. Gormley's supporters included many diligent officials, but they lacked the style of Scargill, McGahey and several others on the Left. Whereas in the past the NUM's institutions had tended to make mutually reinforcing decisions, now the scope for discords was greater. Thus, the attraction of procedural manipulation grew. Union constitutions inevitably contain ambiguities which can be exploited in factional manoeuvres. Within the NUM in the late seventies, the tactic took an especially acute form. Winners and losers each cited appropriate sections of the Rule Book and added their own interpretation. In all of this Vincent as a vocal member of the NEC's Right played a significant role. The Lancashire connection suggested a close relationship with Gormley, not least in the eyes of the NEC Left. Certainly Vincent's verdicts on procedural and policy issues were highly flavoured by factional antipathies and were relayed to largely sympathetic audiences in his own Area.

The incentives imbroglio not only heightened factional rivalries and eroded confidence in the Union's procedures, increasingly it was seen by many as fracturing the solidarity of the early seventies. Clearly the Incentive Scheme produced sizeable discrepancies in wages between and within coalfields. Many in 1984 argued that the Union's problems owed much to the Incentive Scheme and therefore could be blamed on the NUM officials who had plotted its introduction.

In fact the issue is complex. It would be simplistic to suggest any direct relationship between high bonus earnings and expectations – and industrial quiescence. This has not been the uniform experience in other industries and cannot account either for the pattern of local militancy in the NUM pre 1966 nor the varying degrees of enthusiasm with which pits entered the 1984 struggle. The introduction of the scheme lessened the likelihood of deep and widespread anger over wages, but it did not initiate such a development. It was one response to a situation in which significant figures in the Union, the Coal Board and the Labour Government wished to wrest the initiative from the NUM Left. The Government's incomes policy provided both the need and the opportunity. The latter flowed from a widespread desire to give the Government the benefit of the doubt and to avoid further strikes – if only some other basis for increases be achieved. The logic of this predicament signposted some sort of incentive scheme. Officials such as Vincent welcomed this; it fitted with their assessment of internal Union politics, their wider political expectations, and Area concern about the levelling impact of the National Power Loading Agreement.

Whatever strength the NUM possessed was the result of creative construction to offset the industry's endemic sectionalism. The Incentive Scheme did not inaugurate such sectionalism, but it removed a defence, one moreover of particular significance entered as it was around the central preoccupation with wages. But the NUM Left had already begun to discover the limits of a strategy centred around wage campaigns. The problems were increasingly evident before the events of late 1977. But if the wage agitations represented an increasingly unpromising prospect for the Union's Left, what other issues offered themselves as bases for mobilisation?

Notes

1   Interview, Pendlebury NUM.
2   S. Vincent interview.
3   NWA Executive, 9 October 1972.
4   For summing up see Allen, *The Militancy of British Miners*, pp. 174–5.
5   *Ibid.* pp. 165–6.
6   NWA Special Executive, 14 January 1972.
7   NWA Conference, 5 February 1972.
8   NWA Special Conference, 21 February 1972.
9   NWA Executive, 31 July 1972. A response to a left inspired proposal for reform of the NUM's structure.
10 NWA Conference, 17 November 1973.
11 NWA Special Conference, 26 January 1974.
12 NWA Executive, 6 December 1973 including Vincent's report of NEC meeting with Heath and other Ministers on 28 November.
13 NWA Executive, 29 January 1974.
14 *Ibid.*
15 NWA Special Conference, 9 February 1974, includes Vincent's report on the previous day's NEC Meeting.
16 *Ibid.*
17 *Ibid.*
18 NWA Conference, 19 October 1974.
19 For debate see NUM Annual Conference 1975, pp. 394–409.
20 *Ibid* p. 400.
21 *Ibid.* p. 408.
22 NUM NEC, 17 January 1975.
23 NWA Executive, 21 July 1975; Conference, 16 August 1975.

24 NWA Conference, 13 December 1975 (Ashton and Haydock Craftsmen Delegate).

25 NWA Executive, 5 May 1976 had agreed Vincent prepare a statement for the Annual Lancashire Conference, supportive of the Government/TUC policy. This was read aloud to delegates at the Conference. See Report.

26 *Ibid.* (Golborne Delegate).

27 *Ibid.* (Ashton and Haydock Craftsmen Delegate).

28 *Ibid.* (Plank Lane Delegate).

29 NUM NEC, 13 May 1976.

30 NWA Executive, 29 July 1976 contains Vincent's report on the pre-Conference NEC meeting. For Vincent's statement see NUM Annual Conference 1976, p. 302.

31 *Ibid.* p. 467.

32 *Ibid.* p. 484.

33 NWA Conference, 21 August 1976.

34 Much of the document is to be found in Jonathan Winterton and Ruth Winterton, *Coal, crisis and conflict: The 1984–85 miners' strike in Yorkshire* (Manchester University Press, 1989), pp. 10–11.

35 NWA Annual Conference, May 1972.

36 NWA Annual Conference, May 1973.

37 NWA Conference, 20 April 1974.

38 Resolution from Sutton Manor Branch, NWA Annual Conference, May 1976.

39 NWA Composite Resolution on Wages. Original resolutions from Ashton and Haydock Craftsmen and Leigh Craftsmen.

40 NWA Executive, 19 September 1974. The Yorkshire Delegation walked out of the Special National Conference on 26 September after their demand for a vote on the agreement was ruled out of order. See also contributions of Vincent and Donaghy to that Conference, pp. 28–9 and p. 35 of the Report.

41 See NWA Special Executive, 31 October 1974.

42 NWA Conference, 2 November 1974.

43 NWA Conference, 11 November 1974.

44 NUM Annual Conference 1977, pp. 414–15 (Toon); seconded on p. 416 by J. Roberts (North Western Area). For the opposing view see the South Wales Resolution moved by Des Dutfield, p. 416, ending 'it believes that the reintroduction of the piecework system would destroy the unity in the union which the day wage system has created'.

45 *Ibid.* p. 422.

46 NWA Conference, 16 July 1977.

47 NUM NEC, 14 July 1977.

48 NWA Executive, 15 July 1977.

49 NUM NEC, 1 September 1977.

50 See Vincent's report back to NWA Executive, 13 September 1977. Evidence for tacit consent is sparse in the 1977 NUM Annual Conference Report. The NEC's Report was accepted by Delegates at p. 483; earlier at p. 427 when dealing with the relevant pages, Gormley is cited as saying,

'Page 36? 37? I take it you are accepting 38, 39?'
51   NUM NEC, 13 October 1977.
52   NWA Weekend School, 15 October 1977.
53   See Allen, *ibid.* pp. 276–7.
54   Vincent at NWA Executive, 11 November 1977 for a right-wing view of the proceedings: NUM NEC, 10 November, for the formal decision.
55   NWA Executive, 11 November 1977 and Conference, 19 November 1977.
56   See *National Union of Mineworkers Rules, Model Rules, Standing Orders.*
57   See his Presidential Address to NWA Annual Conference, May 1978.
58   Text NWA Executive, 11 November 1977.
59   NWA Conference, 19 November 1977.
60   *Ibid.*
61   *Ibid.*
62   *Ibid.*
63   NWA Conference, 17 December 1977 (Hapton Valley Delegate).
64   *Ibid.* (Pendlebury Delegate).
65   NWA Executive, 13 December 1977.
66   Allen, *The Militancy of British Miners*, pp. 280–1.

4

An unsolved problem: pit closures, 1968–81

The Left within the National Union were influenced heavily by the mass closures of the 60s and by the passivity of the dominant leadership; but significantly the impact of the Left on the Union decisions never came through campaigning against closures. Instead, the lift-off came initially on the surface hours question and then on wages. Neither the NUM Left nor the Union as a whole managed to formulate an effective strategy on the closure question.

In the 1960s the Union's opposition to closures had never passed beyond attempts to influence Government policy through representations by National Officials – a strategy that produced little amendment of Government policy. The possibility of effective industrial action against closure seemed utopian. Such a tactic would be likely to facilitate the run down of the industry. Several Officials seemed to accept the necessity for uneconomic pits to be closed. In 1968 a Kent resolution proposing opposition to any closure, except on grounds of exhaustion, was defeated at the Annual Conference after Paynter had suggested that it was at odds with a previous decision to seek a slow down in the closure programme. Moreover, the National General Secretary claimed that such a policy would not be acceptable in all Areas. 'That kind of policy is unlikely to be operated in a large number of coalfields – a large part of this Trade Union organisation – and that does not make for unity.'[1]

Nevertheless in the changing energy situation of the early seventies and with the Union recovering its self-confidence, policy on closures shifted, on paper at least, to a firmer position. In 1972, the National Conference, in passing a wide-ranging Durham resolution on fuel policy, declared opposition to closures 'resulting

from reasons other than exhaustion of seams or safety'.[2] This
declaration was contemporaneous with the development of a new
method of considering closure candidates, the Colliery Review
Procedure, another legacy of the 1972 strike settlement. Increasingly
it became clear that this procedure offered no effective protection
for miners if the Board were committed to closing a pit. Machinery
introduced after a successful strike still left the last word with the
Board. The only worthwhile safeguard would come from an
informed and effective Union.

The obstacles to such solidarity were all too obvious. Once a
prospective closure was identified, then the threat was localised.
Arguments about sympathetic action could be met by doubt that a
principle was involved after all (anyone could have a transfer); belief
that closure was inevitable (pits close all the time, don't they?), or
perhaps more surreptitiously, thank God, it isn't here. The
butchery of the sixties left not just anger but also pessimism and a
feeling that on closures the Board would get its way; it always did
and therefore why risk a secure pit? Would they do it for you?

Such sentiments were not killed by the strike successes of the
early seventies. In the Lancashire coalfield, with the number of pits
down to nine, Area Officials opted for collaboration with the Board
to stabilise employment. The strategy was facilitated arguably by
the close relationship between Gormley and the Board Chairman,
Derek Ezra – the celebrated Derek and Joe act. Perhaps one
consequence of this was that Lancashire became recognised within
the Board as a place where closures should be avoided if possible.
Nevertheless, the spectre of further closures was never far from
Lancashire Area discussions in the seventies. How could it be
otherwise, given the experience of the previous decade? Slowly the
question of a policy on closures came increasingly to preoccupy the
National Union, until it became the dominant issue. How did
Lancashire respond to the cases taken up by the National Union in
the light of changing expectations within the Area?

The early months of 1976 offered a stark demonstration of the
difficulties in developing concerted action on the closure issue. As
long ago as March 1975, the Union had decided to appeal against the
Board's proposal to close Langwith Colliery in North Derbyshire
on the grounds that its reserves were thin and dirty and that
extraction would be uneconomical. The issue had dragged on, with
the Board refusing to reconsider its position, until the NEC's

January 1976 meeting took a significant decision. Already the Derbyshire Area had imposed an overtime ban; now the NEC decided on a further meeting between the National Officials and the Board, but if this failed to produce a shift in the Board's attitude then there should be a national overtime ban. This resolution, passed by eighteen to seven, was moved by Vincent.[3]

When the NEC met again in February, it was clear that the Board was still refusing to test the workability of reserves; some within the NEC pushed for the implementation of the overtime ban, but others acknowledged the relevance of economic factors – 'the Union could not logically insist on the production of coal at any price.'[4] Vincent's own position looked back to the sixties and forward to the implications of a Langwith closure: 'If they close a profitable colliery like Langwith, something of a similar nature could happen in Lancashire at some of our pits that have been making losses . . . if this Union had made a stand against pit closures, especially in the 1960s we would have had a far bigger industry today.' But how to develop effective action? That remained the problem. Vincent suggested a resolution that the issue of an overtime ban be the subject of a Branch vote. This was ruled out of order by Gormley who was clearly unsympathetic to any action. Similarly McGahey was sceptical; he did not think that they could carry an overtime ban in Scotland in connection with Langwith . . . they having had many pit closures in their Area which they had dealt with themselves.[5] Nevertheless he agreed to recommend a ban if the NEC agreed on one. They did by the thinnest of margins eleven to ten with McGahey amongst the two abstentions. Moreover, two absentees would have been predictable opponents of such action.[6] The result did not produce unity 'After this decision there was uproar. Many of the ten who had voted against said it was impossible to implement such a decision.'[7] On this issue Vincent stood with the Left. He returned to Lancashire and in a lengthy Executive meeting persuaded his colleagues to support his stand. Indeed, the Executive criticised Gormley's anti-ban public statement and resolved that when Lancashire Branches met in Conference, they could not decide *whether* to implement the ban, only *how* to do it.

There were two such meetings, the second, on the day the ban was due to start faced evidence of disunity within the NUM.[8] The Nottinghamshire Area President had opposed the ban and the Nottinghamshire Area Council had rejected implementation by 150 votes to 105. Nevertheless some Nottinghamshire pits had accepted the instruction. From Durham too there was a report of opposition to the ban. Vincent appealed for Lancashire to stand solidly behind NEC policy, and support was given by thirteen votes to five. But increasingly, evidence of opposition to the ban produced a special NEC on the fourth day of its supposed implementation. This was called by Gormley on the grounds that there had been widespread criticism of the ban. The National President suggested that the vote for a ban had been fortuitous – 'a small majority and certain members had been absent and others had abstained.' He also had another reason for reconsideration. The Secretary of State for Energy, Tony Benn, had asked whether the action could be reconsidered, since the following day discussion would be held with the Electricity Boards in an attempt to raise their coal burn. Gormley would not represent the NUM at the discussions unless the ban was lifted. An attempt to retain a commitment to the action after further negotiations was defeated; instead it was decided to end the action and ballot the membership, asking if they accepted this abandonment. The ballot had a relatively low turnout. The problem of mobilising support on this issue, the fact that the ban had been called off, and the NEC recommendation, combined to give a 61 to 39 per cent vote for no action. Only Yorkshire, Scotland, South Wales and Kent – the heartlands of the Left – demonstrated a readiness to fight on. In Lancashire the position of its NEC representative and the decisions of its Conference and Executive were not reflected in the ballot vote – only just over 30 per cent supported action. The Lancashire miners were not ready to see industrial action to save a specific pit as the defence of an important principle.

The NEC minutes for the meeting that had called off the action included a sobering presentation of the gap between formal Union policy and effective action. Defenders of the ban pointed to the Durham resolution of 1972 as a justification of their strategy. Opponents highlighted the reality 'Many closures had taken place since 1972 by agreement in the Areas, and the decision of the Annual Conference had virtually gone by default. Obviously decisions had to be taken in the light of reality including economics.'[9] The ballot result and such an assessment placed the hopes of solidarity in a sombre perspective. Vincent had told Lancashire delegates, 'the Union should show some teeth and make a stand somewhere against pit closures.'[10] but the fiasco of the overtime ban only illuminated the continuing problem. Jim Lord of Agecroft might say, 'today it was Langwith and tomorrow it could be Agecroft, Sutton Manor, Hapton Valley and Cronton.'[11] but there was a yawning gap between rhetoric and reality. This point was underlined when the 1976 National Conference debated the closure question in the context of a composite resolution reaffirming the 1972 decision and asking the NEC to provide guidelines for Areas facing closures.[12] Peter Heathfield, obviously chastened by the Langwith experience, was sceptical about the NEC's resolve: 'Pass the resolution but it is your vigilance that will determine whether you are sold down the river like the miners at Langwith.'[13]

The next closure case to become a national concern provided an even less satisfactory outcome than Langwith. Teversal in the Nottinghamshire Area first became the subject of discussion late in 1977 – once again ostensibly on account of the difficulty in developing reserves. The case worked its way through the machinery, and it was early 1979 before the Coal Board confirmed closure. The NEC decided that rather than a national ballot, only the Nottinghamshire Area should be balloted on industrial action. Vincent suggested to a Lancashire Conference that this indicated an underlying pessimism about the result of any national ballot. He also suggested that pits could be safeguarded more effectively by judicious interventions at Area level.[14]

When the Nottinghamshire miners voted by almost three to one against action to defend Teversal, the reaction in Lancashire was bleak: 'It would give the Board license to do what they wanted in connection with pit closures.'[15] Despite the concern within the NUM, until 1979 the Board was concerned with lifting production. Although Langwith and Teversal were indications of future problems, the reduction in capacity was below the two million tons per year envisaged in that widely quoted 1974 document, *Plan for Coal*. But just as production rose, the world of the seventies collapsed. Industrial recession on a scale not seen since the inter-war years became the new environment for an industry faced also by a new Conservative Government ideologically hostile to the public sector.

By mid–1980 NUM officials were increasingly suspicious about the Board's intentions. Vincent reported to a Lancashire Conference on a NEC/NCB meeting: 'I don't think there was one person present at the meeting . . . who did not think that the NCB had a plan for closures that they would not reveal.'[16] The immediate context was the Government's introduction of a Coal Industry Bill designed to make the industry self-supporting by 1983/84. When Lancashire delegates discussed the threat, a recurrent problem was highlighted – the carrot of redundancy payments. Set against this was the warning by one delegate that 'this Government is closing in on us.'[17]

Stocks were mounting at the pits; by that autumn the Board claimed the Lancashire level stood at 1.8 million tons. Given the recession, it was reckoned this could double in the fiscal year 1981/82. When Lancashire Officials met the Area Director at a Colliery Review meeting that October, they heard demands for cost reductions through natural wastage and early retirement.[18] The storm cones were already hoisted at Hapton Valley where the Board's 'optimistic' scenario envisaged jobs cut from 490 to 280 within eighteen months. The Area Director cited Agecroft and Sutton Manor as pits where sales had dwindled to practically nothing, and argued that continuing heavy losses at the latter pit blocked any programme for long term investment. The Cronton Branch Secretary, John Hensby, summed up the frustrations of 1980: 'We are going to have to fight like hell to maintain jobs.'[20]

This growing sense of foreboding was the prelude to the celebrated meeting of 10 February 1981. The parameters laid down by the Coal Industry Bill pushed the Government to a target of four million tons cut in capacity for 1981/82, well above the rate in previous years. Suspicions fuelled by the tightening of the screw locally led to this meeting between the Board and all three mining unions. The broad outline of cutbacks was revealed with Ezra, under pressure, acknowledging a target of 'twenty to fifty pits' over the next five years. The result, Vincent informed his Area Conference, was dramatic: 'Within ten minutes you could have cut the air with a knife. It was the most rumbustious meeting that I have ever attended. There was shouting and threats being bandied about the room.'[21]

The details were provided six days after the national confrontation, when the NUM officials met the Western Area Director. He said the Board had imposed a reduction of about 600,000 tonnes for 1981/82. Geological difficulties seemed to indicate the inevitable closure of Hapton Valley, and if there was no economic revival then an equivalent cut could well be needed in 1982/83. Moreover, hard choices had to be made about the employment of the sparse capital available. The Board's prognosis was stark. Apart from the Hapton Valley problems, there was a more fundamental threat: 'There are several pits in Lancashire which will have to improve this year if they are to stay in business in future years.' The following day, the Lancashire Executive supported any forthcoming call for a national strike and anticipated a strenuous campaign to achieve the appropriate result in a national ballot.[22] But, as in 1969 and 1970, elsewhere responses were moving ahead of the constitutional timetable. By the time the Lancashire Executive met, half of South Wales coalfield had stopped work; Kent stopped that day, and were followed next day by Scotland. There were soon 10,000 Yorkshire miners out. The picketing was beginning to spread; the prospects for a near-complete shutdown before any national ballot became clear.

In this crisis the government acted; a meeting with the Board and the mining unions was brought forward. The Minister for Energy pledged fidelity to the Plan for Coal, suggested some relaxation of financial parameters for the Board and acknowledged the need to cut coke imports. The NCB Chairman agreed to withdraw the closure proposals. Superficially it could seem like 1972 and 1974 all over again; the Miners had flexed their muscles, even this tough government had climbed down – and at a time when trade union successes were sparse.[23]

Strikers were divided by the turnaround. Some immediately returned to work; those more sceptical of Government promises remained out. Their doubts were expressed at the following day's NEC where eight members opposed a resolution welcoming victory for NUM policy and commonsense and instructing strikers to return to work. Vincent was amongst the fifteen voting in favour and confessed himself 'astounded' by the opposition.[24]

Although some scepticism was expressed in Lancashire, generally the mood was buoyant. Instead of discussing a pending strike, conference delegates could celebrate an apparent victory. This could be given a partisan gloss. It was one more example of Gormley, the master tactician, employing a left-wing mobilisation to achieve his own objective. 'Whatever the Left and other people keep saying about this fellow he does a tremendous job . . . Joe can take them to market and sell them any time.' The delegate's conclusion would be cruelly undermined 'the Tory Government have been shown to be paper tigers.'[25] Disillusion soon came. Within three months, the Lancashire President, Bernard Donaghy, was making a telling comparison with Red Friday in 1925 'Our fate is still uncertain. It wouldn't be the first time in our history that a Conservative Government appeared to surrender and later resumed its onslaught.'[26]

February 1981 settled nothing for the NUM. Perhaps in retrospect it could seem the great lost opportunity for the Union to defend jobs, although it remained questionable whether the unofficial stoppages would have been the prelude to a favourable verdict in a national ballot. The reality behind the rhetoric had not been tested but what is clear is that, for the moment, the leadership in Lancashire and several other coalfields were prepared to accept what was on offer. Its irrelevance was soon apparent; by June 1982, fifteen of the twenty-three pits in the immediate list had closed, usually with Branch acquiescence encouraged by redundancy terms. The Western Area Director had made a significant comment at the February meeting: 'I preferred the 'salami' technique when dealing with economic and social problems – as a slice at a time improves the digestion.'[27] and, of course, erodes the prospect of collective resistance. As yet the Union had no effective answer.

Notes

1   NUM Annual Conference 1968, p. 236. The text of the Kent resolution is on p. 233.
2   NUM Annual Conference 1972, p. 205.
3   NUM NEC, 8 January 1976.
4   NUM NEC, 12 February 1976.
5   This and the previous quotation from NWA Executive, 13 February 1976.
6   Ken Toon of South Derbyshire and Frank Smith of Leicestershire.
7   NWA Executive, 13 February 1976.
8   NUM Special Conference, 14 and 16 February 1976.
9   NUM NEC, 19 February 1976. This time Toon and Smith were present.
10   NWA Special Conference, 14 February 1976.
11   NWA Conference, 14 February 1976.
12   The resolution reflected, amongst others, one tabled by Lancashire reaffirming previous policy on closures and instructing the NEC to carry out the policy. For the Composite see NUM Annual Conference 1976, p. 416. Seconded by a Lancashire Delegate, C. Davies of Parkside, pp. 418–19 and moved by Des Dutfield, pp. 417–18.

13 *Ibid.* p. 421.
14 NWA Executive, 15 February and Conference, 16 February 1979.
15 NWA Conference, 17 March 1979.
16 NWA Conference, 21 June 1980 on NEC/NCB meeting of 18 June.
17 *Ibid.* (Cronton Delegate).
18 NWA Executive, 3 November 1980, reporting on a Colliery Review Meeting of 27 October.
19 NWA Executive, 8 October 1980, Appendix A on Meeting with Board regarding proposals at Hapton Valley.
20 NWA Conference, 20 December 1980.
21 NWA Conference, 21 February 1981.
22 NWA Executive, 17 February 1981. See also NUM NEC, 12 February 1981.
23 For Gormley's view, see his *Battered Cherub*, ch. 10.
24 NUM NEC, 19 February 1981.
25 NWA Conference, 21 February 1981.
26 In his Presidential Address, NWA Annual Conference, May 1981.

5

Life without Joe

The 'victory' of February 1981 was Joe Gormley's swansong. He
had led the Union yet again in a crisis where it had seemed set to take
on, not only the Coal Board, but also the Government. In one sense,
his involvement was ironic, since he frequently attacked the NUM
Left for their underlying political motivations. They sought to use
the Union's industrial strength to bring about wider changes. This
strategy should be rejected: 'You are going to produce an ogre that
none of you will be able to control. You will produce something that
will destroy the Labour and Trade Union Movement in Britain.'[1]
This viewpoint was echoed readily within the Lancashire NUM. It
was hardly surprising that, shortly before his retirement, Gormley
acknowledged the significance of the Area in his career. 'He was
proud of the Lancashire miners who went stamping around the
country to propagate his election campaign; he was proud of the fact
that the Lancashire Area had always supported his point of view.'[2]
The Left within the NUM believed that the relationship was
significant for factional successes and failures within the Union. As
Vincent noted at Gormley's last National Conference, 'Emlyn
Williams on Friday said, "If Joe wants to get anything through, he
starts talking to Sid and there is a vote and that is it, and it has gone:
pull the lever." '[3] Despite Vincent's disclaimer, there was a
significant underlying truth. During the Gormley years, Lancashire
was aligned at every level with the Right within the NUM. Vincent
had worked with men such as Les Storey of COSA, Len Clarke of
Nottinghamshire and Tommy Bartle of the Durham Mechanics to
organise the right wing faction on the National Executive. He had
regularly booked a room in a London pub to discuss policy on the
night before the monthly NEC meeting.[4] The dominance of the

Right had generally survived, despite the apparent boost given to its factional opponent by the successes of the early seventies.

Yet the Right's control at the end of the Gormley era was under severe pressure. The NEC majority depended on the support of small over represented Areas which might have a questionable future as viable units. Arguably there were long term developments – economic and political – in a coalfield as traditionally orthodox as Durham, which might produce a shift to the left. More generally the harsher climate of the Thatcher Government might not only provide the need for a more combative union, it might also exorcise recent complacency. The events of February 1981 could be interpreted as a significant contribution to such a radicalisation, but such a signpost was ambiguous. The crisis did not produce a more thorough radicalism within the NUM, whether on pit closures or any other issue.

Much more significance came from the fact that the Right's dominance owed much to Gormley's guile. He overshadowed his supporters; but on the substantive issues, articulate representatives from the Left dominated debates within the Union.

Gormley's dominance had one significant negative legacy for the Right. There was no widely agreed heir-apparent. Ironically one of Gormley's internal reforms had helped to settle that question for the Left. In 1978 the National Annual Conference had passed a rule-change preventing anyone running for a full-time official's post over the age of fifty-five. By the time Gormley announced his retirement, one credible Left candidate, Michael McGahey was excluded. The mantle fell on the much younger Arthur Scargill.[5]

Any right wing candidate would face therefore an Official from the Union's largest Area, someone who was widely known and whose rise to prominence was identified closely with the victories of 1972 and 1974. He was an orator in a long standing working class tradition – emotional, humorous; he made a virtue of principled stands, as against the pragmatism and the cosy relationship with the NCB that he presented as hallmarks of the Gormley era. The NUM Right managed to convert a difficult situation into a shambles. An initial choice, Trevor Bell, of COSA was handicapped by memories of Sidney Ford's Presidency. The only previous National President from the white collar section had presided over the mass closures of the sixties. Moreover, Bell could be labelled, perhaps unfairly, as not really a miner. After vacillation a second Right candidate emerged – Ray Chadburn, the Nottinghamshire Area President, but the prospect of a straight contest between candidates from the NUM's two largest Areas never materialised. Bell was already committed to his candidacy and Chadburn even failed to secure the formal backing of his own Area. The Notts Area Council preferred Scargill by fifteen votes to nine.[6]

Despite Lancashire's association with the Right, it seems that the prospects of a formal resolution backing either Bell or Chadburn were dubious. Indeed, there seems to have been some indication that Scargill could secure significant support at some pits. Many Lancashire miners were prepared perhaps to ignore traditional Area loyalties and back a well-known and credible candidate. When the time for formal nominations came in October 1981, Cronton Branch submitted one for Scargill. In response the Area leadership adopted a blocking strategy. When the circular requesting nominations arrived from National Office, it was not circulated to the Branches; rather it was considered the 'property' of the Lancashire Executive. This policy allowed the Cronton letter to be stigmatised as 'jumping the gun'; moreover, its nomination was for an outsider. When the Executive met, Vincent appealed to coalfield chauvinism 'The Area and its membership should not be placed in the position of being second class citizens within the National Union of Mineworkers.'[7] The Executive agreed overwhelmingly to nominate the Lancashire President and Agent, Bernard Donaghy. Despite criticism by the Cronton Delegate, the nomination was backed strongly by the subsequent Lancashire Conference.[8]

Donaghy's brief campaign included a broadsheet, *The Lancashire Miner*, written largely by Vincent. The advocacy of Donaghy's merits was overshadowed by an uninhibited attack on Scargill. Under the heading 'A Catalogue of Disaster', longstanding controversies were revived – the bitter arguments over safety and the incentive scheme, the spectre of Yorkshire dominance of a national union in which smaller Areas would lose their autonomy, the claim that Scargill's politics were inflexible and divisive. This onslaught was produced without Donaghy's knowledge; the Lancashire candidate was utilised as a stalking horse in an attempt to pay off some factional scores. Even the fixing of the printing contract for *The Lancashire Miner* was controversial. It was arranged with a North Wales firm; the intermediary was Stewart Oliver, the Coal Board Western Area's Press Officer.[9] The discovery of this transaction was a bonus for the Scargill camp; as Vincent acknowledged, 'it developed into a dirty campaign.'[10] The contest had a decisive result. At one end, Scargill, 138,803 (70·3 per cent); at the other, Donaghy 6,442 (3·3 per cent). For Lancashire, it was far removed from the heady days of 1971. The Area Leadership had to come to terms with a new regime.

The 1982 National Conference at Inverness saw the Left firmly in command and the Right barely visible. Scargill's inaugural Presidential Address put down markers for the future, especially on pit closures. The NUM leadership's record on this during the sixties was stigmatised as 'abysmal'. February 1981 had demonstrated that actions could be effective, but since then, there had been a closure programme by stealth.[11] At Inverness Vincent swam with the tide: 'the right-wing majority had gone . . . I have decided if you can't beat them join them,'[12] but back in Bolton, he told his Area Executive that Scargill had bent the rules on three occasions![13]

Soon, resentments against the new National President and his supporters focused on a specific and a much more significant question. The lengthy dispute in the National Health Service had already produced one-day sympathy strikes in Lancashire pits.

When the NUM delegation to the 1982 TUC discussed the TUC Day of Action on the dispute, proposed for 22 September, they gave unanimous support. The procedure was complex. The delegation included the Union's National Executive which effectively took the crucial decision. The resulting circular called on all members to stop work on the Day of Action. This was amplified in a second document co-ordinating action with NACODS (the National Association of Colliery Overmen, Deputies and Shotfirers) who had also agreed to stop work.[14]

When the NEC met in mid September some members criticised the absence of a ballot. The Lancashire Executive had previously backed the national decision,[15] but a Delegate Conference provided an occasion for abundant criticism. Several speakers focused on the lack of a national ballot, with Vincent responding disingenuously, 'No way do we want to ballot the membership on this particular issue because you will split the membership down the middle.'[16] Delegates argued that their members were complaining about the lack of consultation, although some Branches reported that they had balloted in favour of the strike. One speaker explicitly introduced the personality element 'It has been said by the membership . . . and

I quote, "Scargill's not getting me on strike without a vote."' But as the same speaker acknowledged the strike decision was not the unilateral act of the National President: 'It's Sid and others who have taken this collective NEC decision to throw the Rule Book through the window.'[17] For some the individual ballot was the heart of democratic consultation. 'I don't believe in dictatorship whether it is the twenty seven men on the National Executive Committee or anyone else, the lads in the coalfield pay the Union for the right to ballot . . .'[18] The one-day stoppage went ahead, but the preceding controversy had illuminated the degree to which leading figures in at least one NUM Area were at odds with the new style.

Within weeks, the Left had the first significant setback since Scargill's election to the National Presidency. A national ballot for industrial action combined two issues – wages and pit closures. In Lancashire Branch delegates were critical of this combination and of the rapid introduction of an overtime ban.[19] The result of the ballot was a decisive rejection of strike action, although in Lancashire the pro-strike 44 per cent was greater than in many traditionally cautious coalfields. Post-mortems were overshadowed by an awareness that the result could encourage the Board to push for further closures. Vincent was scathing about the national campaign for a 'Yes' vote for industrial action. 'We had massive rallies all across the country which were like Nazi rallies . . .'[20]

Throughout 1983, the evidence mounted of a deteriorating situation – the 'No' vote over action to fight the Lewis-Merthyr Tymawr closure, the re-election of the Conservative Government with a greatly increased majority, the clear evidence in Lancashire that the Board wished to cut back further. In the midst of these pressures in September 1983, a Lancashire NUM Conference engaged in another bout of Scargill-bashing. This time a vote of censure was proposed.

When the National Executive met on 15 September, it had followed a decision on the need to campaign for membership support on closures, with a lengthy discussion, begun on Scargill's initiative, about recent press attacks on him. These included reports on comments allegedly made by him in Moscow; his supposed reactions to the shooting down of a South Korean airliner by the Soviet Union, and a letter to the Workers' Revolutionary Party newspaper, *Newsline*, in which he allegedly characterised Polish

Solidarity as 'an anti-Socialist organisation designed to bring down a Socialist Government'.

The NEC passed a resolution, drafted by McGahey, accepting Scargill's explanations and condemning the press campaign; but unanimity was achieved only with the insertion of a sentence emphasising the Union's commitment to 'freedom and human rights in every country in the world'.[21]

When Vincent reported back to Lancashire the result was a barrage of anti-Scargill comments from Conference delegates. Some reflected a simple political animus: 'The speech made by the National President in Moscow was considered by some members to imply that the members of this organisation were unpatriotic and had attacked the Prime Minister of the country . . .' This was supplemented by a Gormley style view of the NUM's role: 'The membership consider the National Union of Mineworkers as an Industrial Union, not a political wing of some far left political ideology . . .'[22] There was also concern about the National President's power – an emphasis more commonly heard in Lancashire since the retirement of Gormley: 'Arthur Scargill should be put in his place publicly so that the country would be aware that it was the membership of this Union that made the decisions, not Arthur Scargill.'[23] Demands came from the floor that Scargill be censured but this produced opposition. John Hensby a Scargill sympathiser, an Area Executive Member and the Cronton Secretary located the controversy in a wider context:

> We would falling into the Press and medias' hands once again . . . the National President was one of the first people to openly condemn the Polish action against the miners . . . it would be tragic to pass a vote of censure on the National President. It would be a far better idea to get back to the pits and rally the membership behind the leadership against pit closures.

Donaghy argued a more pragmatic case – a vote of censure was worthwhile only if carried overwhelmingly, and the press would still use it to damage the NUM. Such arguments, along with Vincent's unwillingness to push any censure, proved decisive, but the episode demonstrated more than any other the extent of suspicion and resentment amongst Lancashire Branch Officials towards the new national leadership. It offered little expectation of support for any militant action closely identified with that leadership.

As the industry's crisis was deepened, with the Union already pursuing an overtime ban, one last episode seemed to highlight the factional loyalties of the Lancashire leadership. Lawrence Daly announced his retirement as National General Secretary in November 1983. The Left candidate was already identified as the Derbyshire leader, Peter Heathfield. The Right faced a crisis. After its disastrous mismanagement of the National Presidential contest, there was no immediately credible nominee. Eventually, the North Yorkshire Agent, John Walsh, declared his intention of running, despite having no hope of a nomination from his own coalfield. So did Les Kelly, once employed in the Lancashire coalfield and now Branch Secretary at Point of Ayr Colliery on the North Wales Coast. Heathfield had an abundance of nominations; his two opponents had just three between them. One of these for Walsh came from Lancashire.

The initial decision was made by the Area Executive at its November meeting.[25] The next Delegate Conference was not held until after the deadline for nominations, but this did not prevent criticism of the Executive's pre-emptive strike.[26] The Cronton delegate continued the argument that had begun with the National Presidential nominations. Why had the Branches not been consulted? Vincent's response combined a characterisation of the factional tensions at the highest level with the time- honoured argument that an enforced timetable prevented a wider consultation:

> The election had been stage-managed to elect a person because he is suitable to the National President himself. The reason why nominations were not asked from Branches was because the circular sent from national level arrived in the office on the 16 November 1983. It only gave this Area three weeks in which to select a nominee. The closing date was . . . six days before this conference.

One Executive member, John Hensby, linked the decision with the 1981 nomination of Donaghy: 'On this occasion the Area President was not putting up for the job and the Area Secretary had to do something else.' In response, Vincent clarified the political choice: 'John Walsh is a common sense man, he is somebody who knows his own mind . . . it was no use being a tool or pawn in this Organisation, unless you have a mind of your own, you have got no chance.'[27]

Once the campaign began, it became clear that Walsh favoured a ballot on the current national overtime ban, a demand not adopted by the Lancashire Area. This dimension to Walsh's candidacy occasioned some debate at a later Delegate Conference, but overall his position proved to be attractive – whether because of dissatisfaction with the overtime ban, or a wish that Scargill should be balanced by a General Secretary of a different political persuasion. Heathfield shaded the election by 3,615 on the second count after Kelly had been eliminated and his votes redistributed.

Table 5.1   1984 Election for National General Secretary

	1st Count	2nd Count
Heathfield	70 154	74 186
Walsh	63 310	70 571
Kelly	13 547	Eliminated

Note: In Lancashire, Walsh achieved first place. Overall he managed this in ten Areas, Heathfield in eleven and Kelly just in his own coalfield.

Lancashire first-preference votes

Heathfield	1 701	35·0%
Walsh	2 242	46·1%
Kelly	919	18·9%

Note: The percentages can be compared with those in two other traditionally right wing coalfields, Nottinghamshire and Durham.

First-preference votes in three right-wing Areas

	Lancashire	Nottinghamshire	Durham
Heathfield	35·0%	41·4%	53·9%
Walsh	46·1%	51·9%	38·8%
Kelly	18·9%	6·7%	7·3%

Source: Adrian Campbell and Malcolm Warner, 'Changes in the balance of power in the British Mineworkers' Union. An analysis of national top-office elections, 1974–84', *British Journal of Industrial Relations*, 1985, p. 19.

Clearly the factors influencing voters' choices extended far beyond the political factionalism within the Union. Walsh's strong performance was based on a decent Yorkshire vote for a local candidate, whilst Kelly's relatively good Lancashire vote could reflect his own origins. But some political aspects were important. Heathfield had large leads in Left coalfields uncomplicated by crosscutting and local loyalties – Scotland, South Wales and Kent. Similarly, if these three traditionally right wing Areas are compared, the Durham vote is the odd one out – and Durham would stop work solidly in March 1984, unlike Nottinghamshire and Lancashire. Less dramatically, Heathfield's stronger performance in Nottinghamshire compared with Lancashire could reflect the fact that Heathfield's base lay next door to Nottinghamshire. Alternatively it could point to a divergence between these two coalfields. By the time of this contest, the Nottinghamshire Area leadership included a significant Left presence, a factor which could perhaps affect victory for an Official, but was less likely to be persuasive in a strike ballot held in fraught circumstances.

Lancashire stands out once again in this episode as an Area where many officials, both full-time and lay were suspicious of or downright hostile to the National leadership. In Lancashire there existed no equivalent of the recently elected Nottinghamshire General Secretary, Henry Richardson: the move to the left in Nottinghamshire had no parallel in Lancashire where John Hensby of Cronton often seemed an isolated figure. And in Durham too, so long a bastion of right-wing orthodoxy, there were signs of change. As the coalfield contracted, some large Lodges became more radical and relatively more influential. In 1983, Durham elected a left-wing rank and filer to the NEC, and more dramatically, the Durham Mechanics, a bastion of moderation, in that same year elected a new General Secretary, a radical, Billy Etherington. It seemed the NUM equivalent of a Sandinista elected to the United States Presidency. But in Lancashire, life without Joe showed little change. Vincent dominated the Area and sat on the NEC as he had done for over a decade. His outlook was shared by most who spoke at Area meetings. Against this continuity there stood a question. How many Lancashire miners outside this closed community had been influenced by Scargill's Presidential campaign and by the subsequent abortive mobilisation for strike action? In Lancashire any such sentiments had little purchase on the Union's formal decisions, but the initiation of a radical tactic from national level could evoke a response in the coalfield – a sequence of events that would produce a novel challenge for the Area Leadership.

In Lancashire, the crisis of February 1981 was soon followed by acceptance of the first pit closure for a decade. The end of mining at

Hapton Valley meant the shutting of the final pit in North East Lancashire. In the end there was little controversy. Many transferred to other Lancashire pits, especially Agecroft: forty-five men went to North Wales. It was a prelude to a deteriorating situation elsewhere in the county.

The problem was not just a matter of closure threats at individual pits. Over time some pits were experiencing substantial cuts in employment. In 1970/71 Agecroft had employed 1,770 men, a decade later it was down to 939, and by the start of the strike, another 100 had gone. Parsonage lost heavily as the implications of the Complex rationalisation became clear. Over the decade from 1972/73 employment was halved from an initial level of 960. After that, with operations now combined with these at Bickershaw, the Parsonage workforce declined further. In August 1980 the Area's membership stood at 9,100; in little more than two years the total had fallen by 1,400.

The lure of redundancy payments was a perennial problem. Officials faced persistent pressures from members, as Vincent acknowledged: 'We have men at every collicry . . . who are wanting to take advantage of the new Mineworker's Redundancy Payments Scheme and when he went . . . into pubs and clubs, he was being accused of stopping these men from taking advantage of these terms . . .'[28] The problem, if anything, intensified. At the end of 1982, Parsonage faced 181 jobs to be cut over the next fifteen months. The Branch Delegate simply acknowledged, 'people are queuing up to take advantage of the benefits offered.'[30] Vincent perceived the damage produced by the carrot 'We are selling jobs. The National Coal Board are reducing manpower and closing pits with the benefits that are being offered. This has got to stop.'[30] But how to force a halt? The construction of any collective solidarity ran against a mass of individuals each pursuing their private benefits. As a Delegate responded to Vincent, 'you cannot advise a man not to take the benefits offered'.[31] In Lancashire incremental decline was set against an ever-present fear of further pit closures.

The devastation of the sixties had left deep scars on those involved in the Union. Although nine pits had survived for over a decade until the Hapton Valley closure, there had never been secure confidence about the future. Sutton Manor had been a recurrent source of concern for several years. The Board had stressed the need for new investment to increase shaft capacity and to modernise surface facilities. However, this would not be implemented until performance improved. In the early eighties, the pit showed signs of meeting the Board's requirements; it was no longer the topic of regular crisis discussions. But the investment did not materialise. Funds were tight; perhaps improvements at 'The Manor' would come only with a cutback in unprofitable production elsewhere in the coalfield.

The finger pointed at three other pits. Bold, after some years of relatively slim losses, had a very poor year in 1981/82. The Union became perturbed about the prospect of heavy job cuts. In November 1982, with the argument over a 'hit list' of closures reaching a new intensity, Vincent raised the Bold case with Coal Board Officials 'He hoped . . . the Board's desire to slim the colliery fell short of anorexia.'[32] The authoritative hint came a fortnight later when the Board responded to NUM pressure by arranging a meeting between the NEC and the Area Directors to clarify the overall closure prospects. When John Northard made his statement on the Western Area, the official NUM record included a specific reference: 'He referred to another five pits which he said were under close examination in respect of economic viability and he particularly cited Bold Colliery.'[34] Such public pessimism would leave its mark on the response of the Lancashire Area.

Vincent's report of this meeting suggested that the Board's scepticism was not just turned towards Bold. Northard had noted 'problems' at Agecroft, with its record of heavy job losses – but the most problematic case was Cronton. Here was a one face pit which had been equipped at one stage with just one set of chocks. The immediate consequence was unavoidable loss of production as each transfer was made from an exhausted face to a new one. Difficulties could be compounded if faulting shortened the life of a face. The most Northard would say in November 1982 was that Cronton's future was uncertain – there could be exploitable reserves.[34]

Over the next seven months the general situation deteriorated. There was more debate at national level; the membership balloted not to strike in support of Lewis Merthyr- Tymawr; there was increasing gloom in the peripheral coalfields. On 12 July 1983, Lancashire officials met the Area Director at a Colliery Review meeting. He was blunt about the market situation. Consumption was stagnant and stocks continued to increase at an unacceptable rate. Moreover, the prospect of new capacity meant that older units would require elimination at a faster rate than anticipated. In this context, Lancashire's recent record was grim. In the financial year 1982/83, the majority of Lancashire's pits had lost money; for the current financial year all but one were scheduled to make profits. But in the first quarter of the new year, three pits were performing at far below budgeted level. One, Parkside, had performed well the previous year but the others, Agecroft and Cronton, would be the subject of ominous special meetings.

Table 5.2   Lancashire pits – Performances and Budgets

	Profits, 1982/3 (thousands of pounds)	Budgets 1983/84 (thousands of pounds)
Agecroft	− 2 701	897
Bickershaw/Parsonage	1 046	260
Bold	− 7 427	247
Cronton	− 747	112
Golborne	1 728	257
Parkside	2 666	1 388
Sutton Manor	− 3 548	− 2 385

Note: Minus figures denote losses.
Source: Material is contained. NWA Executive, 15 July 1983.

These subsequent discussions produced little comfort for the Union. In the Agecroft case, the Board's case was accepted as 'irrefutable'. £4 million would be invested over eighteen months: the result would hopefully be greater efficiency, but production would be concentrated on one face and there would be further loss of employment.[35]

The Cronton predicament was much bleaker. Vincent reported to a Delegate Conference that this was obviously a closure situation since the Board were talking of a production gap from October 1984 to May 1985. The claim was that a planned sequence of faces could not be followed through on account of faulting, and the dilapidated state of the roadways limited the performance of essential tasks. Supplying the face, carrying out development work, repairing roadways – all could not be done simultaneously.

Union Officials wished to develop an alternative plan removing the need for a production gap but they acknowledged widespread pessimism about the pit's future. Moreover, if the Union's proposals were rejected, then Vincent saw little hope in the review procedure. 'He didn't have a great deal of confidence . . . because he couldn't ever remember the Union winning a case.'[36] Speakers from Cronton were bitter and cynical about the Board. The NCB had 'set the stall out' to close the pit. Development work had been hindered, investment had been meagre; cuts in the workforce had been excessive and had undermined the prospect of improvements.

The Union's attempt to develop an alternative plan produced no response from the Board. On October 7 Northard wrote to Vincent in the most negative terms. He characterised local management's assessment of the pit's future as 'very optimistic . . . I see the situation far worse.' He claimed that over the previous nine years, Cronton had lost £11·5 million and the anticipated loss for 1983/84 was now more than £2 million. The closure would benefit the industry: 'Not only do the financial losses curtail investment at other collieries with more realistic and viable opportunities, but, particularly in the present state of our industry, where the lowest possible production costs are required to maintain and increase coal sales, the continued operation of 'no hope' collieries can only worsen the security of all.'[37] The specific implications of this in Lancashire were clear. Vincent had already suggested that the Board would make the long discussed investment at Sutton Manor, dependent on a cutback elsewhere.

When the NUM discussed the proposed closure with the Area Director, Northard's comments only deepened the insecurity. He apparently suggested that perhaps the recent decision to invest in Agecroft had been mistaken. Moreover, the Board was pressurising the Union into accepting the Cronton closure. Vincent recalled the ending of his discussion with Northard. The latter 'gave us an ultimatum'. As far as the National Coal Board were concerned, if the National Appeal was lost, Cronton Colliery would close immediately. 'If you want to negotiate the closure date, then we can do that together.'[38] John Hensby, also present at this meeting, described the Board's tactics. Already management had 'all the documentary evidence regarding the rundown of Cronton, and where men were likely to be transferred, but the price of having that information was to accept pit closure.'

But the Cronton miners would not do this. As their Standing Delegate argued: 'We are fighting for our lives and we do not intend to be beaten.'[39] This stand was backed by the Lancashire Area, but there remained the fundamental challenge of developing an effective response. Cronton would go to a national appeal, but there could be little hope of salvation through that procedure. By now closures were threatened in several coalfields; the search for a united and significant national strategy was becoming desperate.

Four days after the Lancashire officials had their barren exchange with Northard, on 21 October, a Special National Delegate Conference was held. The issues were pit closures and wages: the background one of intensifying pressure and a record of Union failure to mobilise majority support in recent ballots on these issues.

The legacy of failure was important. Since 1981, there had been three ballots in which miners had rebuffed the advice of their NEC. The NUM had submitted a claim for a wages increase of more than 23 per cent in 1981 and the Board eventually offered 9·5 per cent. The NEC decided to hold a Special National Conference and tabled a recommendation that delegates opt for a national ballot backed by advice to vote for a strike. Vincent was consistently in favour of this strategy, a position criticised retrospectively by Gormley as irresponsible pliability in the face of left-wing pressure. 'Even "moderate" stalwarts like Sid Vincent gave way to the clamour and I was apalled.'[40] Gormley made a late intervention on the wages ballot. The day before the voting, 13 January 1982, Gormley wrote in the *Daily Express* opposing the NEC's position. It was one last exposition of the pragmatic perspective that had dominated his Presidency 'I have no false hopes that Maggie Thatcher will cough up for us . . . There's not much likelihood of a strike producing more than a few quid in my judgement.'[41] Similar assessments had come already from some Lancashire Branch Officials.[42] There was a fundamental dilemma. A successful strike would mean only a marginal increase in the Board's offer and seemed to many members a waste of time. But failure to mobilise a pro-strike majority would have wider political implications: 'If we don't support the National Executive Committee's recommendations over- whelmingly, then we are handing Maggie Thatcher a massive vote of confidence.'[43]

Immediately after the ballot one Lancashire Branch Delegate suggested that an adverse vote could not be blamed on Gormley. 'It is one of the most vague disputes I have ever known in my life . . . the

NCB have spent thousands of pounds in advertisements, yet there has been nothing from the National Executive Committee.'[44] The pessimistic expectation was soon revealed as accurate with only 45 per cent rejecting the Board's offer. In Lancashire the pro-strike vote was 5 per cent below the national average. Even before the result was officially known, tempers had flared at a NEC meeting. Vincent reported back to Lancashire: 'The debate . . . was . . . the . . . stormiest I have ever attended . . . two NEC members started to push and shove one another, and a water jug was picked up to use as a weapon and spectacles went flying.'[45] Once the issue became that of factional loyalty, then Lancashire's position was alongside Gormley. Vincent voted to block a censure motion against the National President, a ploy which succeeded by one vote.

Such a personalisation of the issue prevented a deeper analysis of the ballot result. Clearly there existed a discrepancy between the world of National and Area Executives and their Delegate Conferences, and the outlook of many normally inactive members. Within a few months Scargill was firmly established as National President. The Inverness Conference had demonstrated the Left's strength amongst the activists, but there still remained that nagging question, how far were their assessments and priorities shared by the wider membership? Once again wage negotiations encountered difficulties and that summer saw the first exchanges between Scargill and the Board over the closure issue. As demonstrated earlier, the national response – an overtime ban followed by a strike ballot on the two issues of wages and closures – provoked criticism from Lancashire Officials already hostile to the new national leadership.

The combination of the two questions was a fair reflection of the way that the Board viewed the situation. Wages could be higher, if loss making capacity were cut back. But given the fact that each member had just one vote, the linkage could seem clumsy or unfair. It forced miners to answer complex issues through the crude mechanism of a simple 'Yes/No' verdict. Perhaps curiously in the light of later events, there was some feeling in Lancashire that desire for a wage increase would undermine what would otherwise be solidarity against closures. The image of February 1981 still held an illusory promise: 'The members have shown in the past, and they would show again that they [will] take action for pit closures, irrespective of the result of the ballot.'[46]

But the Board could exacerbate an underlying pessimism about the strength of the Union. 'Mr Northard . . . put this information about the collieries, there were large coal stocks, there was no more money in this kitty and if you go on strike you will be taken on.' Vincent had his doubts about the credibility of the NUM campaign.

The New Year would be better: 'When you get an exercise like this near Christmas time, it could be difficult.'[47] Such a doubt was justified. Scargill campaigned vigorously for a 'Yes' vote in a series of regional rallies. Lancashire activists travelled to Sheffield to hear Scargill and McGahey addressing an audience of 4,000. There was enthusiasm, standing ovations, a leadership that appeared as incorruptible.[48] But the applause faded with the event; then came the ballot result, a more decisive rejection of strike action than earlier in the year. Down came the 'Yes' vote to 39 per cent, although Lancashire showed an opposite shift from 40 to 44 per cent.

Events in the coalfield had also indicated dissent about the overtime ban. The decision had been ignored by some members of the small but strategically vital Winders Branch. One disgruntled delegate voiced what would become a familiar criticism: 'The Winders think they are a law unto themselves.'[40] The Winders' Delegate was straightforward about what had happened: 'It was passed unanimously that they would not comply with the overtime ban . . . [I] explained everything to them and I was defeated . . . it was the individual members who forced the issue.'[50] But more generally the disparity between Union policy and the verdicts of the membership was stark: 'The membership are telling us quite plainly that the National Executive Committee are getting it wrong so often. The policy over the last three years has been rejected by the membership, and on this occasion overwhelmingly.'[51]

Against this, the issue of closures would not go away. Two months later, the Lancashire Executive passed a resolution that would be acted on in March 1983 – and once again twelve months later. The decision confronted a major strategic issue. Within its terms there were combined two views on how to construct solidarity, with a judgement made between them. 'If we are picketed or approached by another Area of the NUM for support, we should immediately hold an individual membership ballot of the members of the NUM North Western Area. It was unanimously felt by Area Executive Committee members that these problems should be dealt with nationally.'[52]

The first occasion came quickly on St Davids Day 1983, when the Lancashire Executive met a deputation from South Wales. A few days previously Vincent had received a letter from South Wales Area asking for strike action in support of their battle against closures. The focus had become the Board's decision to close Lewis Merthyr Tymawr. Within days of this announcement miners had sat in at the pit. Strike action had spread across South Wales and from 28 February the whole coalfield had been stopped. Now South Wales sent their activists to other coalfields in a bid to persuade them that this was no narrowly parochial question but one with severe national implications.

After listening to the South Wales' arguments, the Lancashire Executive decided with little dissent to ballot on a strike with the recommendation to vote 'Yes'.[53] Already supportive action and the promise of such action were snowballing. Three pits in North Derbyshire and one in Kent stopped; from Monday 6 March, the Left coalfields Yorkshire and Scotland would be out. Ballots with Area recommendations to back a strike were planned not just in Lancashire but also in Northumberland, Durham and Nottinghamshire.

Within this support, already there could be seen the great rift of 1984. Some Area leaderships seemed prepared to instigate a stoppage without a ballot; others were insisting on such a vote as a necessary condition. Here lay the obvious prospect of fragmentation.

When the National Executive met on 3 March it attempted to bring cohesion through ordering a national ballot.[54] Its members heard a passionate appeal from Emlyn Williams and Vincent returned to Lancashire claiming that this vote could prove decisive 'We are at the brink . . . this is the last chance . . . it could be Lancashire's turn next.[55] But some delegates to the Lancashire Conference were sceptical about the likely response of many members. The Board in its propaganda had claimed that no principle was at stake. Just one pit was to be closed and there would be no compulsory redundancies: 'This week the National Coal Board has fastened to everybody's lamp a leaflet stating the NCB facts about Tymawr Lewis Merthyr. This Delegate suggested that the problem went beyond the specific issue to a corrosive insecurity that could destroy any hope of collective action. The 'victory' of February 1981 seemed far away 'They are afraid of pit closures, they are equally afraid of going on strike and losing money that way.'[56] The likelihood was a negative vote; as one speaker acknowledged: 'When you look at the facts the NCB have produced on the one pit issue, with transfer payments and nobody losing a job, then no miner will vote for a strike. We have a hell of a lot of work to be done to swing the vote the other way.'[57] Whatever the effort by Lancashire's activists, the outcome underlined their worst fears. Nationally the proportion favouring a strike stayed at 39 per cent; in Lancashire it fell back five points to precisely the national average.

This vote was perhaps decisive. Hard-pressed miners in South Wales, Scotland and the North East would find difficulty in believing that their pits could be defended by a national stoppage sanctionned by a national ballot. The disparities between coalfields in that last ballot – the large Nottinghamshire coalfield had polled only 19 per cent for a strike – seemed to demonstrate that miners in seemingly secure coalfields would never stop work to help their threatened colleagues. The normal mechanisms of the union seemed to have broken down.[58] But at most, March 1983 was the sombre clarification of a longstanding problem. The NUM had never succeeded in developing an effective national resistance to pit closures. The Langwith fiasco had shown the problems even in the relatively secure mid seventies; in 1983, with economic insecurity all pervasive and a mounting toll of trade union failures against the Thatcher Government, effective resistance seemed even more problematic.

Clearly a continuing adherence to normal Union procedures was likely to mean no effective challenge to pit closures. The result in some coalfields would be a devastating contraction and more generally the sapping of the Union's credibility. Were there other methods by which closures might be resisted? That May, Scargill spoke for the first time at a Lancashire Annual Conference. He suggested that a conventional all out stoppage might not be the best response. Instead:

> Let the NUM say that if the NCB intend to close 30 of the most uneconomic pits, then we will ask the 30 profitable pits, such as Selby, to come out on strike. We will ask the rest of the miners to continue working and to pay a levy and provide the take home pay they would have had. We can keep a war of attrition going for two years, inflicting maximum damage on the Board and the minimum damage on our members.[59]

This was hardly a statement from someone dogmatically blind to all options other than the all-out stoppage and the mass picket!

Arguably such a tactic would have confronted the Union with organisational problems; would it have been a sufficient response to the sectionalism revealed by the recent ballot? If effectively implemented, would it have left an increasingly hawkish Coal Board short of an answer? Would it have provided an escalation into a solid national strike? Such a strategy became one more speculation, as the options continued to narrow. The overwhelmingly Conservative victory in the June 1983 election destroyed any hope of a political redressing of the NUM's difficulties. Instead the imminent arrival of Ian MacGregor as Coal Board Chairman suggested an intensification of the closure programme.

Less than a month after the Tory victory, the NUM held its Annual Conference at Perth. Delegates agreed a resolution on closures and job cuts, instructing the leadership to launch a vigorous campaign. It was supplemented by a suggestion whose ambiguity would become significant: 'The NEC . . . is instructed to conduct a National Ballot of members on the question of pit and works closures at a time deemed to be most appropriate . . .' Michael McGahey presented the Union's task in a speech free of comforting illusions: 'We have had two ballot votes in which our members have rejected the leadership. There is a credibility gap.'[60] The National Vice-President spoke out of a Scottish experience wherein the Board's style of management was becoming increasingly authoritarian. At that moment, the pressure-point was Cardowan, the last pit in Lanarkshire. Jack Taylor, the Yorkshire President, in seconding emphasised that any campaign could not take too long: 'Every day this Union and this industry grows weaker.' Beneath the road show, the demonstrations attended by the activists, there loomed the problem of the uninvolved members. 'We can have standing ovations while we are blue in the face. It doesn't make a blind bit of difference . . . at the end of the road you get into a situation where you are entertaining rather than convincing.'[61] Hopefully the hard slog of persuasion would produce solidarity: 'It has got to be together.'

The debate brought a range of testimony about the Union's stark predicament – from South Wales, Des Dutfield a central figure in the resistance at Lewis-Merthyr-Tymawr; from Scotland, David Hamilton of Monktonhall, the pit destined to be an early battleground as the Scottish NCB tightened the screw; from the same coalfield, George Bolton speaking of managerial duplicity at

Cardowan. These voices all came from the NUM Left's traditional heartlands. But Peter Heathfield, a political ally but from a very different industrial and cultural environment, sounded notes of caution. Old simplicities were irrelevant 'We have got to stop basking in the glory of 1972 and 1974.' But above all, effective action did not depend on the strongholds of the Left 'This Union's ability to launch a worthwhile campaign will depend on attitudes and reactions in the Midlands coalfields.'[62]

Confirmation of this necessity came from Heathfield's neighbours, the Nottinghamshire President, Ray Chadburn. He acknowledged that there was a problem in his Area, much of the difficulty resulting from the coalfield's role as absorber of miners displaced from older districts. They could articulate the individualism that could kill any attempt to develop any united action against closures: 'I hope you understand it is a difficult situation when people say 'I come from Scotland', 'I come from South Wales', 'I come from Kent', 'I come from Durham'. 'Where did they fight for my job?' That is the problem that Notts faces whether you like it or not.'[63] Beneath the interrogation, 'Where did they fight for my job?' there lay another one less often articulated but generally understood, 'Why should I fight for anyone else's job?' It was not the sum of the Nottinghamshire problem, but Chadburn at least had suggested honestly that the national strategy faced obstacles in that coalfield. This was more than some of his counterparts from other Areas seemed prepared to do. These inconvenient questions were raised in Lancashire where the closures of the sixties had not been the subject of national campaigns. But when Vincent spoke in that debate, he suggested no difficulties. Instead he proclaimed that his longstanding Area strategy had encountered a new style of management: 'I saw my job as primarily to keep pits open and see that lads had a good standard of living . . . But I am very much afraid that we have wasted all that co-operation.'[64] Thus the bewilderment of an Area official who found the assumptions on which his trade union career had been developed, subverted by an increasingly abrasive management. But such declarations side stepped the problem of mobilising support for national strategy inside Lancashire. On this crucial question, Vincent said little or nothing at national level. In his Area he articulated and defended national policy on pit closures, but he seems not to have carried uncongenial messages in the opposite direction. Perhaps this is understandable since many Lancashire doubts were specific expressions of factional loyalties and suspicions that Vincent and Gormley had done much to promote and maintain. The consequence was a sharp disparity between the tone of discussions inside Lancashire and, at least after Gormley's retirement, the way in which Lancashire opinion was presented nationally. Vincent had said, 'If you can't beat them, bloody join them', but joining was interpreted as not facing real problems of mobilising support.

The NUM faced a determined opponent. It did so on an issue where solidarity had always proved elusive, and where the prospect of effective action was hampered further by internal factionalism. It is a portrait far removed from the frequently -presented image of a radical national leadership hell-bent on aggressive confrontation with both management and Government.

Notes

1   NWA Annual Conference, May 1981.
2   NWA Conference, 20 March 1982.
3   NUM Annual Conference 1981, p. 324 (in moving vote of thanks to President's Address).
4   Sid Vincent interview.
5   For a discussion of Scargill's emergence see Allen, *The Militancy of British Miners*, pp. 288–91.
6   Michael Crick, *Scargill and the Miners* (Penguin, Harmondsworth, 1985), pp. 89–94.
7   NWA Executive, 13 October 1981.
8   NWA Conference, 17 October 1981.
9   Bernard Donaghy interview.
10   NWA Conference, 10 December 1981.
11   NUM Annual Conference 1982, p. 337. The address also included the statement on p. 343, 'This Conference is and must be the supreme authority of the Union' – a contrast with Gormley's argument for flexibility as between this and other means of making decisions.
12   *Ibid*. p. 356. Note Huw Beynon's comment on this Conference in his introduction to *Digging Deeper: Issues in The Miners' Strike* (Verso, London, 1985), p. 9: 'It wasn't so much that "the right" was in disarray, they simply hadn't fielded a side.'
13   NWA Executive, 26 July 1982.
14   The procedure is documented in NUM NEC, 16 September 1982, and Annexes I and II to these minutes.
15   NWA Executive, 13 September 1982.
16   NWA Conference, 18 September 1982.
17   *Ibid*. (Ashton and Haydock Craftsmen Delegate).

18 *Ibid*. (Mal Gregory of Bold).
19 NWA Special Conference, 8 October 1982. For background see NUM Special NEC, 23 September 1982, and Report of Special Conference, 4 October 1982. Vincent spoke against the linking of the two issues (p. 725).
20 NWA Conference, 20 January 1983.
21 NUM NEC, 15 September 1983. See also Vincent's account of this meeting, NWA Delegate Conference, 17 September 1983.
22 *Ibid*. (Ashton and Haydock Craftsmen Delegate).
23 *Ibid*. (Parsonage Delegate).
24 *Ibid*.
25 NWA Executive, 21 November 1983.
26 NWA Conference, 17 December 1983.
27 *Ibid*.
28 NWA Conference, 20 June 1981.
29 NWA Conference, 18 December 1982.
30 *Ibid*.
31 *Ibid*. (Cronton Delegate).
32 NWA Executive, 22 November 1982, for Vincent's report on a meeting with Board officials on 9 November.
33 Vincent's report back to Lancashire on the national meeting can be found in NWA Executive, 7 December 1982: the reference to Bold acknowledges 'problems' on account of geological difficulties. The national records contain the comment on economic viability. See NUM version of Minutes for meeting between NCB and NUM, 23 November 1982.
34 NWA Executive, 7 December 1982.
35 NWA Executive, 9 August and Conference, 20 August 1983.
36 NWA Conference, 20 August 1983.
37 Copy of letter from John Northard contained in NWA Executive, 9 October 1983.
38 Vincent's account in NWA Conference, 22 October 1983.
39 *Ibid*.
40 Gormley, *Battered Cherub*, p. 208.
41 *Daily Express*, 13 January 1982.
42 See the comments in this vein by Mick Noonan of Parkside and by the Plank Lane Delegate, NWA Conference, 19 December 1981.
43 *Ibid*. by the Plank Lane Delegate.
44 NWA Conference, 16 January 1983 (Cronton Delegate).
45 NWA Executive, 20 January 1982 – Vincent's report on the previous day's NEC.
46 NWA Special Area Conference, 8 October 1982 (St Helens Craftsmen Delegate).
47 *Ibid*.
48 For the description of the Sheffield rally see Beatrix Campbell, *Wigan Pier Revisited: Poverty and Politics in the Eighties* (Virago, London, 1984), pp. 112–13.
49 NWA Conference, 13 November 1982 (Golborne Delegate).
50 *Ibid*.

51   *Ibid.* (Ashton and Haydock Craftsmen Delegate).
52   NWA Executive, 21 December 1982.
53   NWA Executive, 1 March 1983. March 1983.
55   NWA Special Conference, 5 March 1983.
56   *Ibid.* (Ashton and Haydock Craftsmen Delegate).
57   *Ibid.* (Plank Lane Delegate).
58   For a presentation of this response see Huw Beynon (ed.), *Digging Deeper, Issues in the Miners' Strike* (Verso, London, 1985), pp. 9–13.
59   NWA Annual Conference, May 1983.
60   NUM Annual Conference 1983, p. 482 for text of resolution, p. 483 for McGahey's comment.
61   *Ibid.* pp. 485–7.
62   *Ibid.* p. 498.
63   *Ibid.* p. 499.
64   *Ibid.* p. 494.

6

A discordant overture

Wage negotiations soon reached an impasse. Late in September the NCB offered 5·2 per cent and emphasised that further negotiations would be fruitless. When Vincent reported back to a Lancashire Conference, he suggested that this offer would probably be accepted in the ballot: 'On this occasion even the National President and Vice-President believe that the membership will accept the present offer . . . but don't actually say it.' On the closure question an effective response seemed as elusive as ever: 'The Union has been discussing at length new strategy and everybody seems to think that there is no answer . . . there are men quarrelling with one another over redundancies even though your pit may not be threatened. Unless the Union can get the membership to give us the power to call strike action then we can't do a thing.'[1] Predictably, faced with these frustrations some Lancashire delegates looked back to what they characterised as the Golden Age of Gormley, a time of shrewd bargaining rather than slavish and sterile adherence to political priorities: 'One thing in Joe's favour was that he used to negotiate.' But now burgeoning discontent could be a means to wider personal objectives. 'Arthur Scargill was frightened to go back to the Board and reach an improved offer because he just wanted to get the membership out on strike to see to his own interests.'[2]

Whatever the developing strategies of the Government and the Coal Board, many Lancashire officials continued to understand their predicament through the prism of factional loyalties.

The Board's decision that Cronton should be closed was immediate, a local representation of the general crisis. Significantly, John Hensby, Cronton Branch Secretary and well to the left in the Lancashire NUM argued that wages and closures should be taken separately. The wage rise should be accepted, thus clearing the decks for a battle on closures, beginning with an overtime ban.[3] It was an intelligible response given the Cronton predicament, but it raised the perennial question – how could such a battle be effective?

The separation of issues was accepted as a strategy by the Lancashire Area, but when a Special National Conference met on 21 October, this distinction was lost. The dominant sentiment amongst speakers seemed to be that the Board was linking wage increases to further cut backs and thus the Union must respond in kind. The NEC resolution rejected the wage offer and called for a complete overtime ban on both wages and closures. Vincent spoke about the Board's ultimatum on the Cronton closure and ended with a call to action: 'Let's play the bloody game properly and let's bring the Board to their knees.'[4] It might have been comforting Conference rhetoric but it studiously avoided the difficult questions. Vincent did not articulate the Lancashire concern to separate the two issues, nor did he suggest there had been some pressure for a ballot in his own coalfield. In contrast, Ray Chadburn did clarify the limits of the Nottinghamshire response. There had been 'a majority of one Branch to support an overtime ban and possibly that is a good breakthrough in my Area . . . But . . . the vote represented about 5 per cent of the Nottinghamshire miners.'[5] It was all too easy to marginalise such admonitions and to believe that rhetoric plus a clear-cut Conference decision were sufficient. But there remained two fundamental problems. How would the mass of miners respond? Would an overtime ban serve, like in 1974, as the effective prelude to a successful strike ballot? And what resources did the Union have, given the depressed demand for coal and a combative Government? Was bringing the Board to its knees a realistic objective?

Whatever their reservations, the vast majority of Lancashire miners demonstrated no overt opposition to the strategy. This commitment entailed the loss of around 1,000 overtime shifts in each week. Yet there were always potential flashpoints, and beyond these there was an awareness of the ban's Achilles' heel. Pressures for a ballot restricted to the wages claim had to be resisted, otherwise the whole strategy would crumble. Predictably, there was early tension in Lancashire between some winders and other members. Thus, at Cronton: 'There is an uneasy truce . . . which could explode any day because the winders are fighting us all the way.'[6] Even in the early weeks some members expressed individual grievances. One centred around the lump sum available to anyone taking redundancy. This was calculated with reference to the previous twelve weeks' earnings and could be affected adversely by the loss of overtime shifts.[7] As the ban bit deeper, grievances multiplied. The prohibition of weekend work meant that rope cappings had to be carried out during the week, thus reducing the number of shifts worked; water problems were mounting; night-shift men were complaining about the need to return to the pit on Friday, just to collect wages; managerial staff were accused of spreading false information about supposed breaches of the ban.

With the New Year, the NCB turned the screw further and NUM members were sent home at every breakdown. This did not produce a solid mobilisation of the membership against the employer. When the Lancashire Executive met on 11 January, it held a lengthy discussion on the tensions precipitated by the need to cap ropes during the normal working week. Clearly, there was a significant division since it was agreed by 'a majority' to maintain the ban.[8] But the discords could not be dispelled by a resolution. At the subsequent Area Conference, Mick Noonan, the Parkside Branch Secretary, argued unsuccessfully for more flexibility on rope cappings as a means of maintaining solidarity;[9] adherents of a firm line won the day. As one put it: 'We should either lift the overtime ban, or we carry the overtime ban out.'[10]

But a commitment to the ban promised to be a lengthy and perhaps at first discouraging business. With the extent of Coal Board resistance becoming clearer, it would be a long haul: 'It should last at least another nine months and in the early stages the improvement would be very slight.'[11] Hanging on for so long could be a bleak prospect: a mounting loss of income with little observable achievement would only intensify the criticisms of the disgruntled. Moreover, pessimism could be deepened by Board propaganda claiming that the ban was ineffective. Already there were anticipations of claims and counter-claims that would be a dominant motif during the year of the strike. 'At Bickershaw Colliery . . . they were losing a considerable amount of coal. The National Coal Board were telling a lot of lies and the National Coal Board were picking up more and more coal from stock . . . it was difficult to obtain the true figures because the National Coal Board were reluctant to disclose them.'[12]

The pressures resulting from the ban were most intensive at Agecroft. Financial losses were massive. A new face had experienced early production problems and much depended on the punctual completion of current development work. Insecurities were intensified when the Board announced in February that the pit would be stopped for a week to allow for repairs and maintenance. The colliery's manager was clearly under pressure from his supervisors. He informed the Union of an instruction from the Board's Industrial Relations Department that men must appear every day to check the availability of work. The press heard of the lay off before official notification was given to the NUM. Then, after the week's shutdown, the manager said the pit would not re-open until the afternoon shift on Monday 20 February. Union pressure about the loss of the day shift produced a revealing response. The manager contacted the Western Area headquarters for their views; he then said that the Area would not give their permission for an earlier start.[13]

The increasing management pressure was complemented by deepening sectionalism within the Union. Early in the New Year, there had been a crisis in North Staffordshire when two winders crossed pickets and broke the ban on weekend work; the result was a walk-out by other miners on the following Monday. By late February, a similar crisis seemed imminent in Lancashire. John Hensby reported on the deteriorating situation at Cronton, to the effect that: 'All week his members were being threatened by winders . . . After all the arguments the winders had come into the Union cabin to tell the local branch that, as from 3 March 1984, winders would be reporting for weekend work as normal.' Despite denials from the winders' delegate, it was claimed that a similar threat had been made at Parkside. Hensby saw the difficulties of any tough response but equally saw no alternative.

> He was reluctant to see a situation where NUM members had to picket other members . . . but . . . it was up to the winders' section to tell their winders to conform with national decisions and for the platform to tell the National Coal Board that if the winders do work normal, then no NUM members will work with them the following Monday.[14]

Here was a sombre anticipation of the next year's conflicts; of the pressures that drove some miners to make a stand in a situation which also produced division.

But this potential flashpoint never happened. Instead, the Cronton appeal reached its predictably negative conclusion and the struggle began to take on a more serious character. The National Appeal Meeting had been held under the Review Procedure on 17 January. Scargill had presented the Union's case backed by Lancashire officials and by NACODS representatives. The heart of the Union's case was that the production gap necessitated by the Board's plans was avoidable and that the pit had been neglected for some years. There were significant good quality reserves and closure would mean their sterilisation. In response, the Board's representatives emphasised Cronton's geological difficulties.

The exchanges highlighted the fundamentally unsatisfactory nature of the Review Procedure. The hearing was chaired by Merrick Spanton, a full-time member of the Board. His role as Chairman did not inhibit him from adverse comments on some aspects of the Union's case. He rejected the 'allegations' that the Board had shown a lack of commitment to the pit and stressed the geological factor. Yet he reacted against any suggestion of partiality: 'The Board representatives always listened carefully to the Union's case and were concerned only to elucidate points . . . [I] undertook to report all the arguments made to the full Board for their decision. [I stress] that the Board had no preconceived ideas on these matters and were completely impartial.'[15] Whatever the protestations of fairness, the outcome could have surprised no one.

On 29 February, Lancashire officials met Northard. He outlined the next year's budgets for each colliery and announced the rejection of the Cronton appeal. Production would end two days later.[16]

The Lancashire Executive debated the crisis for a very long time.[17] The Board had carried out its threat to impose a closure date. If the Union used the appeals system, some of Cronton's miners, battered by months of speculation and uncertainty, would no doubt see redundancy payments as a blessed release. Now was the time for choice. 'By this very announcement, this organisation had been thrown in at the deep end.' The events of the past few months, the aggravation of the overtime ban, the increasing evidence of the Coal Board's tough policy, did not seem to have brought unity closer. 'It was made abundantly clear that whatever decision was made would not seem right to some of the members of this organisation.'

One signpost pointed: stand up and fight for Cronton. It represented a principle and besides, if closure was not resisted, then some other vulnerable Lancashire pit would come under threat. But against that, other signposts indicated excuses: it's a hopeless case, the overtime ban's cost me enough; it's the wrong time of year; why bother?

Nothing had changed. The Union seemed as far as ever from an effective strategy on closures. In the end, the Lancashire Executive reached a unanimous decision preserving the principle of opposition to closures, but the hope offered to Cronton miners was dimmed by the verdicts of past ballots. The Executive would ask the following week's NEC to permit a coalfield ballot for strike action on the Cronton closure. Nothing in Lancashire's recent history suggested a majority for a strike; the value of a coalfield stoppage was unclear. Some involved in the decision have claimed in retrospect that they had no expectation of a majority for a coalfield strike on the Cronton closure. Once again, espousal of a principle seemed unsupported by a practical response. But by the time that fateful NEC meeting was held, responses to Cronton had been overtaken by events in other coalfields.

Increasingly abrasive management, a confused membership and a new style of leadership within the National Union meant disorientation for Lancashire officials. A familiar world was crumbling; the long-expected crisis seemed about to break. One Branch Secretary recalled the response of his Manager to MacGregor's appointment: 'Mr MacGregor's the best thing that's ever happened to this industry. There'll be a good living for those of us who are left.'[18] Yet such confusions were not limited to traditionally right wing Areas. Scotland had been long associated with the NUM Left, its commitment symbolised by its President, Mick McGahey. The Area's miners had been strong supporters of left positions in ballots over many years. But late in 1982, faced with an autocratic Area Director, Albert Wheeler, this commitment began to fracture. Scottish miners failed to back industrial action in support of the threatened Kinneil Colliery. The pit shut. In the March 1983 ballot on Lewis-Merthyr-Tymawr, Scotland narrowly failed to poll a majority for strike action – a sharp decline from the October 1982 vote when Scotland had polled over 68 per cent for strike action. In the summer of 1983, the Scottish miners failed to prevent the shutdown of Cardowan, the last pit in Lanarkshire. This was followed by an eight-week strike at Monktonhall in Lothian to prevent cessation of development work. In the face of macho-management, the Scottish miners were far from united. Officials and activists were continually frustrated in their attempts to secure effective support across their coalfield. The overtime ban brought continual problems for the Scottish leadership. At several pits weekend cover was often provided as managers played specifically on the doubts and sectionalisms of their workforce. Behind these decisions lay the fears of further closures, fears that crystallised early in 1984 at Bogside and at a development pit, Polmaise. When Bogside was flooded, the Board blamed the overtime ban. In neither case did the Scottish Area officials, nor leaders from threatened Branches, succeed in generating effective backing for individual action across the coalfield. Instead, from 21 February, Polmaise struck. Clearly a traditional Left Area was no nearer a solution to the problem of solidarity over closures; both Scotland and Lancashire faced similar seemingly intractable problems, although clearly the political predilections of officials influenced rhetoric and responses.[19] Yet the repertoire of strategies still seemed limited by the ballot requirement, whether at coalfield level as with Cronton, or nationally, as had been attempted unsuccessfully with Lewis-Merthyr-Tymawr.

No doubt by carly 1984, activists had often become sceptical about the ballot requirement. A South Wales miner reflecting the previous summer on the Lewis-Merthyr-Tymawr failure, had highlighted the problem and a solution: 'If they are going to start holding ballots again, then I'm afraid we're going to lose ... the only strategy if the pit is nearing to close ... is to come out on strike and get the rest of the coalfield and start picketing the pits out. That is the only way you will get miners out on strike now.'[20] There was the strategy in a nutshell, presented by some critics as a conspiracy to evade the NUM's Rule Book, but essentially borne out of a sombre realisation that, on such a divisive issue, a ballot majority was improbable, and that traditional certainties were buckling under managerial pressures and encroaching pessimism.

In such a predicament developments in the largest Area, Yorkshire, could be decisive. Its shift to the left had radically affected the political balance within the NUM, a change symbolised by Scargill's election to national office. Yet within the coalfield, a

Left Area leadership tended to obscure the political variations – the forceful radical Branches of Doncaster and Barnsley, the traditionally cautious pits of North Yorkshire and, somewhere in between, the South Yorkshire collieries. As tempers had frayed during the overtime ban, a range of local disputes had broken out in Yorkshire; some had hopes that they could provide a springboard for a more general stoppage, that at last, divisions could be transcended. One began to take root. A clash over managerial alteration of snap times in order to dilute the impact of the overtime ban on production started at Manvers and acquired support in some South Yorkshire pits.[21] But the uncertain mobilisation was engulfed by another. The day after Northard had announced the immediate closure of Cronton, the day when the Lancashire Executive were pondering what to do, a meeting was held at the South Yorkshire offices of the NCB. The Area Director, George Hayes, told NUM Area Officials that Cortonwood Colliery would close in five weeks. It was an overtly economic closure; the Yorkshire leadership decided a stand must be made.[22]

When the Lancashire Executive met again on 9 March, Vincent reported on some fateful meetings; a national dispute was now clearly in the making. Three days earlier he had attended a meeting of the Coal Industry National Committee. Ian MacGregor had announced a cut in capacity for 1984/85 of 4 million tonnes. This reduction was against the actual output for 1983/84, which was itself 8 million tonnes less than had been projected. The consequential job losses would be 20,000. During the lunch break, Scargill presided over a NEC meeting and claimed that these cutbacks were no more than a first step. The long term prospect was the loss of 100 pits and 100,000 jobs. During the afternoon session, the Board's representatives acknowledged that the next year's closures would be concentrated in Scotland, South Wales and the North East.

This prospect combined with the threats to Cronton, Polmaise and above all, Cortonwood provided the essential agenda for the monthly NEC meeting two days later. The Lancashire request for a coalfield ballot on Cronton stood alongside requests from Yorkshire and Scotland that coalfield stoppages be licensed under National Rule 41. In neither case was there any suggestion of a preceding coalfield ballot. The Yorkshire Area Council, responding to the Cortonwood challenge, had already backed a stoppage from the end of that week. Legitimation could be claimed from a coalfield ballot held in 1981 on the principle of strike action against any closure on economic grounds. Then, the vote for the principle had been 86 per cent, but in the two later ballots where closures were an issue the pro-strike Yorkshire vote had been 56 per cent and 54 per cent. In Scotland, no ballot was needed, a joint Executive meeting of Miners and Craftsmen had responded to the news of the Board's planned cutbacks by calling a coalfield strike.[23]

Vincent and most other NEC members agreed to sanction the Yorkshire and Scottish requests. The resulting resolution reflected a strategic perspective publicly elaborated by Michael McGahey: 'We are not dealing with niceties here. We shall not be constitutionalised out of a defence of our jobs. Area by Area will decide, and in my opinion it will have a domino effect.'[24] The NEC's support for the Yorkshire and Scottish strikes was thus coupled with a general recommendation that: 'Other Areas should encourage their membership to take similar action to Yorkshire and Scotland, and any such action would be given National Backing.'[25] With the adoption of this tactic, Lancashire's request for a ballot on Cronton became a dead issue. As Vincent reported back, 'The . . . Area letter was overtaken by these decisions.'[26] It was superseded also by developments at Cronton where production had ended and transfers were beginning.

Only three NEC members opposed this decisive resolution; they preferred a national strike ballot under Rule 43.[27] The adopted strategy was identified closely with the Left and yet many members long associated with the Right went along with it. To some extent this reflected the weakening of the Right over several years, and especially since the retirement of Gormley. They had long lost the intellectual initiative and were now deprived of the Machiavellian resources of the former National President. Some represented coalfields where closures would bite deeply and were prepared to acquiesce in any attempt to mobilise opposition. Several, no doubt, believed that eventually there would have to be a national ballot and that perhaps action in some Areas might raise awareness of the issues, producing a stronger pro-strike vote. More sceptically some, pessimistic about opinion in their own Areas, could comfort themselves with the assurance that they could protect themselves with their own Area ballots, and the results could legitimise either involvement in a spreading strike or working on.

The Lancashire Executive listened to Vincent's reports. There must have been considerable anxiety about the NEC decisions, which would be articulated forcefully at the following day's Delegate Conference. Executive members responded to the new situation by calling for an early Area ballot with a recommendation to support strike action. Many members may well have been sceptical about the likely outcome.[28]

The following day, a Special Delegate Conference was held in Bolton. The atmosphere was largely hostile to a strike; many speakers poured cold water on the NEC strategy and aired the prejudices of several years. Significantly, delegates from Branches where the stoppage would gain only limited support were already employing arguments that would become very familiar. The Parsonage delegate conjured the spectre of Yorkshire invaders: 'The Yorkshire area resolution is intimidating to our members. We are not prepared to be intimidated by any other Area . . . the only way to get an answer to this problem of pit closures and rundown in manpower, is through the ballot box.[29] Similarly, his Agecroft counterpart was already anticipating his members' response to Yorkshire pickets: 'We do not want bully boy tactics on the gates of Agecroft colliery if we vote for no strike.'[30] The democratic theme was taken up by the Agecroft Branch Secretary, Jim Lord: 'These are bully boy tactics and dictatorship and this is taking the place of democracy.' But the solution which he would advocate for the next twelve months he acknowledged to be self-defeating: 'The only way out of this situation is a national ballot. Unfortunately it will defeat everything that we have done so far.'[31] The argument that a national strike ballot was the only democratic way forward was complemented by a pragmatic claim that such a ballot was essential for a solid strike, and such cohesion was a necessary condition for effectiveness. But there was little belief that such a ballot would generate the required majority. One Delegate acknowledged that his members had little interest in the wider political arguments of the Union's national leaders, but they were concerned about the national strategy: 'They [are] not interested in the Tory Government's attempt to do away with trade unions, or the Chairman of the National Coal Board butchering their industry, they seem to be very concerned suddenly that they are being given the run around amongst our own leaders.'[32] And there was the lure of redundancy payments, just improved as a lubricant to accept Coal Board cuts:

'When the National Coal Board announced £1,000 per man for every year's service, there is no way we, as Branch Officials, could refuse them.'[33]

Against this pessimism and acquiescence, a few voices were raised. Mal Gregory from Bold reminded delegates muttering about Yorkshire intimidation that, in 1981, action across the Pennines had helped to protect the whole industry. His reservation was simply one of timing – hold to the overtime ban until November and then a ballot could be won. Such a vista, perhaps widely held in the NUM, made debatable assumptions about whether the ban could be a radicalising device rather than a splintering one, and whether even after twelve months without overtime a ballot majority could be achieved on the divisive closure issue. Most crucially this was no longer a feasible option. Polmaise, Cortonwood, the announcements about cuts in capacity, were a sequence that seemed to require an early response. In Lancashire, Cronton was effectively shut and John Hensby articulated the bitterness and despair of those who had already lost out: 'The Cronton people feel they have been sold down the river because there have been a lot of people in this hall who have supported us . . . to no avail . . . the men are that sick and fed up . . . we have men who are good workers in their early twenties who are not going to any pit . . .' Hensby focused on a crucial feature of the Lancashire ballot. The identification of Cronton as a target for closure had lessened the feeling of threat elsewhere in the coalfield. The membership should have been balloted earlier when a closure threat was anticipated but the targeted pit had not been identified. 'That was the time that this Area should have targeted a ballot when every pit was in the same boat.'[34] But it was too late for 'shoulds'. At this decisive moment, as some Yorkshire Branches were starting to think about picketing targets, the Lancashire delegates seemed preponderantly hostile to any stoppage spread through picketing. With one dissenter, they voted for an Area Strike Ballot five days later on Thursday 15 March, and for this to be accompanied by a very strong recommendation of strike action. Delegates also approved a policy of attempting to work normally until the ballot had been held. What such attempts should involve was obscure; how should Lancashire miners, about to hold a ballot, respond to large numbers of committed Yorkshire pickets? On this vital question, the Conference was mute.

Notes

1 NWA Special Conference, 8 October 1983.
2 *Ibid*. (St Helens Craftsmen Delegate).
3 *Ibid*.
4 NUM Special Conference, 21 October 1983, p. 845.
5 *Ibid*. p.849.
6 NWA Conference, 12 November 1983.
7 *Ibid*. (Jim Lord).
8 NWA Executive, 11 January 1984.
9 NWA Conference, 21 January 1984.
10 *Ibid*. (John Hensby).
11 *Ibid*. (Ashton and Haydock Craftsmen Delegate).
12 *Ibid*. (Leigh Craftsmen Delegate).
13 See the discussion in NWA Conference, 18 February 1983.
14 *Ibid*.
15 NWA Minutes of Final Appeal Meeting, 17 January 1984; also the report by Vincent to the Area Conference, 21 January 1984.
16 See Appendix A to Executive 1 March 1984.
17 The minutes for this Executive Meeting are a little more detailed than usual, suggesting the lengthy and uncertain character of the discussion.
18 Brian Eden (Golborne NUM) interview.
19 The Scottish dilemma is presented clearly in the minutes of the NUM (Scottish Area) for 1983 and the first two months of 1984. See in particular Minutes of two Scottish Conferences – 23 January 1984, on the widespread failure to observe the overtime ban, and 13 February 1984, demonstrating the problems in mobilising support for Polmaise.
20 Cited in R. Samuel *et al.*, *The Enemy Within: Pit Villages and the Miners' Strike of 1984–85*, p. 65.
21 See *People of Thurcroft*, pp. 43–4.
22 See Michael Crick, *Scargill and the Miners*, pp. 11–12; *Thurcroft*, pp. 44–7; Samuel *et al.*, *The Enemy Within*, pp. 67–71.
23 NUM NEC, 8 March 1984; also Vincent's report to the Lancashire Conference of 10 March on this round of meetings; for the Scottish decision see the Special Meeting of the Area Executive, 6 March 1984.
24 *Times*, 7 March 1984.
25 NUM NEC, 8 March 1984.
26 NWA Conference, 10 March 1984.
27 Ray Ottey (Power Group), Trevor Bell (COSA), Ted Mackay (North Wales). See Ottey's account in his *The Strike: An Insider's Story* (Sidgwick and Jackson, London, 1985), ch. 3.
28 NWA Executive, 9 March 1984.
29 NWA Conference, 10 March 1984.
30 *Ibid*.
31 *Ibid*.
32 *Ibid*. (Golborne Delegates).
33 *Ibid*. (Pendlebury Delegates).
34 *Ibid*.

7

Pickets and ballots:
the strike takes root

The pits of North Yorkshire are linked with their Lancashire counterparts by the M62. When pickets began to make that short journey on Tuesday 13 March, they were effectively initiating an almost year-long strike for some Lancashire miners.

Yet, that first week the dispute had a brittle quality. No-one really knew how long it would last. Even in the traditionally left-wing Areas, there was initially often an uneven response. Both in South Wales and in Scotland, there was some resistance to the strike call. In the former Area, the Lodges voted eighteen to thirteen against a strike, but by the end of that Monday picketing had stopped the coalfield; in Scotland, three pits worked on the first day. Within forty eight, hours all had been picketed out. Yorkshire responded more cohesively; and in historically cautious Durham, the strike soon secured firm and widespread backing. After all, the North East had been targeted in the recently announced cutbacks.

But in Lancashire and other areas, ballots had been ordered – in the Midlands, Northumberland, Nottinghamshire, South Derbyshire and in the miniscule Cumberland and North Wales Areas. In each case, as in Lancashire, the Area had a right-wing tradition and this was likely to be expressed in the ballot. Amongst the balloting Areas, only Peter Heathfield's North Derbyshire had demonstrated much political sympathy for the Union's new leadership.

Before the ballots could be held, pickets began to arrive most dramatically in the large Nottinghamshire coalfield. Miners, initially often from the Doncaster Panel, made the quick trip down the Great North Road or the M18 and the M1. The resulting incidents provided divisive motifs for the next year and beyond – Harworth women encouraging their men to cross picket lines, miners crawling under fences to avoid facing pickets, fear of 'invaders', contempt for men who refused to listen to the Union's case on closures, mutual misunderstanding of motives – all contributed to increasingly abrasive exchanges, culminating rapidly in tragedy – the unexplained death of the young Ackton Hall miner, David Jones, outside Ollerton Colliery.[1] The escalation occurred in the presence of large numbers of police and was accompanied by a shrill campaign in the national and local media. Ironically, given NCB policy, this focused on the Nottinghamshire miners' 'Right to Work'. At the end of the first week, the announcement of the Nottinghamshire ballot result – 73 per cent against striking – spotlighted a fundamental problem for the NUM.

If the strike was to be effective, then the support of miners in the large and profitable Nottinghamshire coalfield was critical. NUM officials and activists; journalists and historians – all have pondered over those critical days. Did the early Yorkshire picketing inflate the anti-strike ballot vote? In fact, Nottinghamshire showed more support for a stoppage in March 1984 than it had done in the Lewis-Merthyr-Tymawr ballot twelve months before, although perhaps the shift was restricted by those early altercations. Alternatively, the initial confrontations could provide miners with a credible excuse for working on, when the reasons for their distance from National Union policy were something else. Could the Nottinghamshire leadership have given a more vigorous lead in support of strike action – or were they aware, in a fashion unavailable to outsiders, of the priorities and the prejudices of their members? Such questions are basic to any understanding of the strike, but answers are elusive. Any adequate account must focus on strategic choices – miners were not simply the prisoners of local geology, market circumstances and an inherited political culture; but it must look also at the extent to which such circumstances limited choices. In order to penetrate some of the issues, the focus should move once again to Lancashire – a much smaller Area than Nottinghamshire, economically more vulnerable, but over many years clearly committed to the NUM Right. In fact, by March 1984, the Left had been far more successful in securing Union positions in the Nottinghamshire coalfield. A deep-rooted Lancastrian hostility to any Yorkshire 'invasion' had been expressed forcibly at the 10 March Area Conference; the ballot was presented as the centrepiece of democratic practice. It seemed that there were all the ingredients of a mini-Notts.

Critical Lancastrians might see the Yorkshire invasion as evidence of a well-planned conspiracy emanating from the top of the NUM. But viewed from the other side, the deployment of pickets was often haphazard.[2] Initial planning in North Yorkshire was based on outdated information; some pickets were initially sent to the closed Hapton Valley Colliery. Security was often rudimentary. Some of the first pickets came to Lancashire in coaches and soon proved to be an easy target for police road blocks. Hired coach drivers threatened with prosecution needed little persuasion to turn back. Such road blocks high in the Pennines several miles from the Lancashire pits could prevent even the most committed from carrying on alone. Quickly, coaches gave way to cars. The long battle to evade road blocks and hoodwink the police began as Yorkshiremen made very early starts to funerals and fishing matches.

Initially the Yorkshire pickets travelled with optimism. The atmosphere was that of an outing or, for the more zealous, a mission. Either way, the Lancastrian colleagues would be persuaded; there was no expectation of confrontation. Even after the Lancashire divisions had become clear to the Yorkshiremen, the latter's view of Lancastrian miners was never as dismissive as their increasingly harsh condemnation of the Nottinghamshire men. The Lancashire men were still seen as essentially good NUM members, undermined perhaps by weak or devious leadership, but nevertheless, they remained within the pale.

One factor facilitating this was that from the first, Lancashire Branches responded to the crisis in contrasting fashions. Bold NUM Branch met the day following the Area Conference. Vincent spoke, advocating a ballot vote for a strike, but also arguing that members should work on until the ballot result was known. This advice was firmly rejected. That Sunday, Bold miners made a firm decision not to cross picket lines.[3] It was soon tested. Two days later, a handful of pickets arrived from Castleford, the night shift refused to go in and the response was repeated next morning when the day shift arrived. From that moment, the Bold Branch were out solidly. Some began to join the Yorkshiremen on the picket lines. Similarly, at the nearby doomed Cronton pit, four Yorkshire pickets turned back 90 per cent of the Branch's members. A Yorkshire picket met John Hensby and had a misleading introduction to Lancashire. Briefly, he assumed that other Lancashire leaders shared Hensby's radicalism. His diary was buoyant: 'Picketed Cronton all right. Sixteen hours success.'[4] But at Sutton Manor, with the pit stopped for repairs, picketing could have no immediate impact. Already in the St Helens section of the coalfield, many miners were sympathetic to the strike and were ready to respect picket lines and, in some cases, attempt to spread the strike.

To the east of Bold loom the concrete shafts of Parkside, Lancashire's largest pit. Early picketing made its mark there. Production was stopped that first week on two days, Wednesday and Thursday. On the latter, 1,300 miners went in to ballot, but only sixty remained to work the day shift. Mick Noonan, the Parkside Branch Secretary, commented that he would have preferred the Yorkshiremen to leave until the ballot had been held, but he acknowledged the authority of the picket line for most members: 'The majority have gone home reluctantly because they will not cross the picket lines.'[5] Down the road at Golborne, the most westerly pit in the Complex, work ceased on the Wednesday. The day shift crossed a picket line, but then met in the canteen, and two thirds decided to go home. Most afternoon men did not work, but next day there were no pickets. Men went in, balloted and worked as normal.[6] These early successes were paralleled at the Complex's other pits. Wednesday proved a good day for the Yorkshiremen. At Bickershaw, they showed up too late to meet the day shift and 134 out of 240 went to work, but after going underground they decided not to work. Similarly, at Parsonage fifty out of 120 on the day shift refused to go in, and by that afternoon only maintenance men were working.[7]

One significant feature of the early picketing at these pits was that it was amicable. Branch officials might express concern that pickets were there at all, but made no criticism of their behaviour. A senior police officer present at Parkside corroborated this judgement: 'It is to their credit that they have behaved in a responsible manner. We are not aware of any cases where abuses or threats have been made to miners wishing to cross the picket line.'[8] Instead, pickets leafleted the Lancastrians,hoping that they could be persuaded to back the strike.

Here at these Lancashire pit gates, there was employed the strategy whose alleged absence in Nottinghamshire was later seen as a fatal error. Such comradely persuasion did make an impact on Lancashire. Many miners respected picket lines; production was badly affected. Yet there were awkward questions. When pickets were not there, many more men went in. A durable strike required either the continuing presence of pickets, rendering the strategy inflexible, or alternatively some act of commitment by Lancashire miners, either through the ballot or some other means. Beyond the gut response to respect a picket line, there stood the need to secure firm support for a specific collective action. But even this piecemeal acquisition of support was offset by one jarring exception that brought the emotions of Nottinghamshire across the Pennines. This was Agecroft.[9]

The Conference debate on 10 March had shown how some leading figures in that Branch had held bleak expectations of flying pickets even before the event. That Sunday, there had been a Branch meeting of a very different character from that held at Bold. The Agecroft Standing Delegate apparently justified the crossing of picket lines: 'I said to the men that it was up to the individual whether they cross the picket line or not. Many of my members wished to cross that picket line.'[10] When pickets arrived on the Tuesday evening, the night shift turned back, but next morning there were heated exchanges. Despite a sizeable police presence only about a dozen went in. The Branch Secretary was hostile: 'There were 150 pickets this morning and about the same number last night. It was intimidation more than anything and it got very bitter and serious . . . there was pushing and shoving and some abuse.'[11] Thursday was quieter, but on the Friday the animosities returned as several day shift men confronted pickets prior to the balloting. Eventually the fliers left, having gained an assurance that only safety work would be carried out. The result was a vigorous condemnation of the Yorkshiremen at an Area Delegate Conference held to assess the week's events. The Agecroft Delegate claimed that some pickets had wielded knives and pick axe handles. 'We had men hurt, we had pickets hurt . . . we had pit headgear damaged, e.g. damaged boilers, showers and they threatened the winders.' But beyond the attack on the pickets' alleged behaviour, there lay a political chasm. 'It isn't the reasonable men we are out to condemn, it is the men that have tried to push their ideas down our throat, whether we wanted them or not.'[12] The Standing Delegate's articulation of these emotions only deepened divisions. Although others within the Branch leadership were critical about the Union's strategy, they were apparently unhappy about such an inflammatory presentation of the Branch's position. One eye-witness recalls how Area meetings became 'horrific' when the Agecroft Delegate spoke, with other members leaping to their feet and shouting.[13]

From the other side, Yorkshire pickets frustrated at the Agecroft gates were now bitterly dismissive of Branch officials' claims. They saw them as devious, if not simply dishonest. Despite their professed sympathy with the campaign against closures, they seemed to have had little success in persuading Agecroft miners to support the struggle. Perhaps they had not really tried. Local officials seemed to say one thing to the fliers and another in the security of the pit when dealing with their own members. Yorkshire pickets became cynical about claims that men crossing their picket were doing safety work. At Agecroft the first optimism gave way to hostility.[14]

Superficially the Agecroft experience seems to underwrite a frequently heard interpretation of the Nottinghamshire situation, that abrasive picketing produced a bitter response and that the Agecroft confrontations, coupled with the Nottinghamshire shambles, demonstrated that the NUM's strategy was fatally flawed. The method of spreading the strike on an inherently divisive issue was itself divisive. But this would be a crude response. Clearly, some leading NUM members at Agecroft were predisposed to respond with hostility to any protests. At the very least this suggests that pickets had to contend with a mountain of prejudices and priorities. This in itself could be a criticism of the picketing strategy. Any attempt at a domino strategy had to take the dominoes as they were, and not as they might be in an ideal world; how they were was a consequence of the structure of the National Union and the contrasting Area cultures.

One long-serving Agecroft Committee man has suggested retrospectively that the Branch leadership, relatively stable over several years, had become significantly more conservative. Memories of 1972 and 1974, the deadening impact of Union routines perhaps, had obscured this deradicalisation. Only when the crunch came did he realise what had happened. Even though he was thoroughly committed to the strike, he initially honoured a decision by the Committee that its members should be prepared to escort members through the picket. Deeply miserable at his involvement in this he stopped work, but found only one other – very new – Committee man had done so.[15]

This shambles occurred with only a handful of Agecroft miners consistently refusing to work. Some of these point an accusing finger at the Lodge officials, especially the Branch Secretary, Jim Lord. They portray him as renouncing any leadership role, and in an impassioned atmosphere, abdicating decisions to the membership and, effectively, those most devoted to working at all costs. Such members pursuing a narrow self-interest set the style for a wider response in the absence of any coherent Branch leadership. The situation was allegedly exacerbated by the practice of escorting miners past pickets. 'We'll fight our way in' was a slogan that all too easily could become a reality. Images became fixed, attitudes set hard and were often impervious to argument.

Beneath the strategies adopted or neglected there lay structural considerations. In the previous decade, Agecroft had suffered a massive contraction of employment, with over a thousand men having left the pit. The overtime ban had seen the Coal Board battering the workforce. The pit had been stopped for a week. Scepticism had been expressed about the pit's future – but just as the final countdown to the strike began, Agecroft's future was declared by the Board to be bright. Perhaps for some, the desire to work on reflected a judgement on how to protect this pit. Although the pragmatic explanation has been denied by the Agecroft Branch Secretary, he believes that a very lengthy strike could have closed Agecroft. Certainly it was difficult to argue that any threat to Agecroft would hit a specific community. Shortly before the dispute the Branch Secretary claimed that only thirty miners lived close to the pit.[16] One key theme of the strike – the threat to communities – was likely to have little resonance in this cosmopolitan colliery.

The responses of Agecroft miners to early picketing do not permit any simplistic explanation with political moral neatly attached. Rather, they were products of complex circumstances which inhibit easy generalisations. Whatever the weight to be attached to specific elements, the result at Agecroft meant a divided Area with all the consequential problems for the cohesion of the Union and the feasibility of any collective action. Yet when Lancashire delegates met after a week of picketing, they faced not just the consequences of the Agecroft confrontations, but also the arithmetic of the Area ballot. This showed a majority to work – 3,765 to 2,596 or 59.2 per cent to 40.8 per cent. The proportions had barely shifted over twelve months.

The Lancashire verdict echoed those in other balloting coalfields. Little had altered since March 1983; only in Northumberland and North Derbyshire were there sizeable shifts towards strike action, resulting in a thin pro-strike majority in the North-Eastern coalfield and a minute majority against striking in Heathfield's old Area. Elsewhere in Cumberland, South Derbyshire, the Midlands and North Wales, the anti-strike votes were more emphatic than in Lancashire. And that Saturday morning, 17 March when Lancashire miners debated the crisis in Bolton, it was announced that Nottinghamshire had voted heavily to work. That weekend, any national strike strategy seemed a precarious enterprise. This appraisal is essential in understanding reactions in the coalfields but it is easily submerged under knowledge of the dispute's longevity.

At the aggregate level the Lancashire ballot result seemed unambiguous.[17] The Area had taken its traditional place on the NUM Right, but the ballots at individual branches indicated divergent sentiments. Seventeen Branches polled. Two – Billinge, representing a small number of miners in licensed mines, and the North Wales Winders – gave a net vote of sixty to the anti-strike column. They can be disregarded as peripheral to events in the Lancashire coalfield. Of the remaining fifteen Branches, only Bold gave a majority (59.2 per cent) for a strike, but two others just fell short. Sutton Manor had an anti-strike majority of nineteen out of a total valid vote of 475; at Parkside the margin was thirty-one out of 1,321. Apart from these, only Golborne (45.3 per cent) and Kirkless (44.5 per cent) returned a pro-strike vote higher than the coalfield average. Below average percentages ranged from Cronton at 40.4 per cent down to the Winders at 7.5%. Some commentators focused on the low pro-strike vote at the two Agecroft branches – 24.7 per cent at the main Pendlebury Branch and 22.5% at the small Craftsmen's Branch. Nevertheless, it would be mistaken simply to conclude that abrasive Yorkshire picketing abnormally depressed the pro-strike votes. Counter-factual arguments of the 'what would have happened if only . . .' variety are always difficult, but it is worth noting the low pro-strike votes at Parsonage 28 per cent and at Plank Lane 31.8 per cent.

From the Branch votes two general trends are clear. Craft Branches were less keen on a strike than pit Branches. Only one Craft Branch out of six exceeded the coalfield average, but four out of eight pit Branches did so. Moreover, there was generally greater support for the strike in the west of the coalfield. Relatively strong backing came at the St Helens pits, Parkside and Golborne. Cronton constituted a partial exception, but effective closure and demoralisation could make the dispute seem almost irrelevant. An equivalent pattern can be found in the Craft Branches, with the strongest support at Kirkless, and in the pits, relatively high support from Craftsmen in those more favourable to a stoppage. The explanations for this divergence remain unclear. There is no plausible account emphasising Branch Officials' political styles that would fit into this picture. An alternative account might focus on the existence in some pits, especially Bold, of a section of young radicals, influential amongst some miners. Certainly one Area Official has argued that contrasts in age distribution between workforces mattered. The western pits had relatively high proportions of young miners for whom redundancy payments offered only a meagre carrot and who were attracted often to a strategy of fighting for their jobs.[18] The conservatism and sectionalism of the Craftsmen certainly struck the Yorkshire pickets, coming as they did from a coalfield where separate Craftsmen Branches were unknown. One flier recalled: 'If you stopped a Craftsman's car, you always had the same answer, 'What's it got to do with me?'[19]

Whatever the explanations, the ballot result brooded over the remainder of the dispute. For some, in the absence of a national ballot, it was the last word, but the Bold result could legitimise that Branch taking strike action rather than just being picketed out. Moreover, the ballot had revealed very substantial pro-strike minorities at some other pits. Many of these were unlikely to cross any picket line and some seemed likely to work with Bold activists to spread the stoppage.

The atmosphere at the Delegate Conference on 17 March was highly charged. The Hall was more crowded than at any time since the 1974 strike. Since this was a calendared meeting, routine items were also on the agenda and the membership listened to discussions of Area finances and other bread-and-butter matters. But even amongst these items, the Cronton shutdown reared its head with bitterness expressed about management tactics, a disillusion bred of awareness that the NUM had been impotent: 'We never accepted the closure . . . as far as the National Coal Board are concerned it is finished.'[20] After the routine came the time for displaying the passions of the previous seven days. The Agecroft Delegate went

beyond the widespread demand for a national ballot. He urged
that the Lancashire Conference should vote, 'AND THAT VOTE
BE A VOTE OF NO CONFIDENCE IN THE NATIONAL
EXECUTIVE COMMITTEE COUPLED WITH A DEMAND
FOR A NATIONAL BALLOT'. For him the Lancashire ballot
result was legitimacy enough. 'Come hell or high water on Monday
we are going to work.'[21] He insisted that Agecroft members be there
en masse to escort their workmates past the pickets; if this failed,
then all Conference delegates should lend assistance. As a subsequent
speaker noted this 'is virtually a declaration of war'.[22] The demand
for a national ballot was voiced by others and one speaker argued for
a vote of no confidence in the National Officials.[23] But other voices
were heard, John Hensby claiming that whatever the Area ballot
result, many Lancashire miners would respect any picket line: 'Just
imagine Parkside Monday morning two Yorkshire pickets, you
have 676 men at Parkside who want to go to work and 645 who don't
want to go to work. These 645 aren't going to cross the picket line,
irrespective of what is said here today.'[24] His solution was
dramatically opposed to the 'work-at-all-costs' faction. Despite the
ballot result, the Conference should 'instruct' all Lancashire miners
not to cross the picket lines.

   Vincent formulated a resolution which he hoped would unite
delegates. This condemned the violent picketing, noted the Lancashire ballot result and asked the National Officials to convene an
immediate NEC with a view to calling a national ballot. So far, the
wording reflected many of the criticisms voiced in the Conference
although stopping short of censuring the national leadership. But
the concluding section showed a significant shift from the previous
week. Now the authority of the picket line was to be respected: 'WE
ENDEAVOUR TO WORK NORMALLY ON MONDAY BUT
WE WILL NOT CROSS PICKET LINES.' As Vincent noted,
this was the 'meat of the resolution', a point taken by the
Agecroft Delegate who moved deletion of the last seven words.
After all, he had talked of working 'come hell or high water.'
His attempt failed; on a card vote, the original resolution was carried
by ninety-two votes to sixty.[25] The majority was provided by the
seven Branches which had returned the highest pro-strike percentage in the ballot. Lancashire had reached a decision but the
debate and the vote only demonstrated the deep divisions within the
coalfield.

For some, a strategy for a united Area involved two tactics. If Lancashire miners did not attempt to cross picket lines, then the confrontations of the previous week could be avoided, tempers might cool and solidarity be re-established. Such a truce could be facilitated if pressure for an early NEC with the prospect of a national ballot seemed likely to have an impact. Then acceptance of the pickets' authority could appear to be a temporary accommodation until the situation was regularised. But the construction of such a consensus faced major obstacles. Beyond the coalfield it depended on whether National Officials could be pressurised into holding a special NEC and whether this would result in a majority voting for a national ballot. The next scheduled NEC was almost a month away and the Right at national level had been thoroughly ineffective since Gormley's retirement. Within Lancashire, powerful sections threatened such a consensus. Some remained committed to working on, using the ballot vote as justification; but others, impatient at the caution and ambiguity of Area and Branch Officials, were dedicated to spreading the strike. In some branches, rank-and-file activists, taking the lead from Sheffield and not from Bolton, were taking matters into their own hands. Already a phenomenon central to the Lancashire strike was emerging – activists, especially at Bold, were taking their own decisions, liaising with Yorkshire fliers, pressurising Branch officials and beginning to by-pass the Area structure.

Signs of such an alternative structure had been evident even in the first week. Some Bold miners had picketed Sutton Manor; a Branch Official had threatened them with the police.[26] As a response to such activity, officials emphasised that the respect for picket lines referred only to Yorkshire pickets on official strike, and not to pickets from Lancashire Branches.[27] But the shape of things to come was emerging. At each working pit on Monday 19 March, the Yorkshiremen would be back; they would be aided by some from within the coalfield.

The first shift on that Monday morning brought picketing successes. Over the weekend, Bickershaw miners had voted to respect picket lines, and when pickets appeared they did so. Golborne miners split, and at Parkside, production stopped as few face workers went in.[28] The most spectacular development occurred at Sutton Manor. Most men were respecting picket lines, although safety cover was provided. When some others went into work and entered the cage, a banksman refused to give clearance for them to be wound down. The management sent everyone home and the Union Branch withdrew safety cover. Many saw this as one more manifestation of an increasingly harsh managerial regime; one Area Official was more sceptical, seeing it as a tactic by activists eager to widen support for the strike. Whatever the explanation, Lancashire now had two pits completely stopped.[29]

In contrast, Parsonage miners had voted to cross picket lines and many did so,[30] whilst Agecroft witnessed the kind of scene becoming commonplace in Nottinghamshire – a massive police presence, most pickets unable to get near the pit gates, those who did so rendered ineffective by the police, and most miners going through the picket escorted both by the police and by their own officials.

Within a few days it was all too apparent that the coalfield was more divided than ever, and on Thursday 22 March, yet another Conference was held in Bolton in an attempt to achieve that elusive consensus. On one issue agreement came readily. The Cronton miners had effectively accepted the closure. Many were due for redundancy. It was agreed that salvage work should be allowed to go on there in order that redundancy payments should not be affected.[31] But the division on the fundamental issue seemed unbridgeable. Some delegates argued that members would not accept the previous Conference's decision not to cross picket lines on the grounds that: 'The resolution . . . had one fatal flaw . . . if you advise people to work normal but not to cross picket lines it meant effectively you were on strike without a national ballot . . . the only way you would get a national ballot was by continuing to work normal.'[32] This justification was couched in pragmatic terms – a national ballot was needed for effective action. But other speakers from Parsonage and Agecroft were arguing in terms that evoked Lancashire's longstanding prejudices. One said that: 'As far as his members were concerned . . . national officials were not concerned with the rights of the ordinary miners. For them it was a big political battle and the miners were merely being used.'[33]

Beneath the rhetoric there was a fundamental issue that emerged at intervals inside the NUM. What was the status of a Conference decision compared with a coalfield ballot? For some the previous Conference decision constituted a mandate; for others that decision had to be subordinated to the coalfield individual ballot. One speaker claimed that attempts to persuade members that the Conference decision on picket lines should be respected ran into vehement opposition. At Golborne 'We were going to hold a mass meeting, but 200 men came screaming into the union cabin and said, 'We have had a ballot . . . and we shall continue to work normal.'[34] The pressures were not always in that direction. At some pits the strike had taken root: 'As far as the men at Bold and members of St Helens Craftsmens' Branch at Bold are concerned we held a meeting and there wasn't one member of either Branch that went against the conference decision.'[35] It was no longer a matter of support simply for miners from other striking Areas. As a Sutton Manor speaker fresh from the clash at his own colliery emphasised, they 'were not to support the Yorkshire Area, but they were asking for support for [their] own colliery'.[36] Once again Area Officials attempted to construct a consensus. This time, the resolution came from the Area President, Bernard Donaghy. Once again the objective was to achieve a national ballot, but now the method would be to stop work for a week:

IN ORDER TO HAVE UNITY IN THIS AREA AND TO AVOID ANY FURTHER DISTURBANCES, WE INSTRUCT ALL OUR PITS AND WORKSHOPS TO STOP WORK NEXT WEEK FROM MONDAY 26 MARCH 1984, TO AWAIT A DECISION ON THE CALL FOR A NATIONAL BALLOT. IF NO POSITIVE REPLY IS RECEIVED WE SHOULD MEET AGAIN ON SATURDAY 31 MARCH 1984 TO RECONSIDER THE POSITION.'[37]

The proposal offered some basis for united action but clearly licensed divergent hopes. Some could focus on the fact that it involved an instruction to stop work; once the coalfield was out, then perhaps the strike would prove durable. Others could emphasise the commitment to a future meeting in nine days time, when there would be either a pending national ballot or an opportunity to return to work. At best, the resolution was a holding exercise in the hope that a shift would occur at national level; in the absence of such a development, it offered no long-term means for healing Lancashire's divisions.

Indeed even at the 22 March Conference, the resolution proved contentious. It was passed only by nine votes to six.[38] At Agecroft, the proposal was highly unpopular. A mass meeting agreed a week's stoppage, but only by 208 votes to 179. But the terms in which this

decision was packaged were significant, namely: 'to preserve unity
and for a national ballot to be called. We shall be back at work next
Monday irrespective of what is happening.'[39] Jim Lord expressed
what was becoming an immutable position: 'If there is no national
ballot during that time they'll need tanks to get us out.'[40] There was
similar reluctance at Parsonage: 'We had quite a stormy branch
meeting . . . and my men were disappointed to say the least at having
to strike this week . . . the men will be back on Monday and if we
have to face up to the pickets when we get there, then that's fair
enough.'[41] At Golborne, a week's stoppage was agreed, but on the
understanding that there would then be a return to work. Similarly,
at Parkside the shutdown was endorsed, but Branch Officials
anticipated that it would not last.[42]

For a week a superficial peace reigned in Lancashire, although
this could not disguise the continuing deep rifts. Any hope of
avoiding yet another demonstration of disarray depended on some
rapid progress towards a national ballot. During the week's
shutdown, Vincent became involved in a disastrous attempt by the
NEC Right to organise an Executive majority for a ballot. Here was
the ultimate in open conspiracies, a meeting at the Brant Inn,
Groby, in Leicestershire, covered by television cameras and given a
heavy emphasis on that evening's television news. Vincent's
involvement in the planning and his presence recalled his role as a
caucus organiser within the NEC. But, unlike some of the others
attending such as Ken Toon of South Derbyshire and Jack Jones of
Leicestershire, Vincent came from an Area where the strike had
significant support. He had to show awareness of this and could not
be seen as involved in a meeting that could be characterised as an
attempt to sabotage the Union's resistance to closures. So he
responded vigorously to the presence of a television crew, 'I shall
get bloody hung in my Area.'[43] Arguably his position differed from
some of his co-conspirators. He had a long-standing opposition to
closures and was preoccupied with the need to reunite his divided
Area. Alongside this he had a longstanding factional identification
with the Right and had expressed and encouraged political criticism
of the National Officials within Lancashire. Some at the Groby
meeting had a less complicated agenda. They wished to block the
strike mobilisation and to dent the prestige of the Left. They faced
no sizeable pro-strike element within their own membership.
Nevertheless, all participants could agree that a national ballot

should be held. Vincent was therefore a party to the press statement read out by Roy Ottey of the Power Group. They claimed that a majority on the NEC wanted a ballot and that a special Executive meeting should be convened.

One section of the statement could legitimise the position of working miners in a coalfield such as Lancashire: 'It is agreed unanimously that a message be sent out from this meeting to all members where a democratic vote has been taken not to strike, or where the members have been advised to continue working until a national ballot is taken, to endeavour to work normally whilst continuing to apply the overtime ban guidelines.' This proposition ignored the central issue that had exercised and divided Lancashire's miners for more than a fortnight. Did an endeavour to 'work normally' justify the crossing of picket lines? A subsequent section of the press statement suggested that, once an Area ballot had been held and the result had gone against a strike, then that decision should be respected: 'We are unanimously of the opinion that the national officials should recognise the validity of the democratic decisions taken in various areas and whilst appreciating the right of areas to take strike action under Rule *41*, they should also recognise the decision by other areas not to strike.'[44] Such an emphasis on the force of a majority verdict within an Area ignored an element that was becoming significant in Lancashire – the development of a pro-strike stronghold, such as Bold, using its own ballot result to legitimise support for the strike.

Clearly Vincent, whilst in the company of these NEC members, backed arguments similar to those espoused in Lancashire by Parsonage and Agecroft Officials. This raises the fundamental question of his position. Did he blend in with the priorities of men who had long been his factional associates, or were these his real views, subordinated within Lancashire to his desire to maintain a united Area? Did he have a fixed position other than his basic predisposition to oppose closures, or did he shift in accordance with his estimate of the balance of forces within his Area and within the National Union? He was coming to the end of his career as a NUM official and was keen to leave with his reputation intact. Within the National Union, financial considerations and self-esteem fed such a priority. The most reasonable interpretation would be a concern with political management rather than with any specific objectives.

Whatever the objectives espoused by the Groby conspirators, they perished in the nationwide publicity. The only legacies were to the Left. Activists were confirmed in their suspicions about many full-time officials. They simply could not be trusted to prosecute a strike effectively and might seek to sabotage the strategy of the National Union. Yet balancing these suspicions, there was the evidence of the NEC Right's incompetence. What had the Left to fear from such crass opponents?

Nevertheless the Lancashire stoppage had to be reconsidered at the Delegate Conference scheduled for 31 March. On the preceding day the Lancashire Executive met in Bolton and drafted a lengthy resolution for presentation to the Conference. This condemned violent picketing and argued that this had been exacerbated by the 'massive' police presence. It reiterated the pressure from Lancashire on the National Officials regarding a national ballot. Three requests had produced one 'inconclusive' response. Since this principal element in the Area leadership's strategy had failed, the recommendation to Conference was predictable. In its neglect of the picket line issue, it reflected the Groby press statement: 'AS A CONSEQUENCE WE ARE LEFT WITH NO OPTION BUT TO ENDEAVOUR TO WORK NORMAL IN THE NUM NORTH WESTERN AREA ON MONDAY 2 APRIL 1984 AND CONTINUE TO ABIDE BY THE OVERTIME BAN GUIDELINES.'[45] When the Delegates met next morning, they began by listening to two speakers from the Yorkshire NUM. One was Frank Cave, an Agent from Doncaster, the other was John Walsh, recently defeated by a narrow margin in the contest for the National General Secretaryship and in that contest, nominated by Lancashire. They emphasised how Cortonwood had forced Yorkshire into resistance. In contrast to Lancastrian claims about bully-boy tactics, Cave's account of picketing emphasised police repression: 'If this policy was operating in Communist Poland all hell would be let loose in this country.'[46] Above all they emphasised that in Yorkshire support for the strike had deep roots; whatever the reservations elsewhere, this would not just disappear.

When Vincent opened the debate on the Lancashire situation, he acknowledged that in some branches, the commitment to the strike would prove more powerful than any Area decision: 'It is abundantly clear at Bold that they are on strike, and their attitudes have hardened over the last week; Sutton Manor colliery is also on strike and I believe that they are not going to change their decision.'[47] This perception was supplemented by the claim of the Parkside Delegate that having come so far they couldn't retreat: 'It would be wrong to back down. We have been out for three weeks and it would appear that we are beginning to win our fight.' A Parkside Branch meeting had apparently decided to bite on the bullet: 'I have been instructed by my Branch at Parkside that we do not work on Monday, they want to fight till the bitter end,'[48] but if the Conference decided to return to work, then in the interests of unity Parkside would try to implement that verdict.

These perceptions were counterbalanced by Delegates urging a return to work in the absence of a national ballot. Some speakers implied that their contributions reflected their members' position and not their own. One Standing Delegate found this period agonising. Personally a strong supporter of the stoppage, he also had his role as Delegate to perform. He admitted to his Branch Secretary: 'I don't know how long I can go on with this.'[49] Some pragmatically stressed that a ballot was essential for an effective strike. But the Parsonage Delegate presented a sectional basis for resistance. His pit had seen its workforce cut from 1,300 to 300, and he pointed out that: 'All the rundowns and redundancies had been done by consent. It seemed ludicrous that this whole thing should blow up over a rundown in Yorkshire when we had encountered similar rundowns without any thoughts of strike for a number of years.'[50]

Against the variety of justifications for a return to work, Bold's Delegate voiced straightforward support for the strike. This would hopefully go beyond a refusal to work. Activists' initiatives might acquire wider backing: 'A Branch meeting [will] be held over the weekend and hopefully they will agree to picket other Collieries in this Area.'[51]

When the Executive recommendation was put to the Delegates it was carried by twelve votes to three; the minority were Parkside, Bold and Sutton Manor. Many left the Conference Hall angry at the decision. Effectively the resolution was less supportive of the strike than its counterpart a fortnight previously. Now the advice was to work normally; there was no reference to respect for picket lines.

Verdicts on the decision mirrored the coalfield's divisions. On the one side stood Roy Jackson, Branch Secretary at Sutton Manor, where a return to work seemed almost unimaginable: 'We are meeting tomorrow and we will recommend that the men do not work. This meeting has gone against the National Executive. We have been stabbed in the back.' On the other hand, Jim Lord, his counterpart at Agecroft said, 'We shall be working. We don't want to lose our right to the ballot box.' In the middle was a disconsolate Vincent, his bid for a consensus in tatters: 'We are split down the middle. We are in a terrible mess.'[52]

A Coal Board spokesman predictably called the decision 'a victory for commonsense' but next day Branch meetings at Bold and Sutton Manor showed very solid backing for the strike. At Parkside a mass meeting voted to work by a very narrow margin – 298 against 293. From the Monday, pickets returned there as they did to the Complex and to Agecroft. Now Yorkshire and Lancashire men united on the picket lines but their impact was uneven. At Agecroft, the combination of heavy policing and a widespread desire to work on, limited the pickets' effect, but elsewhere many stayed away from work. A Yorkshire flier encountered problems at Bickershaw: 'Half the day shift down. Half afternoon shift . . . Branch no assistance. They are trying to force a ballot. Refused to allow me to speak to a canteen meeting.'[53] Production fluctuated between pits and over time. On some days a particular pit would produce little or nothing as the faceworkers had largely been picketed out; but if no pickets were present then turnout would be higher. As yet at Parkside, Golborne and Bickershaw, some were thorough supporters of the strike; many more drew the line at passing a picket. One Branch Official with reservations about the national strategy recalled that the pickets were not always there. In their absence he went in, but he could not cross the picket line. Eventually he would back the strike and picket his own pit.[54] Another Branch Secretary had reasoned that the ballot vote meant that he should carry out his members' wishes and work. But crossing a picket line proved impossible: 'I hadn't the balls to do it'. So for the time being he stayed at home in a state of limbo.[55]

But beyond this middle ground of officials, and many members, concerned to stick by their union, but aware of the muddle, there stood irreconcilable factions. The clash was brought out clearly early in April as fliers unavailingly picketed Agecroft. A local official claimed that the strikers were an out-of-step minority: 'The Lancashire pits not working should fall in line with us.' But a twenty six year old picket from Bold put the opposite case. In the end procedural niceties should not count: 'We are engaged in a fight for our jobs. A decent pit man would not cross a picket line.'[56] As between these view points the guile of experienced trade union fixers could achieve little.

In the early days of April, there seemed perhaps one road to unity. The monthly NEC meeting was scheduled for 12 April. Pressure from several Executive members had not produced an earlier gathering, but even the normal NEC could be used to press for a national ballot. Many local officials might look forward to such a development but they differed as to its significance. Amongst the Agecroft leadership it seemed to be the *sole issue*: 'Agecroft are fighting for the democratic right to vote. Scargill has replaced democracy with dictatorship.'[57] Elsewhere in the coalfield, the ballot controversy did not obscure the fundamental challenge: 'It is inevitable that we shall have to take on the Coal Board which is the agent of the Government. It is the feeling of everyone that we want a national ballot.'[58] Yet Vincent had already expressed scepticism about the hope that a national ballot could be secured 'I do not think that a ballot vote would be achieved nationally. I feel that the National President will rule any call for a national ballot vote out of order.'[59] The years as one of Gormley's lieutenants had not been wasted!

April 12 proved Vincent's instinct correct, and with miners from striking pits lobbying NEC members, it demonstrated the base fact that the strike was here to stay. Vincent came back to Lancashire with two key decisions other than the non-decision on the ballot. The ballot issue would be debated the following week on Maundy Thursday at a Special National Delegate Conference. The venue was almost guaranteed to provide a majority for the existing strategy. Yet the second decision suggested that a ballot might just be held. The Conference would also debate a change in Rule *43* governing national strike ballots; the proposal was that the 55 per cent requirement be removed in favour of a simple majority.

The Lancashire Executive met next day and decided that yet another letter be sent into the national office asking for a national ballot to be backed by a strong recommendation for strike action. There was also an overwhelming vote against a change in the 55 per cent rule.[60] These issues were then discussed by the Area Delegate Conference.[61] Some speakers felt that the removal of the 55 per cent qualification should be referred to Branch meetings and their

decisions phoned through to Area Office; others felt that since the
Area had a long standing tradition of accepting NEC decisions, this
should not be broken. Behind the discussion lay a belief that any
Lancashire decision would be academic and that sufficient Areas
would guarantee the amendment's passage. Some delegates clearly
hoped that such a change would make a national ballot more likely
and that in the present climate, that could be won for a strike.

By now there was a significant divide within the Area, not just
between strikers and those who would work until a national ballot
was held, but also between those who wanted an effective strike
achieved through a national ballot and those who were antagonistic
to the national leadership and saw the ballot as *the* decisive issue. On
a show of hands, the vote to support the rule change was tight nine to
eight but on the card vote, the margin was more than two to one.
Division on this was not matched by any disagreement over the
desirability of a ballot. There was no opposition to tabling of a pro-
ballot resolution for the Special National Conference. No one raised
that vital and awkward question – what could be done in Lancashire
if the National Conference rejected all the pro-ballot resolutions?

Maundy Thursday was the day for decision. Delegates from
striking, working and divided coalfields met in Sheffield; so did
thousands of strikers concerned to lobby delegates, saluting the
pro-strike NEC members and heckling those who were critical of
the national strategy. The Lancashire delegation included more
than its share of critics – Brian Bancroft, the Agecroft Standing
Delegate who had raised passions at the Lancashire Conference as
he advocated crossing picket lines, the Kirkless Branch Secretary
who would never back the strike, and the Area President, Bernard
Donaghy, deeply concerned about the Union's predicament.

The change to the ballot rule produced little controversy.
Opposition was led by the Nottinghamshire Area in the shape of its
Financial Officer Roy Lynk; but on this Lancashire voted with the
majority and the change was made with a majority of over three to
one.[62] Then it was the decisive debate, with Peter Heathfield in his
first major speech as National General Secretary opening the
argument. He raised the spectre of the sixties closures when the
NUM had simply let it all happen, but emphasised that this
challenge was tougher: 'We are no longer talking about transferring
miners from one pit to another. We are talking about the scrapheap.'
In that predicament a ballot could kill effective resistance, it could

be 'a veto to prevent people in other areas defending their jobs.'[63]
Here was effectively an admission that a ballot could well fail to
produce a majority for a strike.

The pro-ballot resolutions followed, a Leicestershire one simply
arguing for a national ballot,[64] and then Donaghy moving the
Lancashire alternative: 'Arising out of the present situation in the
industry the Conference agrees to hold an immediate individual
membership ballot vote with a strong recommendation that members
will vote for strike action with a view to co-ordinating the action
nationally to stop pit closures.'[65] He presented the most coherent
case for a ballot heard by the Sheffield Delegates. He attacked the
fear that a ballot might produce a decision not to strike and was
therefore to be avoided: 'If you think at the back of your mind that a
ballot vote will lose and you are still urging your men to come out on
strike, I think you are cheating on your membership.' Then he
turned to the sentiments of men who had been committed to the
strike for six weeks; why now should they have to acquiesce in a
ballot decision? Donaghy's answer stressed the disunity of the
membership; only a ballot could end this disharmony: 'For the first
time since 1926, we have had confrontations between miners and
miners . . . Our forefathers fought too long to have one union and
one industry to throw it away by fighting ourselves.' This bleak and
accurate prognostication was informed with a belief that the tactic
of spreading the strike by picketing would fail. Perhaps with
Agecroft and Parsonage in mind, he reflected: 'It is no good
standing on a picket line if people keep going past you.'[66]

For all its tight reasoning, Donaghy's case failed to meet one
central question in the opposite argument. What could the NUM do
if miners at a threatened pit wished to oppose closure and their more
secure counterparts elsewhere did not? This sentiment was fuelled
by all the emotion and commitment that came from the weeks on
strike. Jack Taylor of Yorkshire penetrated to this silence in the pro-
ballot case: 'You want to go back to work and you will leave dirty
work to Owen Briscoe, Ken Homer and me, when we go down to
Cartonwood that Sunday morning and say "I am sorry lads . . . 800
jobs have gone down the road."'[67] And the disillusioning experiences of pickets in largely working coalfields intensified the
opposition to a ballot. Terry Thomas of South Wales was speaking
with specific reference to Nottinghamshire, but his words could
have been applied to Agecroft: 'I will never believe that a man who

will cross a picket line with a police escort will put a cross on for a
strike when he is hidden round the corner. It is just not on.'[68] These
were the voices of the Left. Given the Union's factional alignments
their position was predictable. But Durham was a traditionally
cautious coalfield threatened under the recently announced cutbacks. Tom Callan, the Area's General Secretary acknowledged
that contrary to the Durham practice, they had struck without a
ballot. It was a last resort. 'We have carried on in the past and
colliery closures have taken place.'[69] This contribution by a
respected figure who had never been aligned to the Left was
revealing. It demonstrated the pressure on miners in a threatened
coalfield, pressures which could overcome long held political
attachments.

In the most fundamental sense, the Conference debate altered
nothing. It demonstrated the deep commitment to the strike in
some Areas, perhaps the desperation that had led some to adopt this
strategy; it showed the concern in some Areas about divisions in the
Union; some possibly were already moving down a critical road that
would lead them out of the NUM. But the debate exhibited
attitudes, it did not change them. On almost all the resolutions for a
ballot, sixty-nine votes were cast against – the minority varied. The
Lancashire resolution with its accompanying commitment to a
strike achieved the largest support – fifty-five. But this was the
effective end of any campaign for a national ballot. Some diehards
would continue to demand one for several months, but it was never
again within the sphere of practical Union politics.

Instead, the majority backed a resolution from the Kent Area.
This supported the strategy of the National Officials as endorsed by
the recent formal decisions of the NEC. The vital passage read,
'Conference agrees to fully endorse the decisions of the NEC . . .
which sanctionned industrial action in accordance with national
Rule *41*. It is further agreed that the National Union call on all areas
to join the eighty per cent who are already on strike and therefore
ensure maximum unity in the Union.'[70] The Conference decision
was announced to the masses of striking miners outside the hall. For
them it was the decisive defeat of a proposal that had threatened to
subvert all that they had achieved over the previous six weeks. Now
the response had to come from the predominantly working
coalfields and from divided ones such as Lancashire. The choice
was at one level simple, but it was complicated by the legacy of

recent events – the Lancashire ballot result and the entrenched position in some Branches that a national ballot alone could persuade them to stop work.

In Lancashire there followed a brief hiatus. The Sheffield Conference was succeeded by an Easter Weekend of warm days , a foretaste of the long hot summer that would bronze the striking miners. When the Lancashire pits reopened after the holiday break, the mere fact of the Sheffield decisions made no impact. The pattern of attendance was a continuation of what happened earlier in April; Bold and Sutton Manor stopped, Agecroft and Parsonage largely working, the remainder divided. In the nearby North Wales coalfield, Easter Tuesday had seen a decision for an official Area strike, despite a ballot vote more opposed to such action than in Lancashire, and despite a strong 'work until a national ballot' movement at Point of Ayr Colliery. Here was an attempt in a traditionally very cautious area to come to terms with the Sheffield decision.

Predictably, a similar attempt was made in Lancashire. Eight days after the National Conference, the Lancashire delegates met yet again in Bolton. Vincent attempted to win support for the Sheffield decision. He argued that the NUM had come so far that the strike could not be allowed to crumble: 'It could destroy this union.' It was not a matter of the Left taking the membership for a ride: 'Two of the most moderate Areas . . . are Northumberland and Durham . . . [they] and Durham Mechanics came out on strike when the Yorkshire Area did . . . these men will not return to work unless they win the fight.' Although the Lancashire coalfield was divided, many members were committed to the dispute; moreover, other unions in the region were giving support. So Vincent concluded with a plea to support the Kent resolution: 'Let's try to get our members to stop work on Monday.'[71] But this proposal provoked an immediate and hostile response from the Agecroft Delegate. For him, the Sheffield Conference altered nothing: 'This Area has a clear mandate, it was 59 per cent ballot vote of the members against strike action. We note this resolution, but I am mandated to say that we continue to work normal until a national ballot is called.'[72] Against this, speakers from strike-bound pits voiced their impatience at such stonewalling: 'I am sick and tired of going to collieries on picket lines trying to get the rest of this Area out on strike, because it is your jobs they are fighting for as well as their own . . . there were many people dodging and hiding behind a ballot being called.'[73] Significantly, the delegate from the Ashton and Haydock Craftsmen who had previously urged a national ballot as a necessary condition for an effective strike was prepared to consider the realistic options in a world where a ballot had been ruled out. The objectives of the strike should be supported and Conference should unite to secure them. The ballot was a chimera and that argument should end.

Resistance to Vincent's proposals came not only in the form of Agecroft's emphasis on the ballot requirement, it also surfaced in the shape of a procedural alternative. Most members of the Leigh Craftsmen's Branch had consistently demonstrated a desire to work. In the Area ballot, only 26 per cent had backed a strike. Now the Branch Delegate suggested a consultation at Branch level before any decision was made, an initiative backed by the Plank Lane Delegate.

Such a consultation could take divergent forms dependent on the attitudes of Branch officials. They could simply report the feelings of members, or they could return to their Branches and campaign for the national decision. How effective such campaigning could be over a weekend was questionable. Meetings were held but, predictably, the results altered nothing. Only at Parkside did the Kent resolution secure a majority of 280 to 188; at Agecroft and Parsonage there were decisive rejections of the proposal, and at Bickershaw and Golborne there were narrow votes to work.[74] The exercise had done nothing to heal divisions within the coalfield. Delegates travelled to Bolton on the Monday to face another divided meeting, but they found that the seemingly timeless routines of Union procedures had been brusquely interrupted.

Many-rank-and-file striking miners had become thoroughly impatient at the interminable attempts to construct a consensus that could include both them and the persistent crossers of picket lines. Bold had been stopped since the night shift on the Tuesday of the first week; Sutton Manor had reached the same situation a week later. As indicated earlier, a significant number of Lancashire miners were not simply honouring picket lines, they were committed to spreading the stoppage.

When they came to Delegate Conference, they repeatedly encountered criticism of strike tactics from some speakers, and what seemed like a paralysing ambiguity from Area Officials. Pro-crastination had some plausibility perhaps until the passing of the Kent resolution. Now, to the committed, the choice seemed

brutally clear. Jack Taylor of Yorkshire had expressed it bluntly at
the Sheffield Conference: 'There is no problem with getting on our
side. You don't have to have any ballots for that . . . You have to put
your feet on the floor and walk across that line MacGregor has
drawn, his side and our side.'[75] or as another Yorkshire speaker put
it in that same debate 'If you are not on strike, you are the problem.'[76]

Lancashire miners were in that vast crowd outside the Sheffield
Conference; they had wined on the heady atmosphere, they were
thoroughly committed to the dispute. Against this *elan*, the return
to the maze of arguments and counter-arguments in their own
coalfield was, for some, a last straw. The Conference's indecisive
outcome had been anticipated by some Bold strikers. They were not
prepared to continue within the Union's routines:

> Three of us from Bold went one night to Birkenhead. In a pub run by a
> blacked docker, there was a big collection of people – many of them
> unemployed. We had a few drinks and came back to Bold, feeling we had
> to do something to make the strike stick – really for all those people who
> were waiting for us to have a go at Thatcher for them.

For some, the strike was more than a simple industrial dispute. It
was heavy with the traumas of the Labour movement during the
Thatcher years. So an indecisive Delegate Conference would be
countered by a radical act against a network of conventions.

> We decided that if the Delegate Conference came to no clear decision to
> back the National leadership and just kept saying go back and get
> support in the Branches, we would sit in. We planned it with the lads
> from Sutton Manor and Golborne. The Delegate Conference came out
> with the same old line. So we went ahead. Horsfield, the Agent didn't
> like it at all, so we told him 'Get your coat and fuck off'.[77]

The predictable rule-governed world of the official had come into
conflict with the iconoclastic impatience of activists.

The Area Office was decorated with 'Coal Not Dole' banners, a
greeting for Conference Delegates when they returned with the
discouraging news of the weekend Branch meetings. Those in
occupation had said they would stay in the office 'until we get
satisfaction, and our so-called brothers in the Lancashire coalfield
come out on strike.'[78] That Monday they set up a picket line.
Vincent refused to cross this and said that the Conference could not
be held. Jim Lord, armed with the confirmed Agecroft commitment
to no strike without a national ballot, was dismissive of both
demonstrators and Vincent's decision: 'Are we going to give in to

this rabble? It's absolutely ridiculous. This is not democracy.'[79] Against this position, occupiers mingled with would-be delegates chanting, 'Stuff your ballot up your arse.'[80] One activist drew attention to the gulf between officials and rank-and-file strikers 'We want some proper leadership – Sid can take some unpaid holidays to the West Indies.'[81]

The occupation lasted until 9 May. Planned by rank-and-file members, viewed critically and perhaps with trepidation by several Area and Branch Officials, Vincent effectively employed the initiative to develop support for the strike in a fashion paralleling Gormley's utilisation of wage-based militancy. It was not simply that the occupation broke the circle of indecisive meetings; it also provided space for new forces to mould the pattern of events.

One development was the result of liaison between Lancastrian strikers and the Sheffield office, a link which characteristically by-passed the Area Officials. According to one of those included, Scargill and the Northumberland leader, Dennis Murphy were involved in a network of 'phone calls that brought 1,500 Geordie pickets down to Lancashire. One Branch committee man, himself pro-strike, had some awareness of what was planned: 'It was talked about on the grape vine. There were addresses of pubs in Newcastle.'[82] Many were lodged in the Miners' clubs at Bold and Sutton Manor, others in the homes of sympathisers. The rapport with local strikers was close – on the picket lines, the newcomers chanted 'hya we go, hya we go, hya we go' starting a fashion for local miners. Most important, the initiative had its successes. One tough Lancastrian had no illusions:

> These were men brought up on aggression. They'd already been on strike for a long while. The police in Lancashire couldn't cope in part because Notts was the priority . . . Yes, men were brought out by physical methods. After all what else is there to do, if you've discussed it all – he says 'yes he agrees' but then goes into work.[83]

The Geordies' most sensational successes came in the Complex. The Golborne Branch had decided at its weekend meeting against strike action by a majority of just eighteen. By the following Thursday 3 May the pit was subject to intensive and vigorous picketing by 1,200 North Eastern and local strikers. One Area official, unhappy about the whole strike strategy, was shocked by the tactics used. Eight arrests were made but the pit was closed on a decision by the NUM and the Craftsmen Branch.[84] The Golborne

Secretary, Ron Gaskell, impeccably moderate in his politics, was emotional in his response. He was hardly an enthusiast for mass picketing. 'It was terrible. You have to give in to ensure the safety of the membership . . . It is a crying shame that we are having to close, but there is nothing we can do about it.'[85] Yet the picketing left a durable legacy; from that moment, many Golborne miners were solidly behind the strike. Although initially forced out by weight of numbers, often they proved impervious to subsequent Coal Board blandishments and pressures. Picketing had a similar impact at Bickershaw where the North Eastern–Lancashire combination stopped the pit, a particularly significant success since all coal cut in the Complex was wound to the surface there. At Parkside the impact was less thorough, but the numbers crossing picket lines diminished to no more than 10 per cent of the workforce. Only at Agecroft and Parsonage did picketing have little impact, and on account of the Bickershaw shut-down, no Parsonage coal could be brought out. As a result of these May days, the Board could only claim effective production at Agecroft, whilst picketing, had also had a significant impact on Kirkless Workshop in Wigan. Walkden Workshops saw its first significant picketing but to little effect. Some Yorkshiremen recall that assignment as notably unrewarding.[86]

The Area Director, John Northard, might appeal to Lancashire to react against 'strong-arm tactics'[87] but a spokesman for the Board acknowledged that the early May picketing had made a mark: 'These new tactics of suddenly descending in massive numbers on pits seem to be having some effect.'[88] There were swift moves to redress the balance. The police presence was increased 'Afterwards picketing always faced the problem of police outnumbering pickets. Whatever we had, they could get twice as many.'[89] Acrimony on the picket lines increased; arrests began to mount. At Parkside 'they began pushing the lads back and sending in snatch squads.'[90] The Coal Board began its war of nerves. By May, Bold had been completely stopped for two months; a deadlock between NUM Branch and management developed over the latter's claim that a deteriorating face needed urgent repairs. Eventually a deal was struck, but the claims and counter-claims provided a grim foretaste of the psychological battles to come.[91]

If activists' initiatives helped to spread the strike in Lancashire and effectively move the Area towards an acceptance of the Kent resolution, this shift was facilitated by a change in attitude amongst some Branch Officials and Committee men. At Parkside, by early May Branch officials were on the picket line. They had decided to stay out until the strike ended, regardless of how their own members acted.[92] Similarly, at Bickershaw the Plank Lane Committee began to picket their own pit, despite the narrow Branch vote against the Kent resolution.[93] If the mass picket provided a robust justification for staying outside the pit gates, this commitment by Branch officials could provide a legitimacy.

As the tempo of the battle quickened, so the machinery of the NUM Area remained in limbo, due to the Bolton occupation. This ended on 9 May. Next day the NUM's National Executive met in Sheffield; one of its concerns was the interpretation of the Kent resolution. As noted earlier, this included the passage, 'the National Union call on all areas to join the 80 per cent who are already on strike.' But 'call' was an ambiguous word – would an appropriate synonym be 'request', 'demand' or 'instruct'? This issue had been raised at the truncated Lancashire Conference in late April, but without any resulting clarification. But by 11 May, faced with the assessment of the May NEC, the Lancashire Area officials gave a clear, if debatable, verdict: 'This is a national instruction . . . any Branch or NUM member who is on strike in the North Western Area is officially on strike . . . any other Branch or NUM members who are not taking part should be officially on strike in accordance with a National Conference decision.' Their statement also highlighted the pressures on full-time officials to accept their instruction 'Permanent officials of the National Union who [do] not advocate this policy [will] be in serious trouble, they [are] instructed to act in accordance with the National Conference policy.' Such pressures mattered for the Lancashire full-time officials, all of whom had reservations about the national strategy. The consequence was the relaying of the 'instruction' into the Area: 'The four Officials of the NUM North-Western Area instruct all members and Branches of the NUM North Western Area to come out on official strike.'[94] One of the four has acknowledged that there could be no instruction; it was a ploy in an impossible situation.[95] Moreover, the statement did not result from any properly convened meeting of either the Executive or the Area Conference, nor could it be justified by any earlier decision. Instead, the Officials met representatives of striking Branches at an informal meeting in Bolton.[96]

Irregular or not, the 'instruction' went out to Branches and was accepted by most Branch Committees. These included, not just those which had been out from the early days, or where much support for the strike had been evident, but also other Branches such as Leigh Craftsmen and St Helens Craftsmen where there had been considerable opposition to national strategy. Thus, on Sunday 12 May about fifty craftsmen still working at Sutton Manor were instructed to join the strike, following the decision by the St Helens Branch.[97] But there were significant refusals to accept the 'instruction' – both Agecroft Branches, Parsonage, Walkden, and the small but strategically important Winders – all stood out against this development.[98] Overall Vincent could claim that on a hypothetical card vote[99] there was a decisive majority in favour of the strike, but such an argument ignored some fundamental questions. Did the achievement of this majority violate the Area Rule Book? And was this really a majority anyway? Most members had not been involved in this chain of decisions. Would they be persuaded by such a sequence?

The continuing division was as stark as ever when Lancashire Delegates eventually met in Conference on 19 May. Although Vincent emphasised that the Kent resolution was mandatory, speakers from Agecroft and Parsonage stuck to their old arguments and rhetoric. But other contributions showed that recent events had shifted the balance within the Area. The St Helens Craftsmen Delegate was heavily critical of the lack of a ballot; he espoused the Agecroft and Parsonage argument about democratic rights and objected to the informal and exclusive meeting which had issued the Area's instruction – but in the end, if an 'instruction' was issued, argument should end: 'If this is an instruction from the National President and the Area Officials then I as a Branch Official, will accept that decision . . .' Similarly, Mick Noonan of Parkside argued pragmatically: 'There is no chance that we will have a national ballot, and we will probably fall out about the legalities of the instruction in the years to come – the only way of winning is uniting together.'[100] Once the hope of a national ballot had offered the prospect of unity, now it had to be backing for an 'instruction'.

The raising of the temperature as the strike spread in Lancashire was starting to widen the distance between officials in strike-bound pits and those ready to plead the case of working miners. Whilst the Parsonage Delegate emphasised that he was reflecting his members' views, his counterpart from Bickershaw retorted that Parsonage officials should follow the example of their neighbours: 'If they cannot get their members out on strike so be it, but the officials have enjoyed the good times . . . in this Organisation . . . if only their officials would join the picket line and say that they are not prepared to cross, then perhaps their members would fall into line.'[101] Already Branch Officials who sometimes, after much thought, had committed themselves to the strike were expressing concern about the consequences of continuing disunity. The Area had contacted NACODS in an attempt to persuade them to respect the picket lines. The negative response could make it easier for Lancashire NUM members to defy the strike call; equally, the deputies' actions could secure credibility by highlighting this defiance. Very few COSA members ever stopped work in Lancashire; again, disunity could further license willingness to cross the picket lines. More specifically, the Winders presented a predictable and serious challenge. The Parkside Delegate emphasised a persistent problem at his pit: 'We will never win this fight as long as the winders insist on winding blacklegs down the pit.'[102]

The Lancashire Conference accepted the strike 'instruction' but some Branches remained opposed. Two days later the Area executive made one last attempt to produce a solid Lancashire strike. They agreed to suspend for five years any member or Officer who crossed a picket line. Those affected would have to pay Union dues but they would be disqualified from holding office, attending meetings and receiving benefits.[103] The sanction was justified by reference to Area Rule 35. The vital Rule began, 'If any member or officer willfully commits a breach of these Rules, the Area Executive Committee shall have the power to expel him or suspend him from the membership of the Union . . .' Presumably the breach of the Rule would refer to the ignoring of a national instruction subsequently supported by a Lancashire Conference. The Area's Rule Nine seemed to endow this body with sovereignty: 'Subject to the authority of the National Executive Committee, the general management of, and incidental to the affairs of the Union shall be vested in an Area Conference . . .'[104] By the time the notice of suspension had emerged from Bolton, the Agecroft members had voted heavily once more to work on and had passed a motion of no confidence in Vincent. Already, Jim Lord was hinting that lawyers would be consulted about the constitutionality of the strike instruction.[105] When the disciplinary measure was made public, work ceased at Agecroft and Parsonage, but only until supportive legal action could be secured.[106] The Parsonage Branch Vice President, Walter Speakman, articulated the gulf between strike breaking Branches and the rest of the Area: 'It was a heartbreaking decision to make and quite a number of the Branch officials were visibly upset, but the price we would have to pay would be too high. The men accepted our advice reluctantly although they expressed anger and disgust at the Area's decision.'[107] Already the Nottinghamshire NUM had found itself in a legal battle. Three of its members had issued writs on 15 May; their objective was to lift an instruction that the Notts strike was official. Ten days later the plaintiffs won their case. By then, Agecroft leaders were moving down the same track and had won a temporary injunction. Most men at Agecroft and Parsonage immediately returned to work.[108]

The suspension threat, far from producing unity, had only deepened animosities. Yet for supporters of the strike, there was one bonus. Previously the number of Agecroft strikers had been very small. They had felt isolated, not just from others at their own pit, but also from the broad mass of Lancashire strikers. Occasionally they were displayed at meetings to show that not all Agecroft miners were crossing picket lines, but at least one striker felt that they were still regarded with some suspicion. But when the suspension threat appeared, about a hundred came out and never went back. They set up two strike centres, one at the Engineering Union office in Salford, the other in Burnley to cater for the former Hapton Valley men committed to the strike. For several weeks the Agecroft strikers picketed their own pit; soon it became apparent that they would not increase their numbers, but they still attempted to halt supplies. Later, some Agecroft activists moved on to a wider stage and became leading members of the Lancashire rank and file movement. Their commitment to the dispute and to the national strategy would remain total until the end. Ironically, the suspension manoeuvre was typical of the procedural devices employed over many years by the Lancashire leadership; yet the one positive consequence for the strike involved this strengthening of a rank-and-file movement which viewed the officials' manoeuvres, at least with suspicion, and on occasions with hostility.[109]

Although the Lancashire Area was entering a legal labyrinth, the strike had now much more support in the coalfield; the authority of the 'national instruction' , choices made by individual Branch Officials, the mass picketing by Geordies and Lancastrians – all had left their marks. The greatest success had been to shut down the Complex through the picketing out of Golborne and Bickershaw. This clearly concerned the Coal Board, but there seemed some hope that the tide could be rolled back. In one Complex pit, Parsonage, most miners were continuing to work; many members of the Leigh Craftsmen were ready to join them, despite their officials' acceptance of the strike instruction. Moreover, at no time, either in the ballot or in any meeting, had the Plank Lane Branch, organising miners at Bickershaw Colliery, backed the strike. Some had supported the dispute from the start, others would not cross any picket line, but several had ceased work only in May as a result of the impact of the fliers and of the decision by the Branch Committee to back the strike. Throughout much of May, the Plank Lane Branch stayed solid, but this was not evidence of universal support for the strike.

The Coal Board targeted men whom they thought resented the success of the pickets. They reminded them that their Parsonage neighbours were earning regular wages. One official thought that the management were deliberately inflating the income of Parsonage miners: 'the . . . Board are paying a better bonus . . . at Parsonage colliery than they have had over the last twelve months. It is not bonus pay, it is crossing picket line money.'[110] About seventy Bickershaw men responded; they met at Hindley and agreed to return after the Spring Bank Holiday. On the first morning three coaches took them past one hundred pickets. The Board made exaggerated claims about the numbers returning, about the prospects for resuming production at Bickershaw and about the putative domino effect on other Lancashire pits. On succeeding days there were increases in the number of pickets, the police presence and the level of arrests. Hundreds of pickets came from the Bold Miners' Club and from other coalfields. There was no effective liaison with local officials. Whatever the number of pickets, they were matched by the police. The pit yard was full of transit vans; horses were stabled; the canteen was packed with police reinforcements.[111]

Yorkshire pickets recall Bickershaw as marking a substantial escalation of the conflict in Lancashire. Until these early June mornings, policing had been usually more relaxed than in the Nottinghamshire battleground. Now, with the strike settling into a long battle, the Board hoped for an important breakthrough and the full police paraphernalia was turned out. On the other side, the fliers had lost their March innocence. They now responded vigorously to what seemed breaches of normal picket line practice. One Yorkshireman recalls how, with what was by then an experienced eye, he identified snatch squads in the police ranks at Bickershaw. When a striker next to him was grabbed, he attempted to prevent his arrest, only to be arrested himself. He was taken into the pit yard and beaten before pleading guilty at a Magistrate's Court in order to avoid restrictive bail conditions. By now the pickets were resourceful. One morning, a milkman came down the road past Bickershaw. He found unexpected customers. 'He must have thought it was his birthday.' The milk was not the attraction.[112]

One morning pickets breached police lines and delayed the coaches for an hour.[113] Eventually as the Plank Lane Branch Secretary put it 'all hell broke loose'.[114] On 12 June a Coal Board spokesman claimed a 'near riot'. More than a thousand pickets gathered; they threw bricks and bottles at Coal Board vans, they broke into a disused office and took tables and chairs to use as a barricade. The police were accused of using truncheons and horses indiscriminately. Bickershaw offered an early anticipation of what would become a familiar pattern.[115]

The seventy strike breakers never came out again; eventually Branch officials were allowed on coaches to talk to them but they were immovable. But their numbers showed no significant increase. The initial breakthrough did not produce an early and sizeable collapse of the strike at Bickershaw, nor was it emulated at any other Lancashire pit. Instead, the confrontations steeled some strikers for a lengthy and harsh dispute. Having faced truncheons and horses, what else was there to do, but battle on? Most sombrely at Bickershaw, one banksman with no record of union activity became an active picket. Branch officials commented that he would have done anything to stop the buses going into the pit yard. He set fire to one at its overnight parking place, caused considerable damage and was eventually gaoled for six months.[116] The stakes were rising on both sides.

The tensions were compounded in Lancashire by the legal challenge facing the Union. Whilst pickets and police were battling at the gates of Bickershaw, Union officials were taking legal advice and anticipating a struggle in the courts. On the day when the strike breakers were first bussed into Bickershaw, 29 May, the Lancashire Executive met and considered the problem of the Agecroft injunction. Two significant decisions appear in the minutes. One was to apply to the NEC under Rule Forty One seeking approval for an official strike in Lancashire. Hopefully, such approval could protect the Area against legal action. The second decision was simply to resist the Agecroft injunction.[117]

Approval of these steps came four days later at an Area Conference. It was anticipated that NEC approval of a Lancashire strike would permit the implementation of the hitherto abortive suspension procedures.[118] Nevertheless, Vincent appeared in the High Court in Manchester on Friday 8 June and agreed to lift any suspensions. Once the stoppage had been sanctioned by the National Executive then the suspensions could be reactivated.[119] The NEC played its part at a meeting on 14 June,[120] but even now the Lancashire officials found their strategy threatened by a new Agecroft injunction. This argued that a strike in Lancashire approved under national Rule Forty One could be valid only if Lancashire's Rule Forty had been followed. This stipulated that: 'No strike of a pit set or colliery shall be authorised unless permission had been given by the Executive Committee or Conference, subject to the provisions of the National Rules to take a ballot of the men affected, and a 55 per cent majority of the votes recorded have been obtained in favour of ceasing work . . .'[121] The injunction claimed that in the absence of a 55 per cent majority, any putative stoppage could not be 'official' in the sense that members should feel obliged to stop work. The comments of the NEC and Area institutions were insufficient bases.

The injunction's arguments also alleged procedural irregularities in the making of the Rule Forty One application to the NEC. It claimed that the Lancashire Executive meeting of 29 May never decided to propose such an application at the subsequent Area Conference; rather, the only decision had been to take legal advice.[122] Indeed, at that 2 June Conference, the Agecroft Executive member had claimed that any such Rule Forty One resolution must have been formulated after he left. Vincent's explanation hardly clarified the situation: 'I . . . said . . . that it was necessary to protect this Union and that I be allowed to formulate a Minute which would be put before this Area Conference . . . This suggestion was moved and seconded by two members of the Area Executive Committee and agreed.'[123] The means of protection was to be through a Rule Forty One application to the National Executive.

The Agecroft plaintiffs claimed further that the 2 June Conference which had approved this application had been convened improperly since the requisite eight days' notice of business had not been given. These alleged irregularities were placed in the context of earlier Lancashire decisions – that by the Executive on 30 March and by a Conference the following day backing a national ballot and, in its absence, proposing normal working. The plaintiffs contended that this remained Area policy unless changed by proper procedures, and this had not happened.[124]

Fine legal arguments produced a dismissive response from strikers at the 16 June Conference. One who had argued for a national ballot until the Sheffield decisions now drew a sharp distinction: 'There is a degree of hypocrisy that I have never witnessed before in this hall from certain Branches. They call themselves democrats, self-styled leaders of so-called democracy . . . when the majority of Lancashire miners are on strike struggling and bearing hardship . . .' The worthlessness of previous rhetoric was revealed. There had been much talk about the need for action, 'yet when they are given the chance to do something about it, they go and hide behind the judge's skirts.'[125]

In fact, Area officials knew that the injunction was likely to be successful. Their Counsel's advice had been pessimistic,[126] a prognostication borne out by the decision of Mr Justice Caulfield on 26 June. He rejected submissions that an Area strike in Lancashire did not require a ballot. One defence rested on Lancashire Rule Nine, vesting 'General Management' in the Area Conference , the other rested on the precise wording of the Rule Forty which did not link the ballot requirement specifically to an Area dispute. In the judge's view, this position could not be maintained. Lancashire's Rule Forty Three stated that if Area and National Rules conflicted, then the latter should apply. Within the National Rules, a national ballot was needed for a national strike; within the Lancashire Rules, a ballot was needed for a pit stoppage. Could an Area strike be governed by different requirements?[127]

This decision was just one in a series of legal actions lost by the NUM Area – in Nottinghamshire, in North Wales, in North Derbyshire. It made little difference whether an Area Rule Book contained a specific requirement for an Area ballot as in North

Derbyshire, whether it was perhaps unclear on this as in Lancashire, or whether it definitely had no such requirement, as
in North Wales. Whatever the opacity of the Lancashire rules,
there is no doubt that Area Officials had consistently behaved
as if a ballot majority was a prerequisite for any strike action.
Indeed, until the crisis forced them to rethink the situation, they
believed in all probability that a ballot was not simply a convenient
political tactic, but also a constitutional necessity. Certainly they
helped to foster the pervasive expectation that there had to be a
ballot.[128]

The success of the injunction completed the rupture between
striking and working branches. Representatives of the latter had
continued to attend Area Executive and Conference. At the latter
they faced the mounting anger of strikers. A Conference convened
on 29 June, but it proved to be brief. After the roll call, Ron Gaskell,
Golborne Branch Secretary, and less than two months before a
critic of mass picketing, highlighted what for many was both
outrageous and grotesque: 'The overwhelming majority of delegates
and visitors in this hall this morning are on strike . . . we should not
be meeting with delegates from branches who are working.' The
proposal was seconded more aggressively by Mal Gregory of Bold.
The official minutes then conclude baldly 'The overwhelming
majority of delegates and visitors, then rose and left the hall.'[129] The
members from working branches then stayed on for about twenty-
five minutes in the hope that tempers would cool. They did not.
Strikers returned to clear the hall, shouting, according to a
Parsonage official, 'Come out of this hall, it doesn't belong
to scabs.'[130] Allegations were made of boots and fists flying:
Branch officials were chased down the street.[131] As claims of
assault were made to an ever-eager press, Gaskell denied that
there had been any set up. He revealed the chasm that had opened
up, even for a cautious Branch official: 'It is time for us to
stop pussy-footing about with these people. It is a waste of time
sitting with them at Conference making decisions when they are
ignoring the union leadership and taking out injunctions against
us.'[132] From that day, working miners ceased to attend union
meetings. These became gatherings of those professing commitment to the strike.

Notes

1   For early experiences of Yorkshire pickets in Nottinghamshire see People of Thurcroft, *Thurcroft*, pp. 63–70.

2   For material on this and other aspects of North Yorkshire picketing in Lancashire I owe much to the help of some fliers at a discussion in Castleford, July 1987.

3   Discussions at Bold NUM.

4   Steve Vickers's *Diary*.

5   See *Newton and Golborne News*, 16 March 1984; also comments by members of Parkside NUM.

6   *Newton and Golborne News*, 16 March 1984.

7   *Leigh, Tyldesley and Atherton Journal*, 13 March 1984.

8   *Newton and Golborne News*, 16 March 1984.

9   The events outside Agecroft were presented each night on local television and also in the columns of the *Manchester Evening News* and *Bolton Evening News* beginning on 14 March 1984.

10   NWA Conference, 17 March 1984.

11   *Bolton Evening News*, 14 March 1984.

12   NWA Conference, 17 March 1984.

13   Sid Vincent interview.

14   Material for this section gathered from Yorkshire pickets, Agecroft strikers and Jim Lord, the Pendlebury Branch Secretary.

15   Interview Pendlebury NUM; see also, on the impact of this Committee decision, Marge Short, 'One Woman's Story' in *North West Labour History*, No. 11, 1985–86, p. 87.

16   NWA Conference, 17 December 1983

17   The detailed results are given in NWA, Executive 16 March 1984.

18   Bernard Donaghy interview.

19   Comment by a Yorkshire flier at Castleford, July 1987.

20   NWA Conference, 17 March 1984 (S. Vincent).

21   *Ibid.*

22   *Ibid* (Parsonage Delegate).

23   *Ibid* (Leigh Craftsmen Delegate).

24   *Ibid.*

25   *Ibid.*

26   Discussions with Bold NUM.

27   NWA Conference, 17 March 1984; comment from the platform after passing of the resolution.

28   *Leigh, Tyldesley and Atherton Journal*, 22 March 1984.

29   See NWA Special Conference, 22 March 1984; interview with Bold NUM and with Bernard Donaghy.

30   *Leigh, Tyldesley and Atherton Journal*, 22 March 1984.

31   NWA Special Conference, 22 March 1984.

32   *Ibid.* (Ashton and Haydock Craftsmen Delegate).

33   *Ibid.* (Parsonage Delegate).

34   *Ibid* (Golborne Delegate).

35   *Ibid.* (Mal Gregory).

36   *Ibid*. (T. McNicholas).
37   *Ibid*.
38   *Ibid*. (no details of Branch voting given).
39   *MEN*, 26 March 1984.
40   *Bolton Evening News*, 26 March 1984.
41   *Leigh, Tyldesley and Atherton Journal*, 26 March 1984.
42   *Newton and Golborne News*, 30 March 1984.
43   Sid Vincent interview; also the account in Ottey, *The Strike*, pp. 79–85.
44   Copy of Groby Press statement in *ibid*. p.84.
45   NWA Executive, 30 March 1984.
46   *Ibid* Special Conference, 31 March 1984.
47   *Ibid*.
48   *Ibid*.
49   Discussions with Golborne NUM.
50   NWA Special Conference, 31 March 1984.
51   *Ibid*.
52   *MEN*, 31 March 1984.
53   Steve Vickers's *Diary*.
54   Discussions with Plank Lane NUM.
55   Discussions with Ashton and Haydock Craftsmen NUM.
56   *MEN*, 2 April 1984.
57   4 April 1984 (Jim Lord).
58   *Newton and Golborne News*, 6 April 1984 (Frank King).
59   NWA Special Conference, 31 March 1984.
60   NWA Executive, 13 April 1984.
61   *Ibid*. Conference, 14 April 1984.
62   NUM Reconvened Special Conference, 19 April 1984, pp. 110–11.
63   *Ibid*. pp. 113–14.
64   *Ibid*. pp.114–15, moved by Jack Jones and seconded by Ken Toon of South Derbyshire.
65   *Ibid*. p.116.
66   *Ibid*.
67   *Ibid*. p. 122.
68   *Ibid*. p. 124.
69   *Ibid*. p. 123.
70   For text see NWA Special Conference, 27 April 1984.
71   *Ibid*.
72   *Ibid*. As a Delegate to the Sheffield Conference, Brian Bancroft, the Pendlebury Delegate, had given the Report back to Lancashire.
73   *Ibid*. (Sutton Manor Delegate).
74   Discussions with members of Parkside, Plank Lane, Pendlebury and Golborne NUM; *Bolton Evening News*, 4 May 1984.
75   NUM Reconvened Special Conference, 19 April 1984, p. 122.
76   *Ibid*. p. 128 (Dave Douglas).
77   Discussions with Bold NUM.
78   *MEN*, 27 April 1984.
79   *Ibid*. 30 April 1984.

80 *Morning Star*, 1 May 1984.

81 *Bolton Evening News*, 1 May 1984.

82 Discussions with Parkside and Golborne NUM.

83 Discussion with Parkside NUM.

84 Interview with Bernard Donaghy; discussions with Golborne and Ashton and Haydock Craftsmen NUM.

85 *MEN*, 3 May 1984.

86 Discussions with North Yorkshire pickets.

87 *MEN*, 3 May 1984.

88 *Newton and Golborne News*, 4 May 1984.

89 Discussion with Parkside NUM.

90 *MEN*, 9 May 1984.

91 *St Helens Reporter*, 11 May 1984, and later 15 and 22 June 1984.

92 *Newton and Golborne News*, 4 and 11 May 1984; discussions with Parkside NUM.

93 Discussions with Plank Lane NUM.

94 Text in NWA Conference, 19 May 1984, Appendix A.

95 Interview with Bernard Donaghy.

96 This meeting was not minuted but later Conferences minutes contain references, usually by those not invited. See *MEN*, 11 May 1984.

97 *St Helens Reporter*, 18 May 1984.

98 NWA Conference, 19 May 1984, lists the Branches accepting the instruction.

99 *Ibid.*

100 *Ibid.*

101 *Ibid.*

102 *Ibid.*

103 NWA Executive, 21 May 1984.

104 See *Rules of the National Union of Mineworkers (North Western Area)* revised to 15 November 1975.

105 *MEN*, 21 May 1984. The Sanction was announced in NWA Circular 152/84 with Area Rule Thirty-Five as the justification.

106 Jim Lord interview.

107 *Leigh, Tyldesley and Atherton Journal*, 24 May 1984.

108 *Bolton Evening News*, 23 May 1984.

109 Discussions with Agecroft NUM strikers.

110 NWA Conference, 19 May 1984 (Plank Lane Delegate).

111 Discussions with Plank Lane NUM; *MEN*, 29 May 1984.

112 Discussions with Yorkshire pickets.

113 *Leigh, Tyldesley and Atherton Journal*, 7 June 1984; *MEN*, 5 June 1984.

114 Discussions with Plank Lane NUM.

115 *MEN*, 12 June 1984; *Leigh, Tyldesley and Atherton Journal*, 14 June 1984.

116 Discussions with Plank Lane NUM. On his release from gaol, the man concerned returned to work and kept his job.

117 NWA Executive, 29 May 1984.

118 NWA Conference, 2 June 1984.

119   MEN, 8 June 1984.

120   NUM NEC, 14 June 1984.

121   *NUM North Western Area Rule Book*.

122   For the text of injunction see NWA Conference, 16 June 1984.

123   NWA Conference, 2 June 1984.

124   NWA Conference, 16 June 1984.

125   *Ibid*.

126   Sid Vincent and Bernard Donaghy interviews.

127   *Bolton Evening News*, 26 and 27 June 1984; for a discussion of the legal decisions against the NUM see John McIlroy, 'The Law Struck Dumb? Labour Law and the Miners Strike' in Bob Fine and Robert Millar (eds.), *Policing The Miners' Strike* (Lawrence and Wishart, London, 1985), pp. 79–102.

128   As acknowledged by Sid Vincent interview.

129   NWA Conference, 29 June 1984.

130   *Leigh, Tyldesley and Atherton Journal*, 5 July 1984.

131   Jim Lord and Sid Vincent interviews.

132   *Leigh, Tyldesley and Atherton Journal*, 5 July 1984.

8

The deadlock

From the vantage point of June, Lancashire's committed strikers had reason to be pleased. Despite the March ballot result and the criticisms of national strategy by Area and many Branch Officials, most of the membership were not working. Agecroft certainly continued to produce coal; there were relatively few strikers at Parsonage and at Walkden Workshops. But elsewhere the picture was very different with Bold and Sutton Manor completely stopped, and heavy support at the remaining collieries and at Kirkless Workshops. Significantly, Lancashire was not another 'mini-Nottinghamshire'.

The spreading of the strike represented, above all, the triumph of vigorous initiatives taken by a relatively small number of miners who were thoroughly committed to the dispute. This mobilisation had begun at Bold and had taken in sympathetic miners from other Branches. Often these activists were suspicious of their Area and Branch Officials. They worked with flying pickets from other coalfields and their decisions were often independent of their own Area structure. Sometimes they pressurised Branch Officials into adopting more radical positions; always they attended Area Conferences, a solid presentation of the strike's support in the coalfield and a necessary factor in the calculations of Area Officials. But the latter were in some respects simply by-passed. The Bolton office never became a strike headquarters; instead, this effectively stayed at the Bold Miners' Club, a reminder of how the strike had come to Lancashire and of where its roots lay. Vincent attempted to straddle the two worlds of the official union and rank-and-file innovations; another Official simply felt that power had passed into other hands and that the Officials were little more than messenger boys.[1] The marginalisation was the more effective because the rank-and-file members could claim credibly to be the supporters of national policy.

Activists linked with the rapidly developing network of support groups. Sometimes these were close by in the conurbations of Manchester and Liverpool and in other North-Western towns. Sometimes links were made with communities far removed from the coalfield. Lancashire miners campaigned for funds across France and Germany. One, speaking in Dublin, found himself attacked in the press for his alleged expressions of sympathy with the Provisional IRA.[2]

Branch officials watched bemused as standard bearers in left groups competed for dominance within the support organisations.[3] Generally, strikers adopted a pragmatic line towards the support offered by assorted paper-sellers and their comrades. They gratefully accepted the material help but usually responded to the political homilies with tolerance and nothing more. One Agecroft striker listened patiently to contributions from a Socialist Workers' Party Branch before responding, 'We're only trying to win an industrial dispute.'[4]

The entry of miners into unfamiliar worlds could produce new understandings; it could also generate tensions based on class, gender and region. A Bold activist recalled a fund-raising trip to London:

> We were met at Euston by this middle-class woman with a Sloane Ranger name and a sports car. There was only room for one of us in the car so the rest travelled by train. In some ways she was OK. She was arrested whilst collecting. But one lad who'd been down there a while said he'd had a big bust up with her. He said she was on an ego trip – missionary work for these strange men from up there – and this was true.[5]

Lancashire, like other coalfields, developed its Women's Groups. Typically, few were involved; the diffidence found so often in coalfield villages was compounded in Lancashire by the lack of villages dominated by striking miners. For women to come together in a group required a conscious effort by each individual. It was not facilitated by neighbourhood networks. The range of their activities varied.[6] Some tasks were universal and conventional, especially the preparation of food. Tradition might dictate that this was women's work, yet few if any had experience of the large-scale catering required in some food kitchens. Several women activists picketed; some spoke to raise funds. Inevitably, the women had to deal with the NUM, the most male-dominated of trade unions. Cautious Branch officials sometimes found it difficult to cope with women who insisted in taking their own decisions and whose practice was a continuing denial of some customary trade union procedures. A familiar world had been disrupted by the fashion in which the strike had come to Lancashire; now the behaviour of the activists, including the women, only highlighted this predicament. In some Branches, male activists and officials seem to have worked with the women in broadly egalitarian terms with respect for the latter's autonomy. But this was not always the case. Members of one Lancashire Women's Group went to a neighbouring pit. They were dismayed to find the women pressed back into very traditional tasks. 'We were disturbed to find the women not included at all. The Branch Committee carried on in the old way.'[7] Once again there was the contrast between the explosion of activism and the routines of the union.

Early each morning pickets met at the Bold Club. Sometimes they were supported by mass contingents from other coalfields, as in the crucial May days.[8] Often there were women from support groups or sympathisers from further afield. Miners responded creatively to challenges posed by tapped 'phones, possible Coal Board 'moles' and police surveillance. Elaborate decoys were arranged. Repeated attempts were made to shut down Parkside, Golborne and Bickershaw. In one incident at Golborne in late July, the overturning of a strikebreaker's car produced arrests and, for one picket, a gaol sentence and eventual dismissal by the Coal Board. The incident was far from unique; its bitter aftermath highlighted managerial willingness to hammer a prominent activist.

The constant confrontations between police and strikers, and the failure to prevent a hardcore from working, generated frustrations that could readily explode. Early in August, Parkside reopened after the summer break. The working minority faced a thousand pickets, many from Yorkshire. They had blockaded the gates at 4 a.m.; oil and nails were spread across the road; the police escort and the coaches met a barrage of stones, bottles and bricks. Twenty-five pickets were arrested.[9] The pickets remained committed to their task, but after May they failed to extend the strike. The only local encouragement came in mid-August when salvage work ended at

Cronton, and those remaining in the industry joined the strike. Effective picketing in Lancashire meant a holding operation until events elsewhere resolved the dispute.

The conflicts on the picket lines reached down into the towns and villages of the coalfield. In Golborne, by mid-June the old Labour Club had become a soup kitchen and a strike centre. The names of scabs were listed in the windows. Those so stigmatised responded with a range of arguments. This was no 'scab list' but 'a roll of honour of people standing up for their democratic rights'. The Lancashire strike was the result of pressure from 'the Yorkshiremen'. Why should anyone's family be put in hardship 'for a man like Arthur Scargill'?[10] By mid-summer such voices stood outside the pale of the Lancashire NUM, yet similar sentiments had been espoused in earlier discussions by Area and Branch Officials.

The continuing problem of a working minority provided an inevitable focus for Coal Board propaganda and embarrassment for the NUM. During the summer the Board in the Western Area began to develop an effective publicity act. Each morning, figures on the turnout of miners were prepared for the largely uncritical media. Sometimes, figures covered the whole Western Area so that the relative strength of the Lancashire strike tended to be submerged by the figures for North Staffordshire, Cannock, North Wales and Cumberland – all coalfields where the strike was weaker. When claims were presented about specific Lancashire pits, the NCB figures included invitations to media distortion and simplification.

The Board's statements about the numbers reporting for work included NACODS members, a marginal adjustment which inflated the number of working 'miners' but which was not specifically acknowledged by NCB spokesmen for several months. The practice of operating just one shift in largely strike bound pits could license false conclusions. Thus, typically, one day in early August, the Board claimed 353 (or 56 per cent) had reported at Parkside. Quite apart from the fact that this included a significant number of Deputies, the crucial question remains, 56 per cent of what? To the uninitiated the percentage could suggest a significant weakening of the strike. Yet this conclusion ceases to be plausible, given that the membership of the NUM's Parkside Branch, plus the Craftsmen employed at the pit and the few Winders, totalled over 1,500. The percentage related, as so often was the case in the summer, simply to the day shift. It would need to be balanced by a percentage for the afternoon shift which the Board was reluctant to publicise, but which would be very small.

Besides the use of single shift figures to mislead the unwary, there remained another problem with the Board's citing of percentages. Across the Western Area, the NCB utilised a notion of 'normal turnout' which included an allowance for absenteeism. In the above case, the 56 percentage was in comparison with the normal turnout for a Parkside day shift. On other occasions, the Board compared the number working over twenty- four hours with the pit's 'normal turnout' over the same period. The obvious conclusion would be to subtract one figure from the other, thereby arriving at an estimate of the number on strike. When applied to largely strike bound pits, such a practice was distorting since most of those excluded as notional 'absentees' would really be strikers. So long as Lancashire saw little movement back to work, this mode of presentation had little impact, but an effective machine and mode of presentation had been fashioned. Should sizeable numbers begin to go back, then such statistics could well influence, not just the outside observer, but also the individual striker pondering whether to cross the picket line.

Even in high summer, with the line being held, some strike leaders expressed concern about the publicity position. They faced a tough antagonist in the Area Director, John Northard. Although not flamboyant in the style of his North Derbyshire counterpart Ken Moses, he was equally committed to the long haul of a back-to-work campaign focusing on the anxieties of individual strikers.[11] Too many men were only passively involved in the strike for the NUM's comfort. As the Plank Lane Delegate emphasised '40 to 60 per cent of our members at Bickershaw Colliery are doing nothing, saying nothing but only receiving propaganda from the . . . Management.'[12]. But compared with the Board, the Union were severely handicapped in any propaganda battle. The NCB had the address of each employee, it knew exactly who was working; its managers could suggest which strikers would be vulnerable to individual appeals. The Union could not begin to produce a definitive list of working miners. When Union dues arrived from the Coal Board as payments from those at work, they came without names. Always the Union, with its limited resources and with the tensions between Officials and activists, was reacting to events and responding to challenges.

High summer also saw the emergence of the Working Miners' organisations[13] with links between Agecroft and the Nottinghamshire coalfield. One came through the agency of Chris Butcher, the Bevercotes blacksmith who became, for a brief period, the hero of the tabloids. His journeys in search of working miners brought him to Agecroft where he spoke in the canteen; according to one account, this was the source of his subsequent nickname, 'Silver Birch'. Although this highly personalised initiative played a significant role in the development of Working Miners' organisations in Lancashire and elsewhere, Butcher had no weight within the union and soon became a marginal figure. The initiative passed to Nottinghamshire Officials such as Roy Lynk, David Prendergast and Neil Greatrex. Jim Lord travelled to Nottinghamshire for meetings with them, escorted by the police to secret venues. He found these Nottinghamshire leaders congenial people, men with lengthy records of union activity who were deeply critical of Scargill's leadership. All had been, in their own terms, NUM stalwarts, and claimed that they represented the legitimate practices of the NUM. Lord fitted such a profile; he had been Agecroft Branch Secretary for a decade and had served as Area Vice-President. When he was displaced from the latter post in 1982, he was praised by the Lancashire President 'Jim has been an excellent ambassador for the Union . . . no area could have wished for a more loyal and conscientious official.'[14] Despite his affinities with the Nottinghamshire officials and despite their shared predicament, something held him back from involvement in the National Working Miners' Committee. Like Bob Copping, the Barnsley Winder who served briefly as the NWMC Secretary, Lord claims to have been suspicious about the organisation's political ramifications.[15] It was, in his judgement, one thing to voice his members' concerns and to defend his interpretation of the NUM's rules. It was another to go down a slippery slope, becoming entangled in Conservative political associations.

Instead, Lord became involved in a local affair, the Lancashire Working Miners' Committee. Publicly unveiled in August, he served as its Secretary, but the group claimed backing across the coalfield. It had begun as the result of phone calls to Lord by NUM members at pits where the officials were backing the strike. At first, the Agecroft Branch Secretary was suspicious that it was a manoeuvre by strikers, but eventually was persuaded that the calls were genuine and he arranged a meeting. This took place in a bizarre location – the changing room in a Farnworth Cricket Club Pavilion – itself testimony to the atmosphere and assumptions within which some were operating. One result was publicity material seeking to exorcise suspicions of ulterior political motives – 'we are not Tories or Coal Board puppets'.[16] But in the summer of 1984, there was little chance of dialogue between the strikers, and working miners entangled with varying degrees of reluctance in a web of reactionary politics, wealthy backers and legal complexities.

Lancashire striking officials who backed the strike often employed rhetoric that was indistinguishable from the traditional NUM Left; Jack Taylor's April advice had been taken – miners stood either on MacGregor's side or on 'our side'. This came out cogently in August when a Special National Delegate Conference reviewed the state of the strike and the recent fruitless negotiations between National Officials and the Board. Superficially these had come to grief over a handful of words; did the Board's insistence that pits could be shut if there was no hope of beneficial development provide a licence for the closure of uneconomic capacity? In retrospect some Lancashire miners saw these July negotiations as a missed opportunity; if a deal had been struck then, this would not have been a guaranteed protection for miners' jobs, but the NUM would have been in a much stronger position than in March 1985. With the aid of hindsight such emphases are perhaps plausible, but this was not how it seemed to most committed strikers in mid-summer. After so long a strike, many were not prepared to settle for an ambiguous compromise. Alongside those who insisted that 'Total victory is what we want'[17] there went the warning from Tom Callan of Durham that the idea of 'beneficial development' would allow pit closures in the North East: 'For heaven's sake, Arthur, don't allow words to be in where the Coal Board can manipulate them, when you get back to local level.'[18]

In high summer optimism was possible, for example on that July Friday when a demonstration wound its way through Manchester city centre and the Free Trade Hall was packed for a rally and those unable to finds seats stood outside to hear speeches relayed through tannoys. Manchester's Peter Street, with the associations of Peterloo, was closed for the afternoon as the overspill stood in the roadway to laugh with Arthur Scargill and applaud his affirmations of principle. Yet rhetoric had its limits. From a later standpoint,

August 1984 was not even half way, but it could seem an eternity since March. Already, people with long memories or a sense of history were making comparisons with 1926. Such links with the past could give an epic flavour to the struggle, but of course '1926' had ended in division and disaster. The link was double-edged. Already in Lancashire some anxieties were present. Early in August, Roy Walls, the Plank Lane Branch Secretary, expressed a sense of intensifying pressures, but also a deep and dogged determination:

> There are a few more going into work but not many. But we have seen a big increase in the number of people coming in for food over the last week or so. Things are getting very difficult now but we will soldier on. There is nothing they haven't tried in an attempt to drag their men back, but nothing has worked yet and the only thing which will take them back is absolute poverty.[19]

But then came a symbolic rift in the Lancashire strikers' ranks. Bold had been solidly out since the start; its activists had epitomised the determination and *elan* of the strike's' committed supporters. But on August Bank Holiday Monday, six men went back to Bold. The strikers were caught unawares and picketing was only light. Next day was different with a mass picket and many arrests; the following day was a repeat performance.[20] A Bold member admitted, 'in two days the police knocked spots off us.'[21] Despite the hopes of the Board, this first breach of the strikers' citadel did not widen easily, and in general September proved a month when few Lancashire miners abandoned the strike.

It was a time between the confidence of summer and the bitter pressures of autumn. Strikers encountered promising, but ultimately misleading, signposts. At the TUC the NUM had successes and formal victories, but the pledges of support could not be made effective. There were fruitless negotiations between National Officials and the Board. There were indicators that the Deputies might respond to closure threats and managerial pressures by staging a strike of their own. If so, then all pits would close and a victory would seem credible. But despite these prospects, promising but in the event so fruitless, in Lancashire September was a month for criticism and anxiety.

The mistrust of activists for the Area Officials was ever-present. Many strikers identified with the national leadership; they could be bitingly critical of the Bolton hierarchy and dubious of Branch

Officials' commitment. The tangles of the early weeks had made for strange alliances in Lancashire. At moments of frustration, animosities surfaced. The spreading of the strike had been a rank-and-file affair, but activists insisted that support from the top was vital. The September Area Conference was the occasion for some forthright criticism. The Bold Delegate responded to recent events at his pit by acknowledging that rank-and-file members could achieve only so much: 'We have now reached a stage where we have got mounted police and yet we are still trying to organise flying pickets with rank-and-file members . . .' The Delegate voiced the criticism of many strikers that the Lancashire Officials were not really behind the action. They were absent from picket lines and were generally invisible: '. . . it is about time that the three officials got up in a morning because there are two five o'clocks in the day, and tried to bolster up the miners' confidence . . . It is time that the officials came out to the collieries, talked to the scabs, because we cannot get near them.' Vincent defended his own record and acknowledged that morale in the coalfield was poor: 'It will get lower this week because the negotiations have broken down once more'.[22] Here was the pattern for the future – the rising of expectations as more negotiations began, the shattering as they failed. It was a repeated pulverisation of miners' optimism and self-confidence.

Criticism did not stop at the Lancashire Officials. It was also directed at the coalfield's sponsored MPs. One was effectively irrelevant; Michael Maguire had been critical of the strike and he kept away from Union meetings. But Lawrence Cunliffe, the Member for Leigh, was often present, and at the September Conference he came under attack: 'We have never seen the Mining MP on the picket line . . . what has he done in the House, he has never been near the colliery . . .'[23] Cunliffe's response showed how activists and many Union officials and parliamentarians simply lived in different worlds. Thrown together by the crisis, they differed fundamentally on what was politically feasible and desirable:

> There are certain Members of Parliament who feel that their presence on a picket line is going to solve the dispute immediately. In my opinion it's a nonsense. MPs on picket lines in the view of public opinion, does more harm than good and it is far better to direct your efforts in the House of Commons and speaking at meetings outside the House.[24]

Once criticism had started it spread amongst the Conference. The Sutton Manor Delegate attacked, not the picketing record of officials, but their responsibility for the confusions that marked the dispute's early weeks: 'The Area Officials were at sixes and sevens and they had the Area not knowing what they were doing.' Moreover, they bore the responsibility for members' lack of knowledge over what was at stake: 'Previous to the dispute we had a nineteen-week overtime ban and we never set eyes on an Area Official at our Branch. We should have been putting the message across then and we probably would have achieved a national ballot and a strike vote.'[25] Under all the pressures of a lengthy strike, a longstanding tradition of leadership was at least momentarily in dispute.

The issue became much more personalised when Roy Walls of Plank Lane focused the criticism specifically on the Area President, Bernard Donaghy: 'The other three officials have taken some stick on his behalf . . . The members wanted to see our President on the picket line . . .'[26] In fact, Donaghy epitomised the crisis of the Lancashire leadership. Deeply respected as an Agent, he had made a cogent case for a national ballot at the April National Conference. When this proved unsuccessful he accepted the 'national instruction' to strike, but he could not wear these changes of stance with the *panache* of Vincent. He was a principled, cautious official, very unhappy about mass picketing, troubled by the cracks within the union. He went with the tide, chairing Executive Meetings and Conferences, carrying out his duties as Agent.[27] Now his passivity was harshly spotlighted, not by a political adversary, but by someone with whom his relationship had been amicable.

In fact, after this criticism Donaghy's visibility diminished. He chaired the next two Executive meetings, but from the end of September, he attended neither Executive nor Conference. Already ill, he suffered a fall in early October requiring lengthy treatment. He performed some Agent's duties, he visited the Bolton offices but did not take a part in strike activity. As the strike situation deteriorated, activists attacked him as a symbol of weak leadership. It was the most poignant of the Area Union's internal controversies.

The breakdown of yet another round of negotiations led delegates at that September Conference to consider how the dispute could be made more effective. As one speaker suggested, the stakes were now massive: 'This Government has decided to run the miners to the brink, they have decided to take us on and fight us to the finish.'[28] Such a challenge required that, even in a divided coalfield, miners mobilise support from other unions.

This had been difficult from the start. Railwaymen employed to move Lancashire coal to the power stations proved as co-operative as their colleagues elsewhere but the road hauliers provided a demoralising contrast. Despite formal statements of support, the Transport and General Workers Union demonstrated a frequent inability to organise its own members in support of the miners. Drivers claimed that they had not received instructions from union officials; when such directions were given, they were often ignored. Vincent acknowledged this 'The T&G . . . have a mammoth problem because the members are taking no notice whatsoever what the T&G officials are saying, even to the extent of taking their union cards off them.'[29] A typical riposte to miners' pickets was, 'Get your own lot out first'. Many wagon drivers were non-union anyway. By September, the shifting of stocks by road was a demoralising part of the Lancashire scene. This helped to fuel the criticism of Area Officials: 'At Parkside . . . thirty to forty wagons full of coal per day are being driven and unloaded at Bold Power Station and there has been no official . . . near the colliery premises.'[30] But the shifting of coal stocks was unlikely to be stopped by the appearance of an NUM official. Strikers faced fundamental problems of divisions within and between unions, and of the limits on union authority. There could be no simple answer.

Frank King, Parkside President, detailed the situation at his pit: 'There have been wagons called Pearsons going in and out of Parkside with lorry loads of coal.' Some Transport and General Workers Union members who were employed at the pit walked out when instructed to load wagons. It made no impact. 'Pearson's wagon driver, not a member of the T&GW, had deliberately loaded the wagon himself and left the premises to go to Bold Power Station.' King's conclusion was a painful one for many of the strikers' attempts to stop coal movements: 'There was nothing anybody could do.'[31]

The crucial destination of the coal shipments, was of course, the electricity supply industry. This provided even more frustration for the Lancashire strikers. The hostile relationship between NUM national officials and their counterparts in some key unions was a bleak backcloth. However, in the North West there were some hopeful signs. The militant union presence in the massive Fiddlers Ferry Power Station guaranteed sympathy for the miners, but so thorough was the contingency planning by the Central Electricity Generating Board that the station's contribution became marginal. A coal embargo was of little importance.

One trade union officer amongst the power station unions, Fred Howell of the T&GW, wished to take an active role in support of the miners. His power station membership was concentrated in Yorkshire and the North West. The CEGB response was a generalisation of the Fiddlers Ferry method. The issue should not be pushed unnecessarily, a view perhaps shared in the final analysis by Howell. His circular to power station shop stewards was supportive of the NUM, but the guidelines were relatively imprecise and ignored the vital question of oil firing.[32] Although Lancashire strikers did find backing from T&G members in local power stations, the significance of this sympathy was limited by inter-union differences and the threat of disciplinary sanctions:

> The Shop Steward at Westwood Power Station used to work at Bold Colliery and the T&GW members are 100 per cent behind our cause, but the problem is that the GMBWU are putting notices up within the Power Stations saying to work with any type of fuel that comes in. In effect the T&GW shop steward has been threatened with his job if he disobeys.[33]

The NUM might hope to picket power stations, but their own predicament placed severe limitations on what was feasible. The first priority had been attempts to end strikebreaking by the Union's own members; as summer gave way to autumn the emphasis shifted to prevention of any significant return to work. There might be the wish to picket power stations, but persistently there were not the resources. As one striker put it: 'How were the pickets to be organised for the power stations because Parkside could not supply any?'[34] There could be little scope for consistent attempts to block coal movements and to place an embargo on the use of such coal. All that could be managed were sporadic and largely symbolic demonstrations.

September and October were the stalemate months, but the continuing possibility of a Deputies strike gave hope to Lancashire strikers. Local relationships between NUM and NACODS had been poor. Attempts to persuade Deputies to respect picket lines had failed even in strike bound pits. The NACODS presence provided an environment around which strike breaking could seem credible. Late in October, following an 82 per cent vote for strike action, the Deputies reached agreement with the Board. Their complaints were acknowledged and they secured a limited modification of the Colliery Review Procedure. The Deputies' spokesman in Lancashire, Frank Galloway, acknowledged that the deal was credible and that his members would work normally.[35] Nine NUM leaders reacted angrily – Ron Gaskell of Golborne hinted that the NUM position was desperate: 'We are very disappointed and it has not helped us one little bit.' Against the concern, Frank King claimed that the strikers remained optimistic and solid. 'The lads have got their heads up. Their spirits are very high.'[36]

Buoyancy was no doubt necessary in the NUM's predicament. Yet, with hindsight, those late October days did mark a critical divide. The NACODS deal has been demonstrated to be of no substantive value in the protection of miners' jobs. Despite an independent element in the Review Procedure, the last word remained with the employer. Perhaps the precise content of the last word would be influenced by the balance of forces within the industry. The NUM in late October was clearly stronger than after it had experienced another four months' demoralisation. Whether even then it could have prevented a large-scale closure programme through the modified Review Procedure is questionable. What is also debatable is whether a credible deal was ever on offer to the NUM. Both the Government and the Coal Board were clearly concerned to settle the NACODS imbroglio and avoid the closure of all pits. Arguably, many were committed to a very public defeat for the miners: no loopholes could be considered. The union had to be left with nowhere to go.

This was the death of optimism. Amidst all the problems of that summer, there had been a creativity and a self-belief demonstrated in the activists' achievements – the organisation of picketing, the raising of funds, the forging of links with people in such different worlds, the enterprise and the challenge offered by coalfield women to that most male-dominated of trade unions. For a brief moment, there flowered an alternative, reaching out beyond that rule-governed worldly-wise universe of union officials.

But it was a brittle achievement. Now in Lancashire, as in other coalfields, the managerial message was that negotiations were over. It was time for the Board's autumn offensive.

Notes

1 Bernard Donaghy interview.
2 *MEN*, 12 November 1984.
3 Discussion with Golborne NUM.
4 Discussion with Agecroft Strikers.
5 Discussion with Bold NUM.
6 Discussions with Newton and Agecroft Women's Groups.
7 Discussion with Newton Women's Group.
8 This section draws on frequent discussions with strikers involved in the Lancashire flying picket.
9 *Newton and Golborne News*, 10 August; *MEN*, 6 August 1984.
10 *MEN*, 15 June 1984; there is a similar feature in *Newton and Golborne News*, 19 October 1984.
11 This analysis owes much to discussions with the staff of Granada Television during the dispute. For a profile of John Northard see *Financial Times*, 3 April 1985.
12 NWA Conference, 6 August 1984.
13 Jim Lord interview for much of material on this theme.
14 NWA Annual Conference, May 1982 (Bernard Donaghy).
15 On the networks involving Working Miners' Organisations, Mark Hollingsworth, 'Using Miners to Bust the Union', *New Statesman*, 14 December 1984.
16 *MEN*, 10 August 1984.
17 NUM Special Delegate Conference, 10 August 1984, p. 609 (North Derbyshire Delegate).
18 *Ibid.* p. 612.
19 *Leigh, Tyldesley and Atherton Journal*, 16 August 1984.
20 Discussions with Bold NUM; *St Helens Reporter*, 31 August 1984, *MEN*, 28 and 29 August 1984.
21 NWA Conference, 15 September 1984.
22 *Ibid.*
23 *Ibid.* (Bold Delegates).
24 *Ibid.*
25 *Ibid.*
26 *Ibid.*
27 Bernard Donaghy interview.
28 NWA Conference, 15 September 1984 (Ashton and Haydock Craftsmen Delegate).
29 *Ibid.*
30 *Ibid.* (Parkside Delegate).
31 *Ibid.*
32 See M. Adeney and J. Lloyd, *The Miners Strike of 1984–85: Loss Without Limit*, especially pp. 145–7.
33 NWA Conference, 15 September 1984, (Bold Delegate).
34 NWA Conference, 19 October 1984, in the context of a further discussion about the problems of securing support in the power stations.
35 *Newton and Golborne News*, 26 October 1984.

9

Saving the Union

Despite repeated Coal Board expressions of hope, the ranks of the Lancashire strikers had thinned little through the summer and into the early autumn. Little had changed since the first men returned to Bickershaw late in May. But at the end of October, the Coal Board stepped up its campaign and announced that any miner returning to work down to Monday 19 November could make up to £1,400 by Christmas. The NUM called this a bribe; the Board's response was down-beat: 'This is no carrot – this is just a straightforward statement of fact as to the financial benefits of returning to work now'[1]

The advertising campaign was not so laid back. Press adverts were headed, 'It'll pay every miner who's not at work to read this.' The copy emphasised that negotiations were over and more miners were quitting the strike. As yet the numbers were few, but the campaign was designed to change all of that – to create a reality that would feed off itself.

In contrast, the strikers were perhaps more demoralised than at any previous moment. The chance of a breakthrough offered by the NACODS strike ballot had been dispelled, the NUM leadership had been subjected to a campaign of press vilification, virulent by even the standards of 1984, in connection with the visit of a NUM officer to Libya.[2] Most fundamentally the union's officials and activists were aware of the despondency amongst many miners.

This came through when Delegates met for a Special National Conference on the first day of the Board's back-to-work drive, Monday 5 November. They listened to Scargill explaining the failure of recent negotiations but there was not the euphoria and fire of the earlier gatherings. As one Lancashire Delegate subsequently acknowledged: 'There was a very subdued atmosphere and no life whatsoever.'[3] Some of the contributors at the National Conference were pessimistic. Sammy Scott from Northumberland had no illusions: 'When the talks were going on and were breaking down at the weekends our members were . . . very disappointed . . . it is a hell of a job to try and lift them up again once their chins are down.'[4] Vincent threw light on the Board's campaign in Lancashire. COSA members were ringing strikers 'and promising the earth if they will start work . . . One of them rang six people up last Friday . . . six face men . . . he said, "If you will come back to work, today, Friday, you can have a week's wages."'[5] When Lancashire Delegates met the following day there was widespread acknowledgement of despondency. But any response faced the serious problem of how to reach beyond the activists to the passive strikers. Their continuing support was vital if the Lancashire strike was to retain credibility. The Plank Lane President argued that national initiatives for more rallies would not meet the difficulty: 'We keep holding rallies and only speaking to the converted . . . it was about time we got the message across to the members who are sat at home and not on the picket lines.'[6] The back to work movement was just gathering momentum. On the previous day 'Black Monday', November, 5 the Board had claimed that in Lancashire ninety-six miners had abandoned the strike; on the morning that Lancashire Delegates met in Bolton, the claim was for thirty-three more.[7] And so the figures came in day after day; claims of 'new faces', suggestions that many more were about to quit the strike. Pickets on pit gates knew only too well that men were returning, although they argued persistently that the Board's figures were exaggerated and distorted.[8]

The Western Area propaganda machinery went into overdrive. Each morning the press office at Stoke-on-Trent issued the latest totals, and compared these with 'normal turnout'; by Friday 16 November the Board claimed that more than half (2,668) or 51 per cent of the coalfield's miners had worked the previous day.[9] The claim was wrong; the quoted figure included NACODS and COSA members who had always crossed Lancashire picket lines. It was given as a percentage of 'normal turnout', not of the workforce, with a consequential deflation of the strikers' numbers. But the NUM were ill-equipped to win any propaganda war. The situation changed daily; activists found difficulty in keeping up with latest developments and faced the need to maintain the commitment of the strikers.[10]

At particular pits the Board claimed significant breakthroughs – forty-five back in the campaign's first week at Parkside, ninety-three in the second and 184 in the first three days of the third. New faces mingled with longstanding strikebreakers; more and more buses drove past the pickets. Although several hundred men were still out at this large pit, the impact was demoralising. It was becoming more than ever a dogged defensive action. For one Parkside Official, what was at stake was the survival of the NUM.[11]

At Bickershaw too there had been a substantial return to work. The Branch Secretary claimed that some who had been committed to the strike were calling it a day. 'Lads have been phoning me to apologise before going back. I have some sympathy with them.' But the Lancashire NUM had not changed its course: 'The union is still out, and the only way that you can go back to work is without your union.'[12] Elsewhere in Lancashire miners returned to work, although not to the same extent. At Agecroft the ranks of the hardened striking minority were barely dented; at Golborne some went through the gates, but at a pit where the strike had come late, many now stood by their union. In the activists' heartland, there was some erosion of the strikers' ranks at Bold and at Sutton Manor, but at both pits the strikers remained overwhelmingly in the majority. But demoralisation could reach even there. One November Friday afternoon at Sutton Manor, a striker claimed one consolation amidst the disintegration: 'At least I won't have been a scab.' But against that he was sceptical about future solidarity: 'Even some of them on the picket line. It wouldn't take much for them to go back now.'[13]

The Board attempted to provide that something. They staged carefully packaged media events to proclaim the resumption of production. At Bold this occurred on Friday 23 November; television cameras went in through a back entrance to avoid pickets and to film 'newly produced' coal. Strikers were derisive, claiming that neither the quantity nor the quality of strikebreakers could permit such a breakthrough.[14] But the media event became a fact for the record. 'Breakthrough at militant pit' was the headline in one newspaper the next day.[15] Shortly afterwards, the Board claimed that production had restarted at Sutton Manor. Now the claim from the Coal Board's Staffordshire House Headquarters was that no

Lancashire pit was strikebound. This development had been preceded by the announcement of Sutton Manor's long-awaited investment programme, a development that could drive a wedge between the two St Helens pits and perhaps encourage a return to work at the one that appeared to be secure. The members available for the flying pickets dropped in part as some men were forced to deal with their own previously strike-bound pits. Moreover, the police clearly had the upper hand in the ritualistic set pieces.

Lancashire activists were involved also in developments in he nearby North Wales coalfield. Until early November that small Area had been schizophrenic; Bersham Colliery, Wrexham totally stopped, but the strikers in a minority at Point of Ayr. When the first men returned to Bersham, the Lodge controlled by a cautious leadership responded by holding a ballot on the strike. This revival of a central theme of the dispute brought masses of pressmen and television crews to Wrexham; it also brought demonstrators, strikers and women from Point of Ayr and activists from Lancashire.[16] On a soaking wet morning they stood on the pavement outside the North Wales Miners' offices and on the stairway leading to the room where the ballot was in progress. Many feared the worst, but the result was a narrow endorsement of the strike – 154 votes to 145. Yet the minority refused to accept the result. Over sixty already working had not joined in the ballot; others argued that the presence of the Lancashire men had been intimidating. Over the next week, most Bersham miners ended the strike, a mass rally featuring Arthur Scargill failed to stop the flood, and eventually the North Wales Area Executive met to consider a situation where most members were back at work. The precise character of their decision remains controversial; but the North Wales President, Raymond Ellis, announced that the near-collapse of the Bersham strike made impossible further Area support for the dispute. It was the most dramatic turnabout in the Board's campaign.

The reaction of some Lancashire activists was speedy. In an attempt to repeat the Bolton occupation, they drove to Wrexham, evicted North Wales officials from the office and claimed they would stay there until the Area shifted back to support of the strike. But November was not May. In retrospect, one of the occupiers acknowledged that they had little hope of success. 'It was more a sign of support for men who'd been sold out.'[17] The occupation was only brief; it ended when a striking official from Point of Ayr, who was also a trustee for the building, warned that their continuing presence would mean legal complications.[18] The Lancastrians went home. Most North Wales miners remained at work. Local officials used the occupation as a justification for barring the remaining strikers from use of the union offices.[19]

When the North Wales President announced the end of his Area's strike, a jubilant Coal Board official told a television interviewer off the record: 'We've done North Wales, Lancashire's next.'[20] Certainly, the November campaign inflicted serious damage on the Lancashire strike, but it did not seem terminal. A reasonable estimate for Thursday 22 November would place the number on strike as about 3,000 with about 2,400 at work.[21] Although much of the advance made by the May picketing had been rolled back, as yet the strike retained a significant presence. By the end of November, the back-to-work movement had virtually exhausted itself. Outside the Coal Board's Western Area, the campaign had also left its mark. There had been a sizeable reduction in the strikers' ranks in North Derbyshire, so often seen as a barometer coalfield; the near-total solidarity of the North Eastern coalfields had gone, with dramatic returns at some individual pits. Some Yorkshire pits had seen a collapse in strikers' morale, and even in South Wales, for the first time, some men had gone to work. In Lancashire it had always been a matter of sticking it out until the issue was resolved elsewhere; but now, not only was the Lancashire strike weaker, the national balance of power had been transformed.

Lancashire Branch Officials were already highlighting a harsh dilemma for the union. The drift back had been intensified by the lack of negotiations. The only way the NUM could hope to hold the situation was through a rapid return to the negotiating table, yet this was something for which the Board had no incentive. After all, the NUM had few resources to bring to any negotiations. The number of strikers was falling; coal production was rising; support from other unions was no better than it had ever been. What could the Miners offer other than a climb-down? Here was a cruel prospect that would face the union for the next three-and-a-half months.

The weakening was not just a matter of the return to work and declining self-confidence; by early December, the NUM was forced to face some of the implications of legal action by disaffected members. Lancashire had had a limited taste of this six months earlier; now the National Union found itself entering the maze of sequestration.

The far reaching significance of the legal onslaught was as yet unappreciated. For the activists that December, there were immediate problems. How best could the Lancashire strike be maintained? Should the limited picketing resources be used at the pit gates to prevent a further haemorrhage of support, or should efforts be dedicated to the crucial electricity supply sector? There were few illusions about the problems in that area. The Golborne Delegate argued at the December Area Conference that there was no value in merely hanging on with a defeatist attitude. Strikers had to take the initiative; they should place a token picket at the pits and organise themselves to approach power station workers.[22] Once again, activist initiatives would by-pass the caution and animosities of officials. But the huge obstacles to any such campaign were graphically demonstrated a week before Christmas. A meeting with shop stewards in the electricity industry was arranged in Liverpool. The number of delegates was anticipated as 120 to 150. When the meeting began there were eleven people in the room, when it finished there were thirty-three.[23] The hopes and needs of the activists so often had to face a demoralising reality.

This gloomy prospect was offset to some degree by the challenge and the promise of Christmas. In Lancashire, as in other coalfields, seeing it through until Christmas became a symbol of the strikers' commitment; the need for the celebrations to be memorable provided abundant opportunity for displays of inventiveness. Local authorities, support groups, women's groups all combined to provide toys, food, drink and money. Christmas parties for children and dinners for families were glittering demonstrations of the achievement and warm affirmations of solidarity.[24] The supply lines ran, not simply across Britain, but into Europe; Bold received 20,000 Deutschmarks from collectors in St Helens' twin town, Stuttgart.

Yet against these eloquent testimonies to the creativity that had sustained the strike for so long, the holiday offered more opportunity for criticism of a Lancashire Official, this time not the reticent Donaghy, but the very public Vincent. Shortly before Christmas, he flew with a companion to Tenerife for a holiday.[25] At Manchester airport he was recognised by baggage handlers who phoned a local radio station; on the plane he was noticed by another passenger who phoned the Press Association on arrival in Tenerife. The result was an exodus of journalists and photographers to the sun, whilst their less fortunate colleagues were sent to Leigh to produce allegations about Vincent's financial and domestic circumstances. Extensive coverage was given to the escapade of 'El Sid' or 'Sunshine Sid' as he was variously labelled. Contrasts were drawn between a strike leader flying off surreptitiously for some winter sunshine and the poverty of his striking members. Some articles went beyond the immediate episode and argued that Vincent had obtained perks from the union – a rent-free house and a benefit that had not been declared to the Inland Revenue.[26]

After five days' pursuit by photographers, Vincent ended his holiday and came home to criticism from the leaders of the working miners. But in public some strikers played the matter down, either defending the General Secretary's right to take a holiday or suggesting that it was a storm in a tea cup. Clearly, any rift amongst the Lancashire strikers could not be afforded. In private some responses were more forthright. Within the Lancashire Executive, Frank King, the Vice-President, mentioned the accusations of financial impropriety and claimed that there was a damaging consequence for the strike, stating that: 'Hundreds of members who were on strike were saying it was a nice state of affairs when they could not afford to pay their mortgage or rent and the General Secretary was relieved of these problems . . .'[27] Vincent completely rejected these allegations and the Executive unanimously passed a resolution of confidence in him. The decision did not refer to Vincent's Tenerife visit, but this concerned some delegates at the January Area Conference. The principal critic came from Sutton Manor where the Branch had condemned the visit: 'He says he has worked seven days a week thirteen hours a day and so have Branch officials, Committee Members and members, but no holidays for them . . . The General Secretary told the Area officials and conference lies . . . also the Area Executive and the Area Office staff did not know where he was.'[28] But against these criticisms there was the imperative of unity: 'The least said the better . . . we have got to rally round one another.'[29] This was the decisive emotion, strengthened perhaps by the realisation that the Lancashire strike was once again facing difficulties.

Even in the first week of January there had been signs that all was not well. Now that Christmas had passed, the strikers had no clear prospect for the future. Vincent apparently went to the NEC on January 10 and acknowledged that: 'The lull, the vacuum, the absence of negotiations is destroying the morale of our men.'[30] When the Lancashire Executive met a week later they called for immediate talks, whilst urging those still out to stand firm.[31] The combination was itself testimony to the union's predicament. Once again, a return to work movement gathered pace in Lancashire. The next day, forty-nine men went back in the snow at Sutton Manor. This was an unusually high number for a Friday and the Board expressed jubilation at the breakthrough in a strike stronghold: 'the most significant development in the strike in Lancashire for several months.'[32] It did not end there. Men continued to return at Sutton Manor and an increasing number were passing pickets at Bold. By the end of January the number reporting for work at Sutton Manor was about 200 up on the level at the end of the November campaign; at Bold the increase was around 150. The strikers remained relatively firm at Golborne, but at Bickershaw the NUM acknowledged that the majority were working.[33]

The Lancashire NUM, its formal institutions controlled by strikers, now faced acute problems. The majority of the membership were working, and the size of that majority grew each day. There was something increasingly artificial about the situation. A few Branches still had a striking majority, but in general pro-strike Branch Officials found most of their members crossing picket lines. They faced the problem, once the dispute was over, of re-establishing credibility with management and perhaps with their own members. Their own positions in their Branch could be threatened. This prospect became reality in the Leigh Craftsmen Branch early in January. Most members were working, many had never backed the strike, but the officials had accepted the Kent resolution. Now the officials were replaced by men who favoured an end to the strike.[34] The uneasy feeling that the ground could slide from under their feet must have preoccupied many Lancashire Branch Officials who had backed the strike, albeit with some initial reluctance.

Lancashire also faced a problematic relationship with the National Union. In the New Year it was clear that several Areas were looking for a way out of what seemed an impossible situation. But how could this be done without jettisoning fundamental principles? There was also a kind of coalfield *machismo*. There was all the difference in the world between backing an initiative suggested by someone else and having the self-confidence, courage and desperation to voice such a suggestion. A small step down the road could be the kind of insistence coming from Lancashire that there had to be negotiations. There followed weeks of convoluted, often confused, discussions, beginning in mid-January with talks between Heathfield and Ned Smith, involving the TUC and producing a series of misunderstandings. The end came on 28 February with the NEC realising that no likely negotiated settlement could incorporate the union's fundamental position on closures.

Against the fluctuating and feverish expectations about a settlement, the number of Lancashire strikers diminished throughout February. Over 150 more quit the strike at Bold, and similar numbers at Sutton Manor and Parkside. At Bickershaw the number on strike fell to little over a hundred and at Parsonage there were under ten. But at Agecroft, where the strikers had faced so many problems from the start, the numbers showed little decline, and at Golborne, probably fewer than forty abandoned the strike over the month. Across the whole coalfield, however, the number of strikers on the last day of February was no more than 1,500, and arguably a hundred or two less.[35]

By the last two weeks, the remaining Lancashire fliers were desperate. They had failed to stem the return in the coalfield, developments elsewhere seemed grim. Frustration mounted. Some developed a tactic of repaying scores by attempting to catch the police unawares. They took a meal break after the ritual push and shove and returned when the police were perhaps tired. They operated on a principle borne out of bitter experience 'If one or two threw bricks, then they would be done easily, but if everybody did there was safety in numbers . . .'[36] Already in South Wales the notion of an organised return without any negotiated settlement had been discussed and officials from other coalfields, including Lancashire, had informally considered the suggestion.[37] The prospect was hinted at by Terry Thomas, the South Wales Vice-President, when addressing a Special National Conference on 21 February. Although formally the Conference decision was to battle on, there was abundant evidence of difficulties even in solid coalfields. The message from South Wales was that the present impasse would not last much longer: 'South Wales will stand fast for as long as it possibly can, but . . . we will be misleading this Conference to think we can stand as fast as we have forever.'[38] Now in this last week of February, this acquired a new edge as miners in Mardy, the Rhondda's historic Little Moscow, the last pit in the Valley discussed their predicament. Over the twelve months, not one Mardy miner had returned to work; they could claim an authority which few could emulate. The message from Mardy was simple. An orderly return was the only way to prevent the destruction of the NUM.

The South Wales initiative divided the NEC and it divided the strikers. There were conflicting pressures: defence of principles or defence of the Union's viability; the need to gain an amnesty for sacked colleagues; markedly divergent views about what could be achieved or lost through continuing the struggle. South Wales officials might be cynical of officials in largely working Areas who advocated 'Stand Firm'. Their postures were dependent on South Walian solidarity and suffering. In contrast, strikers in predominantly working Areas or pits could be dismissive of South Wales' anxieties. So what if some had gone back down there? This had happened in our coalfield months ago and we'd stuck it out. Why can't they? But against this, there was the insistent, demanding question: what could be achieved by such an endurance test?

The NEC decided 'after a lot of argument and discussion' to hold a Special Delegate Conference three days later on Sunday 3 March.[39] That was the path by which the coalfields had entered the battle; now perhaps it could offer a way out.

The day after the Sheffield meeting the Lancashire Executive met in Bolton. It was a cold soaking St David's Day, so different from those scorching summer weeks that had seen the strike at its zenith. That morning there was a sombre awareness of the union's predicament; Executive members were aware of the strikers' diminishing base in the coalfield and they were concerned by the problems of re-establishing the union in pits where most were at work, but the Branch Officials were not. But against that, everyone knew that a return to work without agreement settled nothing, and it was hard to believe that the Coal Board would be magnanimous. The Lancashire Executive recommended to the next day's Area Conference: 'that we mandate our delegates to the One-Day Special Conference . . . to support an orderly return to work without an Agreement.' There followed a declaration on the most painful of outstanding issues, but one which suggested some wishful thinking, that: 'The Area would do all in its power to get any member of this

Organisation who had been dismissed during the dispute reinstated immediately.'[40]

That afternoon it was becoming clear that the South Wales initiative would secure substantial support. It was endorsed by the North Eastern coalfields and by several smaller Areas where most miners were at work. But Yorkshire's position remained unclear and both Scotland and Kent opposed any return that by-passed the problem of sacked miners. In Lancashire the Executive's position had to be endorsed by the Area Conference. They met next day in the Bolton Conference Hall, scene of so many dramatic debates over the past twelve months. That Saturday morning, the press speculated on whether that weekend would bring an end. The case for an organised return was put succinctly by the Delegate for the Ashton and Haydock Craftsmen:

> We are in a Catch 22 situation . . . if this conference doesn't take a positive step then there will be a flood back to work next week . . . There are men in this room who will stop out on strike forever because they have hearts like lions, but . . . the alternative to a united return to work by the National Union of Mineworkers has no winability.[41]

Some speakers argued that a mass return could lead to a more effective waging of the battle, once the union was back inside the pits. Such false, but perhaps necessary, optimism ignored the union's weak position and in particular the divisions within the membership. As it was, some were only too aware that the dwindling number of strikers could permit the Board to victimise activists and Branch officials: 'We can't stop out on the gates until there is only a handful of men at each pit, because then every Branch Official would be removed, like what had happened at Leigh Craftsmen Branch.'[42]

Any idea that a return to work could be followed by vigorous maintenance of the longstanding overtime ban ignored the basic fact that some Lancashire strikebreakers were already breaching the ban. A *douche* of cold realism came from Mick Noonan the Parkside Branch Secretary. He had been admonished by a member against any sell-out but: 'He asked himself, 'What have we got left to sell?'[43] It was necessary to make the best of a bad job: 'The longer we stop out on strike and the smaller we get, the less impact we'll have when we return . . . we could do more good from within.'

Pessimism about the prospects was in some ways shared by those who urged a continuation of the strike. Colin Lenton, the Bold

Delegate and a leading figure in the vigorous initiatives of the activists was dismissive of any claim that the struggle could be maintained inside the pits: 'If we give in now, we are giving Mrs Thatcher our heads on a platter.' The suggestion that sacked miners would be aided by an organised return was wishful thinking. 'People knew in their hearts that these men wouldn't get their jobs back, we came out on strike, not for a pay rise, but to prevent pit closures and job losses, and yet we are prepared to run away from them . . .'[44] Moreover, the organised return would be particularly bitter for men who had always been in the minority at Agecroft and Walkden. These sentiments clearly evoked sympathy within the conference hall, but as Stan Horsfield, the Agent, emphasised, these present were the committed minority: 'There are 200 delegates in this conference hall and that is the total number . . . actually left at the colliery gates picketing for thirteen and fourteen hours a day.'[45]

The divisions resulting from the strike in the Lancashire NUM were all too evident. There might have been 200 members in that hall, but only nine Branches were represented. They voted seven to two, or eighty-one to twenty-nine on a card vote in favour of the South Wales initiative. Appropriately, the minority came from the two pits where the Lancashire strike had begun. At Bold a majority remained out, and their Delegate claimed that the 'Fight On' policy had been backed by a meeting of 250. From Sutton Manor, where the strikers were now well in the minority, the defiance had a more evanescent quality. As the Delegate acknowledged, 'We had a Branch meeting on Tuesday , and one minute you're mandated one way, then it's altered. You have just got to decide on the circumstances at the time.'[46]

The decisive Lancashire endorsement of an organised return was not emulated to the east of the Pennines. Very narrowly, on a card vote, the Yorkshire Area decided not to back the South Wales initiative. It was a decision that made the outcome of next day's National Conference less predictable, and the confusion was increased on the Sunday morning when the NEC split evenly and failed to offer any recommendation. Miners from all the coalfields had travelled to London to lobby delegates; they were largely committed to the struggle and unhappy about the South Wales solution.[47] The emotional charge, so intense amongst Delegates and lobbyists, was conveyed graphically by a member of the Lancashire delegation: 'There were many heart-breaking words said, and I

don't want anybody here to think that the final voting . . . to support
the Welsh resolution was taken lightly. However, you had to make a
final decision that went against the grain. The men knew you didn't
want it, but at the same time they knew it couldn't be avoided.'[48]

Within the debate, a tough minded recognition of the union's
predicament had been articulated by supporters of the South Wales
resolution, most forcefully by Billy Etherington, the radical leader
of the Durham Mechanics. The truth for him was stark: 'We do not
have a negotiating position.' Through all the discussions, the
National Officials had achieved nothing. It was wishful thinking to
believe that their Area counterparts could do better after an
organised return. The reason for a return was not to achieve
something, but to prevent a bigger disaster: 'We are going back
because we cannot hold our members any longer.' That, in his view,
was proper leadership; he was dismissive of leadership as an
endurance test: 'If you can see no way ahead and there is no
advantage to be gained by stopping out any longer, it is not only lack
of leadership to keep on with the fine rhetoric, it is downright
wicked.'[49] Against this case, there stood the insistence by leaders,
such as Jack Collins of Kent, that the South Wales strategy would
leave the sacked men isolated and would not achieve any of the
union's objectives.[50] The insistence was correct and painful; how to
achieve the objectives remained obscure.

The South Wales resolution was passed narrowly by ninety-eight
votes to ninety-one. Outside in the rain, men committed to the
strike opposed the decision. The dispute with all its pain had
become a way of life. Some wept.

In Lancashire next morning the pickets went out in a last gesture
of defiance. At Bickershaw, the strikers held their last meeting. The
Branch Secretary described it as 'heart-breaking'.[51] Over at the
Bold Miners' Club, the centre of so much activity, many men and
women who had worked together throughout the dispute came
together for the last time. The emotion was almost palpable.
One present recalls something reminiscent of Zola's *Germinal*:
'The tension was so great that if any one had said, "Let's go and
take pit apart, we'd have all gone."'[52] The pride and the passion
went along with resentments – at Coal Board tactics, at the failure of
other unions to give worthwhile support, most bitterly at strike-
breaking miners and NUM officials who had lacked enthusiasm for
the fight.

These resentments were articulated as delegates reconvened in Bolton to hear a report on the National Conference. There was a sharp reminder at this meeting of the rift within the Lancashire NUM. In the absence of any accredited delegation from Agecroft, one of the pit's strikers, Steve Howells, was allowed to speak for men who had always been in the minority. There could be little credibility for the Agecroft strikers in the idea of a dignified return to work. Howells, for one, did not agree with the national decision. 'We don't agree that we are going back . . . Everybody is saying that we shall go back with our heads held high, but I'm speaking for the lads and it will be harder for us to go back with our heads held high.'[53]

The following morning the miners marched back. About 250 went into Parkside, their banner carried by the Newton Women's Group. At Golborne and Sutton Manor, about 200 walked in to each pit, but at Bickershaw, scene of those June battles, only just over a hundred went back that Tuesday morning. The Agecroft return showed the most bitter side of the Lancashire struggle – men unbroken, committed to the fight, returning to a hostile workplace with nothing to show but their own self-belief. At the pit bottom on that first day, they read some graffiti: 'You went out with empty heads; you've come back with empty pockets.' 'No', responded one, 'our pockets are empty but our heads are full.'[54]

Bold had the largest march bac,k over 300-strong – but they encountered a problem. Nine Yorkshire pickets from the radical Armthorpe Branch arrived to argue the case for a national amnesty for sacked men. The strike-breakers went through, but many who had supported the strike until the end were reluctant to do so. Bold officials were unhappy at the pickets' presence, preoccupied as they were with restoring an effective Union in the pit: 'These men have been solid for twelve months and now you threaten to split us. During all that time they have refused to cross the picket lines, but now you have put one up when they are supposed to go back. We know half will cross and the other half won't – and you will have split a good branch.' Eventually one of the pickets agreed to 'phone back for advice, and within twenty minutes the pickets had dispersed.

The ending of the Bold strike offers the most fitting epitaph to one strand in the Lancashire strike:

> The sounds of singing began echoing towards the main gates. Finally they came, the Miners' Wives' Support Group first, singing and clapping. They lined the entrance to the gate and began applauding as

the first miners, with their embroidered banner came into view. They marched briskly, singing, 'Here we go', and halted a moment before the first man stepped through just after 8 a.m.[55]

That March morning the returning Lancashire strikers expressed publicly the epic quality of their resistance. This transcended all the tensions, the uncertainties and the pain. It had been expressed in the creativity with which the strike had come to Lancashire in that long-past springtime, and in the optimism of a fiery summer. In the darker defiant days that followed, it had taken a more sombre form. Now came the final act; that moving climax. Then the men passed through the gates to their uncertain future. Suddenly there could only be memories of what had been and the brutal reality of defeat.

Notes

1 *Newton and Golborne News*, 16 November 1984.
2 As a result the Union's national leadership was criticised publicly by the North Wales Agent, Ted Mackay. Vincent commented, 'I want no truck with Colonel Gadafy[sic]' but the Union needed assistance. *MEN*, 29 October 1984.
3 NWA Special Conference, 6 November 1984 (Parkside Delegate).
4 NUM Special Delegate Conference, 5 November 1984, p. 700.
5 *Ibid.* p. 704.
6 NWA Special Conference, 6 November 1984.
7 *MEN*, 5 and 6 November 1984.
8 See for example the comments of Mick Noonan of Parkside and Ron Gaskell of Golbourne in *Newton and Golborne News*, 16 November 1984.
9 *MEN*, 16 November 1984.
10 The 'over half back claim' was taken on board by a newspaper not normally prey to Coal Board propaganda claims, *Observer*, 18 November 1984; but see the same newspaper, 25 November 1984, for a more sceptical discussion of Board claims.
11 Discussions with Parkside NUM.
12 *Leigh, Tyldesley and Atherton Journal*, 15 November 1984 (Roy Walls).
13 Discussions with Sutton Manor NUM.
14 Discussions with Bold NUM.
15 *Guardian*, 24 November 1984.
16 Discussions with Bersham and Point of Ayr NUM; Point of Ayr Women's Group; *Wrexham Evening Leader*, 8 November 1984.
17 Discussions with Agecroft strikers; see also *Wrexham Evening Leader* 22 November 1984.
18 Les Kelly interview.
19 Discussions with Bersham NUM.
20 Comment at the time from a Granada Television interviewer.

21 Using figures supplied by NCB (Western Area), subject to criticisms made above.

22 NWA Conference, 10 December 1984.

23 NWA Conference, 19 January 1985.

24 Discussions with Newton Women's Group.

25 Sid Vincent interview.

26 NWA Executive, 7 January 1985.

27 *Ibid.* For some public comment, see *Observer*, 30 December 1984.

28 NWA Conference, 19 January 1985.

29 *Ibid.* (Frank King).

30 *Ibid.* in Vincent's report on the NEC meeting of 10 January 1985.

31 *Ibid.* Executive, 17 January 1985.

32 *MEN*, 18 January 1985.

33 *Leigh, Tyldesley and Atherton Journal*, 24 January 1985; *Newton and Golborne News*, 25 January and 1 February 1985.

34 *Leigh, Tyldesley and Atherton Journal*, 10 January 1985.

35 Using the NCB figures supplied for that day and subjecting them to analysis according to criticisms made previously.

36 Discussions with strikers.

37 See comment of Mick Noonan, NWA Special Conference, 2 March 1985, 'We have come clean, we have been tossing this idea about for six to eight weeks . . .'

38 NUM Special Delegate Conference, 21 February 1985, p. 61.

39 NUM NEC, 28 February 1985.

40 NWA Executive, 1 March 1985; also discussions with Branch Officials on the day of this meeting.

41 NWA Special Conference, 2 March 1985.

42 *Ibid.* (Plank Lane Delegate).

43 *Ibid.*

44 *Ibid.*

45 *Ibid.*

46 *Ibid.*

47 Discussions with strikers from Agecroft and Bersham, both pits where most were at work and therefore the concerns voiced by South Wales could seem less urgent.

48 NWA Special Conference, 4 March 1985 (Brian Eden).

49 NUM Special Delegate Conference, 3 March 1985, pp. 96–7.

50 *Ibid.* pp. 93–4.

51 *Leigh, Tyldesley and Atherton Journal*, 7 March 1985.

52 Discussions with Newton Women's Group.

53 NWA Special Conference, 4 March 1985.

54 Discussions with members of Branches concerned.

55 *St Helens Reporter*, 8 March 1985.

10

Splits and shutdowns

As the miners returned to work, Ian MacGregor was in a triumphant and vindictive mood. In a press interview with a prominent supporter of Coal Board policy, he made his frequently-quoted comment on the fate of sacked miners: 'People are now discovering the price of insubordination and insurrection. And boy, are we going to make it stick.' More broadly, as far as he was concerned, the old order had gone. MacGregor's view was that 'there were a lot of people in the industry who did not understand what had been going on for the last year, now we had succeeded we were going to exert our right to manage the enterprise.'[1]

Lancashire miners, like their colleagues elsewhere, soon faced difficult choices. The Union was still endeavouring to implement the overtime ban; within days, miners were sent home from the Bickershaw complex after an attempt to maintain the policy. The NUM Branch had refused to sanction weekend safety work, a stand which ran into conflict with the reality of a divided workforce. Throughout the later months of the strike there had been repeated demands from Union loyalists that strikebreakers who were breaching the ban should be disciplined. At Bickershaw, the Craftsmen involved in this safety work had been strikebreakers. Their attempt to secure union approval for weekend work not only raised questions about the viability of the overtime ban; it also implied retrospective approval for overtime worked during the dispute. Already, local officials faced some negative consequences of the strategy used to terminate the strike: 'This is what happens when you go back without a negotiated settlement. We knew there would be problems, but I didn't think it would be this quick.'[2] Work in the Complex stopped for three days and when Lancashire

Delegates met the following Saturday, there was a sombre awareness
of the Board's post-strike style. Already there were rumours of a cut
in employment at Bold. A leading strike activist at that pit had met
with a tough managerial greeting. He was 'told to go on a job other
than his own job which was on the face. He refused and said he was
going on his rightful job because he was the Chargeman. The
management said if he didn't go on the job, they would all be sent
home. He came up the pit and some ninety men followed him . . .'[3]
The militancy of the strike was not yet extinguished but the
Bickershaw incident highlighted the uncertain prospects for the
overtime ban. Delegates accepted an Executive resolution suggesting
that the ban should be applied with some flexibility. The objective
was to obtain five normal shifts 'in this most exacting situation';
essential tasks should be timetabled to permit this.

The days of the ban were clearly numbered. When the National
Executive met in late March, it voted eighteen to five to call a
Special Delegate Conference and to recommend the lifting of the
ban.[4] Some Conference Delegates were brutally realistic about the
situation in their own coalfields. George Bolton, the Scottish Vice-
President, announced that in his Area there was fragmentation and
the threat of more: 'You are discussing the ending or continuation of
a crumbling overtime ban . . . It is a recipe for intensifying the
potential splits and the divisions of this Union.'[5] Equally, Vincent,
who had so often presented a euphoric view of the Union's
situation, now presented a harsh prospectus: 'If this Conference
does not vote to lift the overtime ban today then you have lost that
one . . . we are now faced with the position of losing control of this
Union.'[6] The ban was called off by 122 votes to seventy-four with
the large Yorkshire Area providing much of the minority.

There remained the wages question that had helped to spark off
the whole confrontation. This was resolved speedily. Following
discussions between the Union and the Board, the old offer of 5.2
per cent for 1983/84 was accepted, followed by an equivalent offer
for 1984/85.[7] There was simply no other response that the Union
could make.

If the Union was to have any hope of dealing with the Board's
tougher policies, then a first priority had to be the reconstruction of
its own unity. The signs from Nottinghamshire were already
ominous. The Area had unilaterally ended the overtime ban; the
hostility between the emerging new leadership in Nottinghamshire

and the national officials was grimly apparent. Yet in some other coalfields the legacy also posed problems. In Lancashire most miners worked during the strike's later months and some Branches had dropped out of the Union's decision-making. Committed strikers were often reluctant to sit in a meeting with men who had worked throughout, and in some cases, taken the Union to court. The priorities of some strikebreaking Branch Officials were obscure. Did they want to re-enter the debates within the NUM? Would they be attracted by breakaway unionism in a larger Area such as Nottinghamshire? Would many of their members be attracted by such outside blandishments? In the middle there were some who wished to rebuild the Lancashire Area on as catholic a basis as possible. They saw this as a necessary condition for coping with the Board. But for them there was a crucial political problem. How much should be conceded to strikebreakers in order to reintegrate them within the Union? How often was it possible to hold back from criticism without denying the meaning of the last year?

One Lancastrian legacy was heavily personalised – the criticism that had focused on the Area President, Bernard Donaghy, after he had vanished from Executive Committee and Conference meetings at the start of October 1984. As the situation deteriorated in the New Year, so Donaghy became the target of repeated attacks by strikers. These focused on the fact that he was still carrying out some of his Agent's duties but was not involved in any strike activities. As yet the anger was largely contained within the institutions of the Union. In the last weeks of the strike, there was a fundamental need to avoid any embarrassing disclosures. Yet criticism came, not only just from activists, but also from Branch Officials politically close to Donaghy. Mick Noonan, the Parkside Branch Secretary, and very much a conventional Lancastrian moderate, felt that Donaghy had simply abandoned his post: 'He is doing everything except acting as President of this Area.'[8] The discussion hinted at a wider lack of sympathy for the strike. It was alleged that there had been duplicity on the part of some employees of the Union: 'Half of the trouble in this Area has been caused by Agecroft Branch, but certain information has been passed on to these strike breakers by our own people.'[9]

This web of rumour and accusation just as the strike was ending highlighted once again the culture of the Lancashire Area, how distant its style was from recent developments within the National

Union and how confused the start of the strike had been. One striker recalled Donaghy's stance at a critical moment: 'After ten weeks on strike we held a crisis meeting in this hall and [I] asked the Area President to come off the fence and join the strike. He disagreed with the dispute and the way it had been handled and the way the men had been brought out on strike.'[10] But Donaghy's opinions on the dispute's origins had not been eccentric within the Lancashire NUM leadership. After all, he had moved the Area's resolution at the Sheffield Delegate Conference in April 1984. But then, lines became sharply drawn, and the positions that men took could not be deduced always from their past records. By the end of the strike, Donaghy, once the persuasive advocate of the Lancashire case for a national ballot, had become for many activists a symbol of weak leadership and a focus of resentments at a time of defeat.

With the return to work and the heightening awareness of the Union's weakness, the attacks continued. The March Delegate Conference insisted that Donaghy attend an Executive Meeting.[11] He duly did so[12] and then on 20 April he chaired his first delegate conference for seven months. He outlined his case – illness, the need for intensive treatment, his regular contacts with Area office, the extent of his work as Agent during this period. On the strike, he had accepted the implications of the Kent resolution: 'Once the decision was made that the strike was official he accepted it, but he did say at the Executive Meeting . . . that he had reservations about the strategy, but he had never encouraged anybody to cross a picket line in his life.' Even earlier when passions had run high at Agecroft, he said that his message at a meeting had been: 'Whatever you think of the Union's strategy, please do not cross picket lines' and that had been his attitude all through the strike.'[13] But he faced on the agenda, a proposition from the Kirkless Branch: 'Our members feel that our Area President, Mr Bernard Donaghy has wilfully neglected his position during our recent dispute with the National Coal Board. We therefore propose that Mr Donaghy be asked to tender his resignation and we ask Conference Delegates to support this proposal.'[14] Donaghy responded that his only objection was to one word – 'wilfully'.[15]

The proposition was withdrawn but Delegates debated a proposal from Bold for an amendment of the rule relating to the election of the Area President. The individual ballot would be replaced by a Branch vote. This would threaten Donaghy's prospects in any future contest, since the decisions in many Branches would be influenced by those who had been most committed to the strike. The amendment was carried by ninety-seven votes to forty-three with the minority consisting almost wholly of predominantly non-striking Branches.[16]

This was not the end of the Donaghy affair. For the next Delegate Conference, the Kirkless proposition reappeared, redrafted to make it clear that the resignation demand related just to Donaghy's role as President and did not cover his full-time job as Agent. The proposition was carried by eighty votes to sixty, the majority composed of Branches controlled by strikers – Bold, Golborne, Parkside, Sutton Manor and Kirkless.[17] Eventually, Donaghy left the Presidency.[18] Apparently he felt that such a move could be therapeutic, removing a focus for recriminations and thereby facilitating a more united Area.[19]

The need for this was all too clear, but so was the extent of the task. The narrow vote against Donaghy indicated the enduring anger of some strikers, but the narrowness highlighted the fundamental problem of unity. From April, Branches led by strike-breaking officials began once more to attend Lancashire NUM Meetings. Already there were reservations about the loyalty of some, and at the April Conference, Delegates debated a variety of rumours about possible breakaways. Some centred on an old adversary, the Winders' Branch, and its members' alleged lack of co-operation with the rest of the workforce. One speaker believed that perhaps some winders were already outside the NUM: 'He had heard that they were paying another contribution to a Union but couldn't provide any concrete evidence to back it up.'[20] More specific allegations came from the Golborne Secretary, Ron Gaskell. At his colliery, there had been a recruitment drive, with Coal Board backing, for the breakaway Durham-based Colliery Trades and Allied Workers Association: '. . . a craftsman at Golborne . . . was going round the pit recruiting for the new craftsmen's Union being formed in Durham, and yesterday there was a notice up . . . saying that anybody suffering harassment or intimidation could contact a free phone . . . number at Staffordshire House.'[21] The Durham based organisation was also active at Kirkless, hoping to find a receptive audience in the wake of defeat. 'They were collecting openly at the workshop for expenses to go to this meeting in Durham . . . There are about sixty people involved . . .

There are obviously men at Kirkless who are disillusioned but
didn't scab all the time . . . but are being pressured by these men to
join a breakaway union . . .[22]

Events at a Lancashire Conference in mid-June showed that the
divisions resulting from the dispute could be easily opened up. The
situation at Kirkless was desperate; the Board had just announced
its closure and would not discuss the decision. The membership
seemed ready to accept this; moreover, it was a divided work force;
ninety-five had quit the NUM and joined the Durham-based
breakaway association. Transfers after any closure could erode
unity elsewhere: 'There are going to be jobs for the boys and the
management are definitely siding with these people to break up the
NUM.'[23] Delegates agreed unanimously to oppose such a development; only NUM members would be accepted as transfers from
Kirkless. The effectiveness of this policy would be tested at
Walkden where only a few men had ever joined the strike and where
a breakaway could have significant appeal. Vincent argued that the
Branch Officials faced a vital task: 'If these men get in at Walkden,
then they will try to destroy that Branch . . . [I hope] that this
message [will] be conveyed to the Walkden members.[24] There
might be unanimity on this issue, but it was overshadowed
immediately by acrimony over the involvement of Lancashire
miners with the National Working Miners' Committee and their
writ against the National Officials and the NEC. Criticism of the
continuing legal threat produced a sharp response from the
Parsonage Delegate. He claimed that his Branch had returned to
Conference after an appeal from Area officials. His reception was
evidently hostile. The official minutes then noted that the 'Parsonage
Delegate asked certain Branches in conference, "Did they want
them present, or not?" ' The rhetorical question clearly produced
an answer since the Delegates from Parsonage, Walkden and the
two Agecroft Branches then left.[25]

Almost twelve months before, the striking branches had walked
out of the same hall rather than sit with strikebreakers. Now the
rift seemed as deep as ever. Ironically, Ron Gaskell, who had
triggered off the 1984 walk out, regretted this new division: 'What
we have allowed to happen in this hall this morning was wrong . . .
we are splitting ourselves up . . . the National Coal Board will be
aware of this . . . we are playing into their hands.' There was only
one priority – unity in the Area including those who had worked. He

would never forgive them, but the Area can't manage without them.[26]

But already some Branches were receptive to breakaway initiatives and soon these would be given a much more credible basis. The principal bone of contention concerned the rewriting of the NUM Rule Book. The roots of this went back before the strike; the Rule Book had seen little alteration since its initial formulation back in 1944. The projected reform of the Rule Book could be seen as one facet of Scargill's concern to modernise the Union. But such brave hopes were engulfed by the industry's crisis. During the dispute, the ravages produced by legal action provided new grounds for the revision of the Rule Book; so did the frustration of strikers who felt powerless to deal with members who crossed picket lines, and in some cases, ignored the overtime ban. One early manifestation came in July 1984 when a Special Delegate Conference approved a new Rule Fifty-One providing a national basis for disciplinary procedures. This was only finalised at the second attempt a month later, after the initial decision had been vitiated by a injunction granted to some Nottinghamshire strikebreakers.[27] The Lancashire Area, preoccupied with its own disunity, backed this move, but further proposals for reform early in the New Year provoked a different response from Bolton.

This time, the purpose was the reform of the National Executive, to be considered along with the possible expulsion of the Nottinghamshire Area. The restructuring strategy involved the merging of small right wing Areas – Lancashire Cumberland and North Wales, for example, would be brought together. The Lancashire Executive opposed this thoroughly.[28] There was a natural desire to defend the Area's autonomy and, cynics would say, the Officials' jobs and status. But the proposals also had a taint of political manipulation in the eyes of the Right. Critics focused on the continuing independence of the Kent Area – small, but on the Left. Even allowing for geographical difficulties, the modernisation drive seemed to be applied unevenly. On this occasion the proposals came to nothing – the harsh crisis faced by the NUM led to the abandonment of the projected Conference.

Yet the issue did not disappear. In the prelude to the July 1985 National Conference, Areas had to consider a new Rule Book. The NEC restructuring was largely abandoned, but the proposals contained elements bound to reawaken the passions and divisions of the strike. Rule Eleven was a response to the 1984 Trade Union Act. This required five-yearly ballots for all voting members of the Union National Executive. The new rule laid down that the National President would have no vote in the National Executive; re-election was thus not required.

The legacy of the strike was seen in the proposed Rule 5b which, by permitting associate membership, would open the NUM, for example, to members of the Women's Support Groups. Rule 26c harked back to the controversial strategy that had underpinned the strike: 'The NEC shall have the power to call industrial action by any group of members whether in one or part of one or more than one Area and such action shall be deemed to be declared official.'[29] For critics, here once again was the spectre of a strike without a ballot, although in that self-same rule, paragraph e retained the requirement that a national strike required a national ballot.

Predictably, Nottinghamshire, South Derbyshire and Leicestershire were in opposition to all or most of the new rules. But in the depressed post-strike world fissures were opening up within the NUM Left. In South Wales and Scotland there were criticisms of Scargill's leadership, concern about the risk of a secession; in some cases the critics claimed the beginnings of a tough-minded willingness to face up to the realities of the Union's situation. Thus South Wales opposed the new Rule 11; they also objected to the NEC's proposed power to call Areas out on strike.

The Lancashire response to the proposed new rules was similar. The Executive and a Delegate Conference considered them. They opposed associate membership; they backed a COSA amendment to Rule 11 that would remove the National President's protection against re-election and they backed deletion of the contentious Rule 26c. But Lancashire supported the new disciplinary procedure.[30] Moreover, the Area found itself involved in a procedural manoeuvre that did much to guarantee the new Rule Book's adoption. In the lead-up to the Conference it might seem that an alliance of the old Right and the newly-discontented Left could block the two thirds majority needed for some of the more controversial innovations. But on the eve of the Conference, Scargill announced that the new Rule Book would be put to Conference *en bloc*. If this proposal received a two-thirds majority, then the same requirement would be needed to remove or amend any of the new rules. This raised the hurdle and destroyed the hope in some sections of the Left that perhaps some contentious proposals would be blocked without left critics having to display their unease too publicly. The need for a two- thirds majority to block any new rule meant that these critics would have to declare themselves in speeches and with their votes. Predictably, they usually preferred to keep quiet.

At the start of the Rules Revision Conference, Scargill moved the new rules. His seconder was not a member of the NEC Left, but Sid Vincent, who perhaps saw in the manoeuvre a procedural flair of which Gormley would have been proud. As a Lancastrian cynic put it: 'Vincent had become Arthur's most vociferous supporter.'[31] The ploy worked. The NEC motion for the new rules was passed by 170 votes to fifty-eight; almost all of the Nottinghamshire delegation then left the Conference, saying that they were mandated not to accept the new Rule Book. This facilitated the acceptance of the new rules: in the event, only the associate membership clause was deleted.

The estrangement of Nottinghamshire proceeded rapidly. Two days later the Area Council voted by 228 to twenty to quit the NUM. There was also the prospect of support for secession in other coalfields. South Derbyshire and Leicestershire had made clear their objections to the new Rule Book and the Durham breakaway association claimed 1,300 members. Lancashire seemed likely to play a significant part in such a move. The Durham organisation already had recruited a hundred members in that coalfield. Old animosities continued at Delegate Conferences and in some Lancashire NUM Branches. Then in mid-July, following the controversies of the National Conference, there came the announcement that Agecroft would consider leaving the NUM. Three months previously, the Branch's Standing Delegate had reassured his first Conference for ten months that: 'They were not involved in any move to break away from the NUM.'[32] But after the alarums and excursions of early June, Jim Lord claimed that the new Rule Book had altered the situation. He reintroduced the rhetoric of the strike: 'Scargill has buried the ballot box. He has taken the voice away from the rank and file.' As in the critical days of the strike he would reflect the majority decision. Personally, he preferred to argue his case inside the NUM, but 'if the men democratically decide to quit, we'll have to adhere to the result'.[33] The responsibility for any split lay, not on Agecroft, nor on the Nottinghamshire men – 'Scargillism' was to blame. However, the

Agecroft Branch Meeting in late July did not follow up its condemnation of the rule changes by an immediate decision to ballot on a breakaway. The Lancashire Executive had reacted to the June Conference walkout and to the pressures of Coal Board policy by deciding to hold a meeting of Branch Secretaries and Presidents that could discuss the obstacles to unity. The Agecroft meeting decided to await the outcome of this, although disenchantment with the NUM national leadership was all too apparent.[34]

Elsewhere in the coalfield the move for secession did not pause until after this 'peace' meeting. The Leigh Craftsmen had been controlled by anti-strike members since January. Already several pro-strike Craftsmen had moved into the Plank Lane Branch and, as a result, the Leigh Craftsmen had become a Branch dominated by sentiments antagonistic to the NUM. Its members balloted decisively to join the Durham breakaway association. More than 150 favoured this step, the Branch was unrepresented when the 'peace' meeting met on 17 August and the next day the Leigh Craftsmen formally decided to leave the NUM.[35]

The 'peace' meeting was informed with a bleak awareness that Coal Board priorities made unity a matter of urgency. The prospect of a new coal terminal in Liverpool posed the threat of cheap imports to the Lancashire pits. The Board's response to any competition was obvious: 'The Board have told me that the only way they can provide opposition is to make our pits economic in Lancashire and getting the price of coal as low as possible.'[36] But the embers of the dispute could easily burst into a blaze. The new Rule Book was presented by its critics as productive of a more centralised Union with initiative drained from the Areas and the erosion of individual members' rights. Here was a controversy that went back over four decades. How far should uniformity go in the National Union? Did centralisation produce a more effective union, or did the NUM operate better as a national union in name but a federation in practice? Vincent's case was that, at Area Level, nothing had really changed: 'The rule changes which are made nationally do not affect this Organisation at all. We are a union in our own right.'[37] This verdict was completely at odds with the assessment of Igor Judge QC, advisor to the Nottinghamshire critics. In his view the new rules fundamentally changed the Area/National balance.[38] This evaluation clearly lay behind persistent querying of Vincent's assessment by Jim Lord. Moreover, other speakers expressed their concern about specific rule changes, but with an acquiescence in the National decisions: 'When a decision was made at Conference, they had accepted it, whether they agreed or not.'[39] Fuelling concern about the rules changes, there were the continuing antagonisms within Lancashire. Bold's delegation articulated the case of the committed strikers. Twelve months' struggle could not be simply wiped from the memory, but hopefully such recollections could be containable Mal Gregory presented his position, 'He would never forget what happened during this dispute, and . . . neither would his branch members, but for the working of the pit and for safety it is essential that we work together . . .'[40]

From the other side some representatives for strike-breaking Branches focused on the card vote system in Area Conference. This could connect with the continuing controversy over the ballot, although within Conference the card vote was a venerable tradition. Indeed, the criticism from Agecroft seemed, not so much against the system, as the anxiety of people who found themselves in a minority under a procedure that they had previously accepted. One stated that: 'In the past, it had been effective.' However, he 'would not like to see three or four pits coming together and ruling this area, because then freedom of speech and opinion would be lost'.[41] More plausibly, Jim Lord focused on the very recent shift in the procedure for electing the Lancashire President, but did so in terms that hardly indicated acceptance of the Union's procedures: 'In normal circumstances the card vote system for election of officials would not have gone through . . . the only democratic way of electing officials is by ballot . . . [my] members [will] not recognise any official of this organisation who [has] been elected into his position by a card vote.' Against this came the riposte from Bold: 'A big branch has got a big vote.'[42]

The debate reflected a general awareness that Area decisions would be dominated by Branches controlled by strikers. Some unhappy about this suggested that the longstanding procedures of the Union – the making of decisions at Branch Meetings, and then by mandated Delegates at Area Conference – was not really democratic. This position was developed by Walter Speakman of Parsonage: 'If a decision is made by way of a card vote, it is not a true majority and the only way of getting to know the members' wishes was by holding a ballot.'[43] This argument would legitimise past behaviour; it underpinned Jim Lord's defence of his actions during the strike. What he did, he said, 'was to carry out a mandate given to him by the men at Agecroft and the mandate given by the majority of men in Lancashire . . .'[44] But it could be employed also to license future actions. Thus, the Parsonage President suggested mass dissatisfaction at his pit: '. . . if they had called a meeting last week, they would have been mandated not to come to Conference . . . the majority of rank and file members at Parsonage wanted to leave the NUM and . . . they wanted a ballot on any decision made.'[45] Future problems were casting their shadows, although for the moment this informal meeting produced a statement arguing for a united front against the NCB, and repeating Vincent's controversial claim that, in Lancashire: 'These rule changes do not make one iota of difference.' Once again, as in March 1984, Vincent sought unity through the development of a consensus that could blunt the edges of the coalfield's antagonisms; but again, as in the strike's early weeks, Lancashire had to react to developments in other coalfields.

In Nottinghamshire the campaign for a breakaway union moved ahead, with lavish advertising, appeals to coalfield parochialism, and attempts to limit the scope given to pro NUM speakers and activists. The Nottinghamshire ballot result was awaited with anxiety elsewhere. Should this large coalfield declare for separation, then there would be a credible reference point for critics of NUM policies and leaders. In mid-October Nottinghamshire voted decisively to quit the National Union. The margin on a 90 per cent poll was 17,750 to 6,792 – 72 per cent for the breakaway. In the small South Derbyshire coalfield, the margin was wafer-thin and controversial – 1,286 to 1,260. Lancashire Delegates met under the shadow of these results, with the Union of Democratic Mineworkers soon to become a reality. Employment prospects in the coalfield were threatened further with the Board's announcement of Bold's impending closure. The premium on unity was rising, yet there were persistent rumours that Agecroft would quit the NUM. The Branch's Delegate presented the Nottinghamshire decision as catalytic: 'On their Minutes of a branch meeting, it was overwhelmingly asked for a ballot at the event of a Nottinghamshire succession [*sic*] and that Minute still stands.'[46] Two days later the press announced a forthcoming Agecroft ballot. Lord expressed once more his preference for sticking with the NUM. Unity was essential, but he acknowledged what he saw as his members' dominant and personalised sentiment: 'The men are fed up with

Arthur Scargill and have demanded a ballot.'[47] Yet on this occasion he was unhappy about the majority position at his pit. He had been contacted by the Nottinghamshire leadership in the hope that he could become the breakaway organiser in Lancashire. The proposal could seem attractive, not least because his prospects within the NUM seemed blighted, but he turned down the offer. Perhaps the inhibitions that had kept him out of the National Working Miners' Committee now held him back from a wholehearted espousal of the breakaways' case.[48]

That same day, the Durham breakaway association, including its Lancashire members, announced an unsurprising ballot result. 98.2 per cent of its members had backed the emerging alternative to the NUM. This produced a BBC claim that '230' Craftsmen at Bickershaw and Parsonage wanted to join the UDM. This exaggerated the secession and also gave the impression of a snowball effect following the Nottinghamshire result. In reality, these former Leigh Craftsmen had made the break several weeks previously.

Yet the snowball seemed to grow. The Agecroft vote took place on 30 October. In the main Pendlebury Branch, the vote went for the breakaway by 322 to 190; in the small Craft Branch, the margin was twenty-two to fourteen.[49] UDM officials were jubilant. Here was the promise of progress beyond the Nottinghamshire heartland.

The Agecroft ballot was only an expression of opinion. A Branch meeting on Sunday 10 November could decide on the next step. Those favouring a split invited Neil Greatrex to put the UDM case; the rank-and-file members committed to the NUM worked hard to stem the tide. They approached the National Officials and were told that either Scargill or Heathfield would come. But at this point, the always delicate question of the relationship between National and Area prerogatives emerged. According to an activist, Vincent declined the offer, saying that he would tackle the breakaway association himself.[50] But only a few days before the meeting he announced that he would not share the platform with Greatrex. Vincent's own account was different and gave no credit to the activists. The Area General Secretary:

> had asked Arthur Scargill would he address a Branch meeting at Agecroft . . . and he agreed. He [i.e. Vincent] wrote to the Branch, didn't get a reply, so he telephoned J. Lord . . . and the Committee turned the request down . . . it was also turned down at the Branch Meeting . . . how could he be expected to attend . . . when this Branch has refused the National President a chance to speak to them?[51]

Whatever the explanation, the consequences were harmful to the NUM. Activists felt that their battles were not supported by effective Area leadership. Their endurance during the months on strike at a largely working pit, and perhaps even more their tough commitment in a hostile environment since the return to work, seemed unappreciated. Those less involved but still basically loyal to the NUM could be a prey to cynicism – 'Why should I bother, if no one cares enough to come?'

At the meeting the Branch President refused to let any NUM supporter speak as a platform opponent to Greatrex. The meeting was in no sense a debate between two rival viewpoints, but a pro-UDM rally punctuated by critical questions. The vote found only thirty-nine opposing secession – a gross under-representation of the NUM's support at Agecroft and a needless propaganda coup for the UDM.[52]

The Agecroft decisions had been supplemented by a ballot at Parsonage in favour of leaving the NUM, but only by the narrow margin of 110 to ninety-one.[53] Now, perhaps late in the day, there was a feeling that matters had been let slide. The Leigh Craftsmen Branch had been allowed to fragment and the result was NUM members who had no Branch. Similar problems loomed at Agecroft and Parsonage. Loyalists felt isolated. If splits came about, they would need organisation; in the immediate crisis, they needed information for campaigning and encouragement in what could seem an uphill struggle.[54]

Walkden provided the one boost for those fighting to maintain a united Area. The great majority of members had ignored the strike call but now they voted 270 to twelve not to ballot on any breakaway.[55] Already Vincent was taking advice on the legal complexities of secession. Could Branches do so? If it was permitted, what conditions had to be met? He had informed an Executive meeting soon after the Agecroft ballot that there were serious legal obstacles.[56] Secession had to be by individuals; a Branch as such could not break away from the Area. So long as some Agecroft miners wished to be NUM members, then they would constitute the Branch. Perhaps most crucially, 'the Branch funds must remain intact and belong to the members of Pendlebury Branch NUM'.

The point began to be taken by those favouring secession, although the threat of a substantial haemorrhage still seemed present. When Parsonage Branch met on 1 December they decided once again to break away. This time, the margin was much more substantial. The Branch President claimed that he'd been threatened with knee-capping if Parsonage left the NUM, but suggested that by the time of the Branch meeting, 170 out of 235 members had already filled in UDM forms. But there remained the legal conundrum. As the Parsonage President acknowledged: 'We will need to look at certain rules and there are legal aspects which need to be resolved.'[57] Such awareness was starting to influence the Agecroft situation. Ten days prior to Christmas, Pendlebury Branch held its Annual General Meeting. The would-be secessionists faced the prospect that the dissolution of the Branch necessitated a five-sixths majority of the membership. This was a precondition for the freeing of Branch funds. The AGM failed to pursue one possible strategy – an appropriate change in the Branch Rule Book. Perhaps this indicated an awareness that members had not been given the required notice of this long-deferred AGM, and therefore any resulting rule change would be vulnerable in the courts.[58]

Within a few more weeks the prospects of rapid growth for the UDM both inside and outside Lancashire had diminished. Perhaps surprisingly, late in January 1986 Leicestershire voted two to one to remain with the NUM. Closer to Lancashire, the UDM found its efforts frustrated in North Wales. At Bersham, where almost all strikers had returned to work in November 1984, there was an overwhelming 327 to forty-two vote to stay inside the NUM. UDM hopes had rested on the bitterness that had followed the rapid disintegration of a solid strike. At the other North Wales pit, Point of Ayr, the balance of strikers and strikebreakers had been similar to Agecroft, but with one significant difference. The Point of Ayr Committee had been controlled and continued to be dominated by strikers. As at Agecroft, Point of Ayr working miners had served injunctions, not just against their Area, but also against their own Lodge officials. Yet a UDM recruiting drive backed by the management failed disastrously. The breakaway was rejected in a ballot by 498 votes to sixty-three. These decisions in a nearby coalfield, also part of the Western Area, could give encouragement to the Lancashire NUM. Even in promising territory the snowball was ceasing to roll.

In the New Year, the anti-breakaway campaign within Lancashire combined propaganda by activists, especially at Agecroft, with the threat of legal sanctions. Late in January activists forwarded a solicitor's letter to the Agecroft officials threatening such measures, should the Rule Book be infringed. The campaigning side of the strategy was seen at the beginning of February when Scargill spoke to a meeting of about 250, including Agecroft and Parsonage miners. How many this included beyond committed loyalists was doubtful, but a significant response came from Jim Lord. His initial comment had been dismissive: 'I said after the strike that Arthur Scargill should have called for unity then, but no, anyone who worked was still a scab' But almost immediately his emphasis shifted. The pressures from management were now the decisive factor 'A split union would be disastrous for this industry. And a split branch would spell disaster for this colliery.' He painted an implausible picture of Arthur Scargill and Roy Lynk meeting to discuss unity.[59] Legal constraints could offer the justification; pressures within the industry could highlight the virtues of a single union.

At Parsonage, the breakaway move had already met difficulties. A week previously, members had met to consider rule changes that they hoped would allow the Branch and its £20,000 in funds to join the UDM. The meeting listened to a letter from Vincent threatening legal action if the dissolution proceeded without the agreement of the Lancashire Executive. Less than one-third of the members attended the meeting and the proposed rule changes failed to achieve the required a two-thirds majority by just one vote. A fortnight later Parsonage abandoned the breakaway campaign.[60] Legal difficulties were advanced as one justification; another suggested was the Board's proposed reorganisation of the Complex under a single management. Even combined with the breakaway Leigh Craftsmen, a seceding Parsonage Branch would be decisively in a minority and would have no negotiating rights. This contention pointed to a weakness in the UDM's position when it attempted to expand at pit level. In the short term, secessionists would lose out – with only the uncertain prospect of majority status, and therefore recognition at some vague later date.

A week later the Parsonage climb-down was emulated by Agecroft. Only about 150 attended a meeting to hear that the rules prohibited a breakaway by the Branch and therefore secessionists could have no access to Branch funds. Some abstained in the crucial vote, but by seventy votes to forty-eight the meeting decided to end the attempt to take Agecroft out of the NUM. This settled the question of whether any Branches would leave the Lancashire Area;[61] it offered no barrier against disaffected individuals. As the NUM leadership acknowledged, they had the right to go. Since the Leigh Craftsmen had evaded the legal safeguards in the confusions of the previous summer, the resulting UDM membership offered a nucleus for the discontented elsewhere in the coalfield. A former member of the Leigh Craftsmen issued a general invitation: 'Our aim is to carry on and spread the word of the UDM in the Lancashire coalfield. We welcome miners – not only craftsmen – from other collieries with open arms.'[62] The target was 1,000 members; under the UDM's rules this would permit the formation of a regional grouping. But subsequent recruiting fell far short of this. At Agecroft about sixty joined the UDM and they were followed later by another one hundred. In other Branches, the ranks of the NUM were virtually undented. Across the whole coalfield, the breakaway never managed to achieve 400 members.

From this standpoint, the Lancashire campaign could count as a success story for the NUM. The coalfield was a potential weak spot in the NUM's defences against the breakaway; a large recruitment in Lancashire would have helped to make the UDM seem more than a Nottinghamshire affair, but this had emphatically failed to happen. This was significant for the credibility of the National Union, but in Lancashire there was a more mixed legacy.

Committed NUM members might be deeply hostile to the UDM and to its supporters, but especially in the Complex the latter had become a fact of life. Loyalists might not want to mix with men who had crossed picket lines and subsequently had left the Union, but in the pit, the managerial allocation of tasks could make limited co-operation inescapable. NUM Branch Officials found that their performance of routine tasks could involve working with breakaway members.

The method whereby the secession had been limited was revealing. Although activists had campaigned hard against the UDM, a decisive contribution had been made by the legal threats emanating from the Area leadership. Parsonage and Agecroft had been kept within the NUM, not so much by a persuasive campaign, but more by the use of the Rule Book. The leadership style characteristic of the NUM Right for so many years before the strike – the use of the machine and of procedure rather than of argument –

had surfaced once again. The weaknesses of this style of politics had been harshly exposed in March 1984, but despite a year's kaleidoscopic happenings, little in this respect seemed to have changed.

The containment of disaffected Branches still posed a fundamental problem for the NUM leadership. Collective decisions had to incorporate them as if the last two divisive years had never happened. This imperative had been acknowledged by the Bold Delegate at a time when a sizeable breakaway still seemed possible: 'They know at Agecroft, that if it fails, this UDM in Lancashire, this Conference will accept them back . . . They will still be able to come back here, because we need them as members . . .'[63]

Area Officials, well aware of this, could be concerned to court potentially secessionist groups and to pay less attention to the NUM loyalists in these Branches. The latter's support for the Union could be taken for granted, they held no official Union positions; the officials who had led the strikebreakers still retained control of their Branches and once more participated in Area decision-making. They had to be reintegrated into the routines of the Area. This need, underpinned by concern about unity, has proved a perennial problem for the Lancashire NUM. The need to re-establish unity has meant that such reconstruction has been significantly on the would-be-secessionists' own terms.

This necessity has helped to maintain a pattern of Area politics demonstrating significant continuities across the apparent Rubicon of the strike. Memories of the year remain sharp, but often a collective self-censorship operates. One Branch Official acknowledged that the strike is rarely mentioned at Branch meetings so as to avoid opening old wounds. The activists who emerged during the strike, often literally out of the ground, have had little effect on the Area's politics. They have found it difficult to gain any substantial foothold within the key institutions. Instead, Lancashire meetings remain dominated by men who took leading roles before the strike. Some stood on picket lines, others crossed them, but beneath this division there were years of broad agreement on political and industrial issues. Such shared values may provide some cement to maintain a coherent NUM; their relevance at a time of managerial aggression is more questionable.

The harshest and most conclusive evidence of defeat came with the accumulating arithmetic of closures and of employment cut backs even where coal production was to continue – all underpinned by a managerial regime demonstrating MacGregor's insistence that the right to manage must be asserted. In Lancashire as in most other coalfields, the future seemed to wither; here was reason enough for a solid union. The day-to- day realities could convince most miners of that, but beyond awareness of this need there loomed other questions. Did the Lancashire Union after a twelve month struggle have the capacity to respond effectively to closures? This was in part a matter of the membership's resilience. But it was also a question of the Area's political style. As normality began to reassert itself, how well equipped was the Lancashire NUM to understand and deal with the Coal Board's new regime?

The first challenge in Lancashire was, as one Area Official recalled, 'a bolt from the blue'.[64] It came not from the Coal Board's Western Area, but from the Workshops Section. For some time, the Area leadership had been concerned about the future of Walkden, but in mid-June 1985 the closure was announced, not of Walkden, but of Kirkless. 300 jobs would be axed, a cut back justified by the Board in the context of the industry's long-term developments. For more than a decade, the number of central workshops had been stable, but their workload had diminished. The number of operating coalfaces had declined and the introduction of new machinery had extended the period between overhauls.

The threatened workers' response was fatalistic. Kirkless had been much more supportive of the strike than had Walkden, but Bernard McGurrin, the Branch Secretary, evinced an awareness of the Union's weakness: 'There seems very little that we can do about it at the moment. We have just spent 11 months on strike trying to stop things like this happening. Workshops are closing down all over.'[65] When the Area Conference met soon afterwards, the Kirkless Delegate highlighted the Board's style: 'A meeting was held in . . . Stoke on the Regional Workshops and Stores . . . it was announced . . . that there would be no further negotiations, but that the Workshop was closing.' Such a predicament might engender a wish for an effective response, but the hope was not bolstered by any reality. 'We wanted our members to take a lead so that the delegation could come to conference and say we want to fight . . . but the backing wasn't forthcoming.'[66] All that the Delegate could suggest was vociferous argument about the industry's plight through the Labour Party and the TUC. Unlike pits, there was no

Review Procedure for Workshops. Lancashire jobs were vanishing as part of a national cut-back and Lancashire NUM members shared the powerlessness of their counterparts elsewhere.

The depressing contrast with the packed Conferences and emotional charge of the year of the strike was emphasised by the Bold Delegate: 'Fourteen weeks ago this conference hall was full of strikers. This morning we are here and we can't raise a gallop, yet we have a workshop that is closing.'[67] Late in October Kirkless closed. Its workforce accepted redundancy or a transfer to Walkden or to Trentham in North Staffordshire. But this contraction was overshadowed by a new threat: Bold, the centre of the Lancashire strike, faced closure.

This pit had had a poor economic record in some of the years preceding the strike. There were plenty of reserves, but the NCB expressed concern about persistent but unpredictable geological difficulties. But as the Return to Work campaign resumed early in 1985, the Board attempted to reduce the ranks of the Bold strikers by painting a rosy picture of the pit's future: 'Speaking hypothetically if the NCB had looked at pits solely from the profitability point of view, Bold Colliery, for example, might have been a candidate for closure. But because the Board could see a future for the colliery it intended to make it a sound and firm proposition.'[68] But as soon as the Bold miners had marched back through the gates, events began to belie this propagandist optimism; already, in mid-March, the Board announced the transfer of 180 men, cutting the workforce from 1,000 to 820. In the language of management wedded to ideals of rationalisation and vigorous competition, it was 'a slimming down'. The cut-back was blamed on the NUM Branch Officials, since they had been uncooperative during the dispute when the pit had faced problems. The NCB spokesman commented sardonically on the Branch Secretary's claim that the pit would shut: 'We can only assume the union officials are relieved that the consequences of their action are not more severe.'[69] The Bold officials argued non-co-operation with the proposed transfers. The Board's strategy was to move men to Parkside, thus allowing the redundancy of older men there. But if Bold NUM acquiesced in this, they would lose credibility with their own older men who were keen on redundancy, but if they obstructed transfers, some members might claim that they were jeopardising the pit. It was a foretaste of the pressures to which Bold

Branch would be subject as the Board sought to exploit potential splits within the membership.

When Area officials met Western Area Management that June they remained dubious about the Board's attitude on Bold. The NCB claimed that development schemes at Sutton Manor and at some Staffordshire pits should increase production levels. If so, where would the compensating cut backs fall? The circumstantial evidence suggested more job losses. Vincent was subsequently dismissive about the Board's projections for Bold: 'They put a plan for Bold which was an abortion and the Branch have been telling [me] for weeks what the Board are doing is trying to destroy the colliery.'[70] The screw was tightening. Relationships between the NUM Branch and the Bold management were poor. Prospects seemed tentative: 'The Colliery Manager circulated a bulletin at the pit that if the colliery doesn't make a profit by a certain date, then the pit will be run on a month to month basis.' The 'slimming down' threatened to become anorexic: '300 jobs have been lost at Bold . . . there is going to be some transfers and some redundancies for the infirm and injured.'[71] Now the hope was that a cut-back to two faces and yet another job loss of one hundred would push the pit towards profitability.

Speculation was replaced by authoritative pessimism at the September Review meeting. The Area Director announced that Bold had 'no future prospects'. Subsequently, on 9 October the Board announced the pit's forthcoming closure. The official justification suggested that the pit was a hopeless case. Production costs stood at £77 a tonne; the NCB claimed monthly losses of £1 million.[72] January and October were worlds, apart so far as the Board's view of Bold was concerned.

The announcement was just one more in a melancholy sequence that had confronted the NUM since the strike ended. Already several closures had gone ahead; in other coalfields miners had accepted redundancy or acknowledged what seemed the impossibility of another struggle. Impotence bred tensions. In June these had exploded inside the NEC in a way that cut through the conventional left/right divide. Vincent reported the scene back to Bolton:

> There was a terrible uproar . . . regarding pit closures and workshop closures . . . Arthur Scargill said there was only one way to oppose these closures and this was industrial action . . . the majority of the National

Executive Committee put forward their views, mainly saying, 'how do you expect the membership to come out on industrial action when they are in financial difficulty from the last twelve months?'[73]

The initial response from Bold NUM seemed to stand out against the prevailing pessimism.[74] Four days after the closure announcement, the Branch voted by a majority of two to one at a meeting of at least 200 to oppose the closure. But as the Branch Secretary, Mal Gregory, acknowledged, any campaign would not involve industrial action. Yet Bold activists began to think through a possible strategy. They could link with other pits where closure threats were opposed. Something of the style of the Bold strike seemed to remain. But any effective response needed a firm and united commitment from the workforce. In the new pessimistic world, problems were soon evident.

One had been foreshadowed at another Western Area pit, Wolstanton in Stoke-on-Trent. The pit Branch and the NUM Midlands Area had decided to fight closure through the Review Procedure but very quickly sections of the Wolstanton workforce demanded a ballot. When this was accepted, 85 per cent voted to accept the closure.

Predictably, the Bold Branch decision to contest the closure precipitated demands for a ballot. These were strengthened by the Lancashire NUM's maintenance of separate Craftsmen's Branches. The St Helens Craftsmen members employed at Bold balloted on the closure questions and decided to accept the shutdown by eighty-five votes to seventeen. Inevitably, this encouraged claims that the Bold Branch vote was unrepresentative of the membership. Such arguments soon achieved concrete from. A petition demanding a Branch ballot secured 293 signatures. Some who had signed had been expelled from the Branch after the strike. Officials insisted that the commitment to fight would stand until the petition contained a majority of proper Branch members. Moreover, they argued that the Branch Rule Book did not require any ballot to fight a closure threat. Pressure came, not just from members, but also from the Board. The earlier agreement to reduce the workforce had resulted in the negotiation of redundancy terms for ninety-eight men. When the Branch opposed the closure, the Board blocked further progress on the issue.

At that moment, Bold offered dramatic testimony to the problems facing the NUM. The Union office still wore the insignia of recent battles. The piles of *Socialist Organiser* and *Newsline* showed the political attachments of individual activists; stickers spoke the emotion that had sustained the Bold strike, 'NUM Fight the Bastards'; the office wall carried a picture of Ian MacGregor implausibly signed, 'Best Wishes to Mal and all the boys at Bold'. Activists crowded into the small office hoping to develop a campaign that could exorcise pessimism and save the pit. But there were other voices in the room, men who came in acknowledging that they had signed the ballot. A harassed Branch Secretary stonewalled; he had to carry out the Branch decision.

But the campaign for a ballot was extending beyond signatures and angry voices. One day 110 men refused to go down the pit unless a ballot was granted. The crowd in the canteen was bleak evidence of the Union's fragmentation. Below ground there were more difficulties. Some facemen began working to rule as a means of forcing a ballot; they seemed to do so with managerial support. The Branch Secretary drew attention to one incident

> The men who came off the face . . . only went back down the pit at 3.30 p.m., but the Manager never telephoned him to let him know of this. If these men had stayed up the pit because of bonus problems, the Manager would have said, 'When are you getting these men back down the pit?' But this didn't happen because the National Coal Board are playing along with it.[75]

The pro-ballot section eventually organised their own poll. Branch officials urged abstention; 251 voted to accept closure, twenty-nine opposed and roughly 250 didn't vote. Following this the go-slow intensified and production fell to barely 3,000 tonnes a week, less than half of the break-even level and under a third of what was technically feasible. When Branch officials saw management about the go-slow, they received a bland response. The work to rule was nothing to do with the Board; those concerned were in dispute with their Union. Even the post-strike regime could be liberal in appropriate circumstances, but such tolerance was not extended to traditional union men. When the Branch suggested that men committed to the pit's future be deployed on a key face, the management hinted at legal action under the Mines and Quarries Act. Tolerance had its limits; after all, there was something called the right to manage.

Rumours multiplied about the scale of redundancy payments. Any future at Bold could seem unattractive to men deep in debt and earning no bonus because of the pit's low production: 'No wonder the men are disheartened . . . some men . . . have been in the colliery office and said, "We want the colliery to keep open but we can't go on any longer. We need a ballot and get to a pit where we can earn some bonus." '[76] As the pressure intensified, it became clear that NACODS would no longer oppose the closure. The Bold Committee decided with a few dissenters to hold a ballot. This took place on 14 November, five weeks after the Board had announced its intention to close. Activists maintained brave faces to the last, but the verdict was decisive – 277 for closure, 148 against. Even the eighty or so abstentions could not hide the extent of acquiescence in what seemed inevitable. The very next day, coal production finished at Bold.

Branch activists viewed the closure as the Board's revenge: 'We are convinced that it is a political closure, the reason being that we have all been naughty boys for the last twelve months.'[77] Other Lancashire pits had lost money, most notably neighbouring Sutton Manor, where deficits had been shouldered for several years in the belief that performance might improve. The Board's sloganising about Bold's post-strike losses ignored the complexities of colliery economics in order to secure easy publicity. Some of the pit's recent losses could be ascribed to the need for the development of new faces. By the autumn of 1985 these were ready, but were never given the chance to demonstrate their capability. It was alleged that Bold had been used as a testing ground for equipment prior to its possible employment elsewhere. Union anxiety about the financial implications of such experimentation had been brushed aside, but the doubts now seemed justified:

> The Manager . . . assured us, 'Don't worry about it, we know what is happening and what it is costing, but it will be wrote off.' They are now using these figures against us and when we ask them about it, they renege on previous promises and commitments. The National Coal Board have deliberately made Bold Colliery a loss pit with the installing of this machinery over the years.'[78]

But in November 1985, the arguments stopped. The one Branch to have backed strike action in the March 1984 ballot, the vibrant centre of so much strike activity, 'Bold NUM', not just a geographical statement on posters and badges, but a declaration of optimism and daring – all this was ended. The Branch had been killed by corrosive pessimism and the glitter of redundancy payments. Several activists took redundancy; others were deployed around Lancashire's remaining pits. One leading figure in Bold NUM remained sacked, despite an industrial tribunal's judgement that he should be reinstated.

A possible focus for militancy within the coalfield had been shattered with perhaps significant implications for the politics of the Lancashire NUM. Before the strike, there had been little effective opposition to the dominant ethos within the Area. During the dispute a familiar world was transformed as rank-and-file members took so many initiatives. Longstanding officials could feel disorientated; others could take hope that old routines might have gone for good. Certainly the grim post-strike situation dispelled any easy left optimism. Some who had seemed to have been radicalised by the strike now took little part in Union affairs; others whose commitment still burned discovered the Union's weaknesses. But Bold still provided a much needed focus with activists' meetings organised at the Bold Club, and the Branch's support for the rank and file paper the *Lancashire Miner*. Closure meant the loss of a rallying point, the end of a Branch where activists' views enjoyed a legitimacy or acceptance within the Union hierarchy. Activists in other pits were often few, their influence in the Branch could be slim; with the end of Bold the rank-and-file movement became more fragmented.

There have been no more pit closures,* but there have been further cuts in employment. Early in 1986 the Board announced a reduction of 300 jobs over fifteen months at Parkside. The NUM Branch accepted the rundown in the hope that other jobs could be protected and in the belief that resistance was impossible.[79] Despite its new investment programme. Sutton Manor's results remained poor. Relations in the pit were often harsh, and after persistent rumours a reduction of 250 jobs was announced; the threat of closure hovered as it has done for so long.

These declines were overshadowed by the closure of Walkden, Lancashire's last workshop in November 1986. This was not presented as a negotiable question, but as an objective the management were determined to achieve. In 1985, the Board had closed Kirkless where the strike had enjoyed significant support; a year later it was the turn of Walkden, where most had worked

---

*This ceased to be true in 1989 when the Golborne section of the complex closed

through the dispute and others had barely settled in after the move from Kirkless. Now management could only offer alternative jobs in North Staffordshire, but the Union acknowledged immediately that any effective anti-closure campaign was impossible. They were reduced to the hope that a local Labour MP, on a visit to Downing Street, could persuade the Prime Minister to encourage a rethink by the Board. Few gestures could be more revealing of the NUM's weakness – except perhaps the accompanying emphasis that these were men who had mostly ignored the strike call![80]

Notes

1   Ian MacGregor, *The Enemies Within* (Collins, London, 1986), p. 358. The insurrection comment is in *Sunday Telegraph*, 10 March 1985.
2   Roy Walls cited in *Leigh, Tyldesley and Atherton Journal*, 14 March 1985; see also NWA Executive, 14 March and Conference, 16 March 1985.
3   NWA Conference, 16 March 1985 (Mal Gregory referring to Colin Lenton).
4   NUM NEC, 28 March 1985.
5   NUM Special Delegate Conference, 2 April 1985 p. 133.
6   *Ibid.* pp. 133–4.
7   NUM Special Delegate Conference, 22 April 1985.
8   NWA Conference, 2 March 1985.
9   *Ibid.*
10   *Ibid.*
11   NWA Conference, 16 March 1985.
12   NWA Executive, 29 March 1985.
13   NWA Conference, 20 April 1985.
14   *Ibid.* Agenda.
15   *Ibid.*
16   *Ibid.* i.e. Four Craftsmen's Branches – Clifton and Pendlebury, Leigh, St Helens and Walkden – plus Parsonage and Pendlebury.
17   NWA Conference, 18 May 1985.
18   He chaired his last Executive meeting on 27 August 1985.
19   Bernard Donaghy interview.
20   NWA Conference, 20 April 1985 (Sutton Manor Delegate).
21   *Ibid.*
22   *Ibid.* (Bernard McGurrin).
23   NWA Conference, 15 June 1985 (Kirkless Delegate).
24   *Ibid.*
25   *Ibid.*
26   *Ibid.*
27   NUM Special Delegate Conferences, 11 July and 10 August 1984.
28   NWA Executive, 17 January 1985.
29   Text of this and other proposals in NUM Report of Special Rules Revision Conference, 4/5 July 1985.

30   NWA Executive, 23 May 1985 and Conference, 15 June 1985. The latter itemises the decisions made. The decisions were made after the predominantly non-striking Branches had walked out of the Conference.
31   Discussion with Parkside NUM. Vincent's seconding is at pp. 662–3 of the Special Rules Revision Conference Report.
32   NWA Conference, 20 April 1985.
33   MEN, 16 July 1985.
34   *Ibid.* 30 July 1985.
35   *Leigh, Tyldesley and Atherton Journal*, 1, 8 and 22 August 1985. Discussions with Plank Lane NUM.
36   NWA Meeting, 17 August 1985 (S. Vincent).
37   *Ibid.*
38   See Adeny and Lloyd, *The Miners' Strike*, pp. 271–2.
39   NWA Meeting, 17 August 1985 (Geoff Clarke, Ashton and Haydock Craftsmen).
40   *Ibid.*
41   *Ibid.* (J. Edwards).
42   *Ibid.*
43   *Ibid.*
44   *Ibid.*
45   *Ibid.* (D. O'Brien).
46   NWA Conference, 19 October 1985.
47   *MEN*, 21 October 1985.
48   Jim Lord interview.
49   Discussions with Agecroft strikers; Jim Lord interview.
50   Discussions with Agecroft Strikers.
51   NWA Conference, 16 November 1985.
52   Discussions with Agecroft strikers; *MEN*, 11 November 1985.
53   *Leigh, Tyldesley and Atherton Journal*, 21 November 1985.
54   Sentiments articulated at the NWA Conference, 16 November 1985.
55   *MEN*, 12 November 1985.
56   NWA Executive, 5 November 1985.
57   *Leigh, Tyldesley and Atherton Journal*, 5 December 1985.
58   Discussions with Agecroft strikers; NWA Conference, 18 January 1986.
59   *Bolton Evening News* 3/4 February 1986; discussions with Agecroft strikers.
60   *MEN*, 10 February 1986.
61   NWA Conference, 15 February 1986; *MEN*, 17 February 1986.
62   *MEN* 22 February 1986.
63   NWA Conference, 14 December 1985.
64   Bernard Donaghy interview.
65   *Wigan Observer*, 14 June 1985.
66   NWA Conference, 15 June 1985.
67   *Ibid.*
68   *Newton and Golborne News*, 25 January 1985.
69   *Ibid.* 15 March 1985.

70 NWA Conference, 15 June 1985 (Vincent).
71 *Ibid.* Bold Delegate.
72 *Newton and Golborne News*, 27 September and 11 October 1985.
73 NWA Conference, 15 June 1985.
74 The section draws heavily on discussions with members of Bold NUM then and subsequently.
75 NWA Conference, 19 October 1985.
76 NWA Conference, 16 November 1985.
77 NWA Conference, 19 October 1985.
78 *Ibid.* (Mal Gregory); discussions with Bold NUM.
79 *MEN*, 8 February 1986.
80 *Ibid.* 23 September 1986. The NUM Area records contain little reaction to the Walkden closure.

11

Legacies

Union routines were re-established in the Lancashire Area, as they were across much of the British coalfield. At least where the NUM remained the sole or the dominant union, the continuities across the year of the strike seemed significant. Superficially, the cycle of meetings suggested a return to that predictability that some officials had missed during the dispute. But beneath the reassuring routines, much had changed.

The apparently familiar world embraced far fewer people. In part this stemmed from closures – Kirkless, Bold, Walkden – but it also reflected reductions in employment at the surviving pits. At the beginning of 1988 these employed only 3,545 people.[1] If members of other unions were deducted, then probably less then 3,000 remained in the Lancashire NUM. This depletion was a microcosm of what had happened to the National Union. But in Lancashire, as elsewhere, the NUM's weakness was not simply a matter of a depleted membership. More fundamentally, the Union could not respond effectively to management demands.

These were at their most intense at Sutton Manor. New investment had not promoted the elusive profitability. In the 1985/86 financial year British Coal claimed losses of over £5,600,000; the next year these had risen to over £8,100,000.[2] As the 1987/88 year progressed, the quarterly deficits suggested even higher losses. The Manor's Standing Delegate presented a sombre picture: 'Men were being blackmailed daily. Men were already divided face by face, shift by shift and individuals were also being approached. We were asked to form a united front, but we had our arm up our back, we were always being asked to compromise our principles and eat humble pie.'[3]

The Union's weakness led some to place their hopes on a change of government. Once, NUM activists had seen industrial action as the most effective response to Thatcherism; now they were reduced to the hope that a Labour administration might rescue a beleaguered Union. But on the morning of 12 June 1987 this slender hope, held in the face of psephological wisdom, was dead. One young Agecroft miner had ended the strike reluctantly. Since his return he had coped with managerial pressures but had never felt at home in a pit where so many had ignored the strike call. Now there seemed no alternative to further aggravation and perhaps dismissal. Margaret Thatcher returned to Downing Street and he took redundancy.

The implications of a third term of Thatcherism cut deep for Lancashire's miners. That 1987 summer, trains loaded with coal ran from the Bickershaw Complex and Parkside to power stations. As they trundled through the flat countryside of south Lancashire, they seemed solid and durable – but the Government was preparing legislation to privatise the electricity supply industry. Ministers left no doubt that any future owners would be free to buy coal in the cheapest markets. Much could come from overseas. A British contribution could be provided by capital-intensive mines in the Midlands and North Yorkshire. Coalmining in Lancashire could be threatened with extinction.

Inevitably management, faced with the prospect of cheap international competition and with a Government requirement that the industry move quickly to a break-even position, resorted to cost-cutting. Lancashire, along with all coalfields, has experienced drives to reduce jobs and to otherwise lower production charges. As yet the coalfield has not experienced direct demands for either six-day-working or extended shifts. When the National Union debated these issues at its 1987 Conference, Lancashire voted as part of the majority opposed to such changes. The decision at Area level had been unambiguous.[4] But opposition by rhetoric was one thing; the development of a coherent and effective strategy on the issue was something else. The pragmatic traditions of Lancashire officials hinted that, should such proposals come to the coalfield, then some accommodation might be found.

The significance of the strike and its aftermath for the politics of the Lancashire Area is not susceptible to simplistic generalisations. The two full-time Agents, Bernard Donaghy and Stanley Horsfield, retained their posts. Here was an element of continuity with

Lancashire's pragmatic past, albeit in a radically transformed environment. Donaghy had been replaced as Lancashire President by Frank King of Parkside, one of those Branch Officials who had given firm backing to the strike in that decisive period following the ending of any prospect for a national ballot. The new President saw himself as a conciliator who was aware of the need to include all tendencies if the NUM was to re-emerge as an effective force. His outlook and strike record was shared by the new Vice-President, Roy Walls of Plank Lane.

Historically the most powerful figure in Lancashire has been the General Secretary. In the Spring of 1986 Vincent retired. The ballot for a successor highlighted some significant aspects of the post-strike Union. The poll was only 55 per cent, suggesting that many members were alienated from their union. Some might have preferred the breakaway organisation but had been blocked by legal obstacles; others wanted to quit the industry as quickly as possible. The list of candidates showed how the strike had blighted or furthered men's prospects of office. Predictably, no opponent of the strike stood and neither did Donaghy who was regarded widely as a competent official. In a close contest, the verdict went to Roy Jackson, the long-serving Sutton Manor Branch Secretary, who had been involved in the strike from a very early date.[5] Prior to the dispute few would have selected him as Vincent's successor. The arrival at Bolton of the genial and somewhat self-effacing Jackson offered a stylistic contrast with the colourful personalised Secretaryships of Gormley and Vincent.

The new Lancashire leadership had to establish an identity within a National Union where old alliances were fragmenting and new alignments unclear. The NUM Left was in disarray. Once it had been able to unite in opposition to Gormley and behind Scargill's campaign for the Presidency. Now the National President's style and his industrial and political judgements provoked controversy. In particular, South Wales and, to a lesser degree, Scottish officials shifted to an overtly critical position, whilst still claiming to stand on the left. Scargill could still count on considerable support within Yorkshire, although this Area too contained its allies with reservations and some thorough critics. But the NUM's traditional Right was weaker than ever. The departure of many Nottinghamshire members had taken away one of its principal props, while the Durham Area, so long identified with the Right, had produced a left leadership. Leicestershire, COSA and the Power Group still articulated the priorities of the Right, but within the Union structures they controlled few votes.

As the Lancashire leadership attempted to come to terms with this new political landscape, they also had to operate within a changed Area politics. Men who had once been allies had found themselves in opposition during the strike. Although many officials sought to mend fences, memories of that year were inescapable. Lancashire decision-makers had to be aware that some members could switch to the UDM, should NUM policy provoke old passions; but equally, Branch and Area officials had to acknowledge the continuing activities of some rank-and-file members who had played such a leading role in the strike. As yet these activities had few footholds in the Area's institutions, but they could be a potent force at Branch meetings. Decisions at pit level could lay down the parameters within which area policy must be made. The shifting politics of Lancashire, internally and in its relationship with the National Union, were demonstrated in two nomination decisions.

Michael McGahey retired from the National Vice-Presidency during 1987. Once pilloried as an implacable revolutionary, he had been characterised post-strike as a sagacious elder statesman offering coded encouragement to South Wales and Scottish criticism of Scargill. The contrast between these two National Officials was apparent in their contributions to the 1987 Lancashire Annual Conference. Both referred to the six-day-working controversy. Scargill articulated thorough opposition on principle; but McGahey's appraisal was not too distant from the traditional style of Lancashire: 'If the North Western Area got an offer of a £90 million development with 800 jobs plus another 800 surface jobs and the Coal Board stated they would like to discuss concepts of shift patterns, would you reject it? Would the Lancashire mining communities not say to you, "Surely you would discuss it?" '[6]

Already the identity of McGahey's successor had been decided and in the nomination process, Lancashire had moved in a new direction. The contest for the National Vice-President was the occasion for the division within the NUM Left to become thoroughly public. Scargill's favoured candidate was Sammy Thompson, a Yorkshire member of the NEC. In opposition, Scotland and South Wales nominated Eric Clarke, the Scottish General Secretary and the Union's representative on the Labour

Party National Executive. Both candidates publicised their positions on a centre-page in the *Morning Star*. The text suggested few disagreements; but the fundamental distinction needed no detailed demonstration. One was Arthur's candidate; the other was not.

When a Lancashire Conference nominated Clarke by a decisive margin – nine branches to three – delegates broke with a mountain of tradition. No Branch backed a third candidate, a representative of the Right.[7] Instead Lancashire went for a Scot who had been close to the Communist section within the Union. It seemed light years from the 1971 battle between Gormley and McGahey. The significance of the decision was complex. Any anti-Thompson nomination could capitalise on anti-Scargill and anti-Yorkshire sentiments. The latter involved, for some, memories of flying pickets and concern about the strength and the politics of the NUM's biggest Area. Moreover, amongst the officials there was a wish to back a credible opponent rather than a no-hoper. For at least one official there was a concern that, faced with Board pressures and confusing Union politics, Lancashire needed allies. Perhaps a new alliance of the peripheral coalfields might be credible. The Area Conference decision was confirmed by the Lancashire membership in a relatively low poll. They backed Clarke over Thompson by a majority of rather less than two to one – 980 to 512, with 374 votes going to two other candidates. It was a contrast to the Scot's overall defeat.

Thompson's victory demonstrated the significant numerical dominance of Yorkshire in any decision where the Area's members were disposed to back one side to a disproportionate degree. Yet across the coalfields Thompson had secured support from miners who identified closely with the Scargill leadership. In Lancashire some rank-and-file members worked hard to achieve a credible vote for the Yorkshireman. The 512 that he secured came as a pleasant surprise.

This tendency in the Union's politics arguably mattered when the second contest unexpectedly materialised. By the autumn of 1987 Scargill faced increasing difficulties within the National Executive. A limited overtime ban over the industry's disciplinary code was having minimal impact, but the Board, true to its *macho* style, refused to pay the second instalment of a pay deal until the ban was terminated. The NEC lacked any coherent strategy. South Walian criticism of the National President grew less coded and he responded in kind.[8]

In this sulphurous atmosphere Scargill informed the November
NEC meeting that he proposed to resign from the National
Presidency and would stand for re-election. The formal justification
was that pending legislation necessitated such a move, but politically
the resignation was a shrewd tactic. Opponents would have to back
an alternative candidate with the risk of defeat, or ignore the
challenge with a consequential decline in their credibility.

Any anti-Scargill candidate faced a tough prospect. He would
begin with a handicap. Several thousand miners who would have
opposed Scargill had joined the UDM. Beyond this, he would face
one of two problems. An alternative left candidate, most probably
from Scotland or South Wales, would face serious difficulties in
cutting into the Yorkshire vote; but alternatively, an anti-Scargill
candidates from within Yorkshire would be identified with the
Right and would lack appeal in traditionally left South Wales and
Scotland. In the event, the anti-Scargillites faced the second
problem. The only candidate to emerge was John Walsh, the North
Yorkshire Agent who had run Heathfield so close at the start of
1984.

In that earlier contest Lancashire had provided one of John
Walsh's few nominations. Even in the heady days of 1981 Lancashire
had not nominated Scargill. Late in 1987, Area Conferences still
resounded to familiar criticisms about the shortcomings of the
National President. The coalfield leadership had one further
ground for opposition to the National Officials, and particularly
Scargill. With the NUM's depleted finances and declining numbers,
the old Area structure, largely unchanged from the days of three-
quarters of a million members, could seem extravagant. In its
failure to parallel the employer's regional organisation, it could
seem inefficient. Pressures for mergers came from the centre and
were resisted by officials who felt their positions threatened and by
many more who evinced local patriotism. The proposals for
Lancashire envisaged the formation of a new Western Area
convering the Lancashire and Staffordshire pits. Nothing had been
decided, but the discussions provided one more basis for anti-
Scargill sentiments.[9]

Another Lancashire nomination for Walsh might have been
anticipated but this did not happen. When a Lancashire Conference
met in mid-December, one delegate suggested that no nomination
be made. This was the response of both South Wales and Scotland,

but in Lancashire the proposal secured no more support. All the other Branches had made their choice; a majority six to four favoured Walsh, but on a card vote the margin favoured Scargill by forty-nine to twenty-two. With one exception, the line of demarcation was that of 1984. Branches that had eventually backed the strike nominated Scargill; those that never did went for Walsh. The choice showed how far the striking Branches were controlled by men who had been committed to the strike. Support for Scargill was a reaffirmation of past experiences and loyalities.[10]

The membership's vote did not reinforce the Conference nomination. The Lancashire miners backed Walsh by a majority of 146. The margin would have been wider but for the losses to the UDM. Yet some pit branches gave majorities for Scargill and the Agecroft vote provided Walsh with a majority bigger than his overall margin.

Table 11.1   Lancashire vote in the National Presidential Election, January 1988

	Scargill	Walsh
Ashton and Haydock Craftsmen	34	94
Billinge	21	19
Clifton and Pendlebury Craftsmen	3	25
Golborne	180	156
Parkside	409	342
Parsonage	112	134
Pendlebury	82	233
Plank Lane	253	189
St Helens Craftsmen	32	58
Sutton Manor	121	142
Total	1,249	1,395

Note: E & B Winders returned no vote.

The Presidential contest solved none of the problems facing the NUM. At most it was reaffirmation of support by many miners for their National President, but his margin of victory 5,668 was significantly less than the membership of the UDM. Moreover his vote was almost 100,000 less than his poll in 1981 – a stark testimony to the industry's contraction and to the reduced power of the NUM. This weakness was demonstrated by more than the arithmetic of the Presidential ballot; the concurrent overtime ban was a harsh demonstration of managerial strength and the NUM's unavailing search for some effective response.

The 1987 Annual National Conference might have divided over flexible working, but delegates were unanimous in their opposition to the employer's application of its recently amended disciplinary code. South Wales, COSA and Yorkshire combined to urge a ballot on industrial action. The objective was to achieve the code's withdrawal, allowing the negotiation of new arrangements. The NUM attacked management for punishing miners on account of alleged offences committed away from the pit. This attack was aimed at union activists; its purpose was to shatter union effectiveness in the workplace.

On this platform the Union moved speedily to a ballot on 'various forms' of industrial action. Miners voted in late July and into August. The result was an expression of thorough resentment at managerial authoritarianism. 77.5 per cent of those voting backed the NEC. Every constituent Area had given a majority – even, by a small margin, the much-maligned COSA. The Lancashire decision was less decisive than the national one, – but at 1,842 to 651 or 73 per cent, in favour, it was still very emphatic.[11] A ballot vote as an expression of sentiment was significant, but how could this decision be cashed into an effective strategy?

The National Executive discussed the problem on 6 September. It was already an acrimonious meeting because of disagreements over Scargill's refusal to be involved in meetings with management alongside UDM members. Similarly, there was argument over the state of play on the disciplinary code. The Union's National officials claimed that British Coal had made no concession in recent discussion. Some NEC members queried this, objecting to the rapid rejection of the latest employer's position without any appraisal by the NEC. In contrast, there was pressure from Yorkshire for an early move to an overtime ban, but South Wales representatives argued for more talks. The result was a decision to seek further discussions; but should these prove abortive then an overtime ban would begin from 21 September – the last permitted date, given the timing of the legitimising ballot.[12]

Meetings followed between the National Executive and British Coal Chairman, Sir Robert Haslam, supplemented by discussions between both parties and ACAS officials. Ultimately, disagreements focused on the Union's demand that some form of binding arbitration along the lines of the old pit umpire system be restored to disciplinary procedures. British Coal objected, insisting that disciplinary appeals were best dealt with through Industrial Tribunals.

The specific disagreement was symptomatic of a fundamental clash over the management's repeated insistence in rhetoric and action on what it saw as the right to manage. Should an Industrial Tribunal rule that a miner should not be dismissed, British Coal still had the right to transfer him to another pit. Any binding decision by an arbitrator would remove this freedom. The employer's insistence on the right to manage was reinforced by the realisation that a weak union could offer little resistance to the exercise of that right. Awareness of a powerful position was evident in British Coal's preconditions for further talks with ACAS. It was stated that the Union must call off their proposed overtime ban and would have to acknowledge the employer's 'ultimate right to determine where a dismissed man was to be re-employed'.[13] Such insistence were reminiscent of the Board's hard line in the last weeks of the strike – an insistence that the Union abandon its fundamental position as a prelude to negotiations.

The NEC discussed this *impasse* amidst conflicting emotions. Some members felt it was time to take a stand, but others were concerned that in some coalfields the Union could not sustain an effective action. Any ban would encourage a UDM recruiting drive. The outcome was agreement on some kind of overtime ban, but debate as to its character. A Yorkshire proposal advocated a ban with minimum safety cover; South Wales offered a more modest alternative. The ban should cover only coal production on faces, and development work. Here was a gesture of opposition to managerial policies which also acknowledged the Union's weakness. Narrowly the NEC favoured this option.[14]

When Lancashire Conference members debated the NEC's decision, some delegates articulated their fears. Sutton Manor was once more the subject of pessimistic rumours and the Standing Delegate was open about his members' predicament: 'Overtime may be vital to Sutton Manor Colliery.' Beneath this local anxiety lay a more thorough pessimism: 'When we were previously in a so-called powerful position we had an overtime ban and strike for over twelve months. Could anyone explain how this limited overtime ban can produce a result when all-out effort failed?'[15]

Despite concerns about the effectiveness of the strategy, Lancashire NUM members followed the ban guidelines. Soon, rumours began to circulate that these were being honoured more in some coalfields than in others and thus miners loyal to their Union could put their jobs at risk. When the NEC met early in October, requests for a Special National Conference, seen in some quarters as a forum that would initiate tougher action, were rejected. Instead the *status quo* was reaffirmed.[16]

Lancashire officials soon encountered the Board's response to even this modest tactic. On 12 October a Colliery Review Meeting provided an occasion for the Area Director and his colleagues to attack the NUM for endangering jobs. Each British Coal Board Area must break even. 'That was not just a target – it was the Area Director's remit. Consequently any unit which was unable to contribute towards that end would be shut. Such was the business reality.' The Area Director claimed that the ban was having a uniquely damaging impact in the Western Area. In the first three weeks 70,000 tonnes had been lost at a cost of £3 million. Other NUM Areas such as Yorkshire were talking tough, but in the pit it was a different story.

These claims were followed by a review of individual pits with Union officials responding to some managerial allegations. A British Coal claim that the Bickershaw Complex was losing 5–6,000 tonnes weekly on account of the ban was queried by Roy Walls. Surely a loss of such dimension could not be explained by a policy of not cutting coal in overtime? The Area Director's response perhaps signposted the shape of future policy. The Area's structural problems with the sizable distances between pit bottoms and faces, necessitated overtime as a feature of viable production practices: 'The Area had in effect introduced flexible working before the rest of the country. Without overtime, the Area's pits were finished. There was no way the Area could survive on coal cut only within the shift.' The game was all about survival. As another managerial representative commented: 'The issue of the disciplinary code was now an irrelevance.' The managerial insistence was that the Western Area must look after its own interests. If production continued at its current level, then redundancies would soon be inescapable.[17]

Beyond this spectre of insecurity was one specific crisis – predictably, Sutton Manor. The Board claimed almost £20 million losses since the end of the strike. Now there had to be instant and consistent meeting of production targets or the pit would close. Despite rumours that closure would happen anyway, output rose. In October 1987 it was 17,000 tonnes, in December, 50,000. At the start of the New Year Sutton Manor achieved its highest ever weekly tonnage. Records were not confined to one pit. Parkside had set a best-ever monthly tonnage in November.[18] The rising production levels in Lancashire had their parallels in many other pits.

The substantive irrelevance of the ban was reflected in the *impasse* at national level. In November, the NEC could not find a majority for any proposal on the policy's future – *status quo* abandonment or a one-day Conference. A month later the vote was decisively for a Special Conference.[19] Any expectation that this could be a springboard for more radical action was unfulfilled. Delegates met as NACODS were beginning their own overtime ban laced with one-day stoppages. The day before the NUM delegates met, the Deputies had closed almost all Britain's pits. Despite this abrasive context and despite Scargill's recent re-election, the Conference on 22 February 1988 did not endorse the National President's preferred option of a tougher ban. Instead, by a narrow margin of fifty-six to fifty-three, they decided that members be balloted on the future of the existing action. The Union's strategic problems seemed as intractable as ever.[20] The result of the ballot – 58 per cent for abandoning the overtime ban – was clear testimony to the policy's failure. In Lancashire the vote for ending the ban was even more decisive 64 per cent.

The Lancastrian vantage point inevitably affords a distinctive angle on the politics of the NUM. Yet hopefully this can be employed to shed some illumination. The National Union, in fact rather than aspiration, has never been the solidaristic strong organisation feared by opponents and fêted by members and would-be allies. Much of the style of the old Federation continued following the formation of the National Union. Areas jealously guarded their autonomy and maintained clear and usually stable political identities. Whilst such diversities acquired a momentum of their own, they also indicated the varied experiences and expectations of miners in different coalfields. The distinctive self-image of each NUM Area was fundamental to the conduct of its internal affairs and to the character of its interventions in the National Union. For over two decades the NUM was governed by a right-wing majority within a well-institutionalised system of factionalism. Such a leadership could operate easily on the principle that the most cautious Areas should set limits on pace and direction.

The misleading image of solidarity has been complemented often by one of industrial strength. But much of the miners' history belies this. 1921 and 1926 were disastrous attempts at effective national action; the sixties saw little resistance to mass closures and depressed wages. Many miners believed that the declining market for coal made collective action futile. The five years from 1969 seemed to present a more optimistic scenario: the unofficial stoppages of 1969 and 1970, the humiliation of the Heath Government in 1972, that Government's loss of office two years later. It was easy to believe that the NUM was the effective spearhead of a trade union movement radicalised by the economic failure of the Wilson Government and by the trade union legislation of its Tory successor. This vision is naive. In January 1972 the NUM took on a Government ill prepared for such a conflict and perhaps unappreciative of the effect that such a stoppage would have on the electricity supply industry. Two years later the Government seemed better equipped, but gambled on an election to legitimise more thorough resistance to the NUM. The Union adopted a much lower profile without the mass picketing that had characterised the 1972 dispute. A myth emerged, embraced by some on both the left and the right, that the NUM had toppled a Tory Government. In fact, Heath was a victim of the vagaries of the British electoral system. More votes than Labour still meant fewer seats in a context where the Liberal vote showed a dramatic rise. The incoming minority Labour Government rapidly settled the strike, and the myth of NUM power seemed plausible. But suppose Heath had won the election. What could the NUM have achieved against a Government whose resolve had been strengthened by the electoral verdict? The awkward question was not asked.

The years after 1974 showed little evidence of the Miners' supposed industrial strength. The rise in oil prices might have helped bring coal out of the doldrums; containment of wage increases might have been a continuing priority for the Wilson and Callaghan Governments, but the Union did not exploit its strengthened market situation. Instead, under Gormley's sometimes Machiavellian leadership, majorities were constructed – perhaps at a National Conference, perhaps in the National Executive, perhaps in a membership ballot – for policies compatible with Government objectives. Traditional factional loyalties were mobilised; arguments might not always be won, but in one form or anther, a majority could be achieved. In all of this containment, Lancashire played a significant role.

Gormley's successes were won in the face of an NUM Left whose base had been broadened with the political shift in Yorkshire and whose confidence had grown in the wake of two successful national strikes. Yet after 1974, the Left saw the gelding of the earlier militancy. The climax of this was the introduction of Area Incentive Schemes and the destruction of the National Power Loading Agreement. Gormley's opponents might cry 'Foul', but these reverses signposted weaknesses in their own position. The NUM's politics in the mid-1970s demonstrate the inadequacy of any expectation that wage-based militancy will lead readily to a more general radicalisation. Indeed, after 1977 it seemed much less likely that the wages issue could generate any sort of effective national action.

Alternative bases for any left mobilisation were elusive. Several of the emerging Left within the National Union had been appalled by the Old Guard's quiescence in the face of the sixties mass closures. But even in the relatively calm waters of the seventies it proved impossible to develop an effective strategy for opposing specific closures. The issue might unify at the level of rhetoric, but when it came to resisting this closure now, the unity disappeared. The divisions of 1984 were not the consequence of incompetent and dogmatic leadership; they were characteristic of the NUM's longstanding inability to respond effectively on the closure question.

Contrary to some prevalent images, the Miners were ill-prepared to cope with the Age of Thatcher – the legislative restrictions on trades unions, the austere attitude towards the public sector, the sharp downturn in industrial activity that contracted the markets for coal. The Government's retreat of February 1981 was misleading, a tactical withdrawal that sustained the myth of NUM power at a time when successive closures were demonstrating the hollowness of that myth.

NUM members – and particularly officials – experienced the collapse of a familiar world. This applied as much to left-wing Scotland as it did to right-wing Lancashire. Traditional relationships with management began to be transformed as Area Directors worked through the implications of Government policies. Yet for Areas committed historically to the Right, the trauma was intensified. The Left had taken control of the National Union. Scargill's election to the Presidency and the emergence of a left majority on the NEC deepened the disarray amongst Right officials. They were unsure whether to acquiesce or to oppose. At least in the security of their own Areas, they could attack the new regime and gain a sympathetic hearing from colleagues who remained committed to their old factional loyalties.

The Union was under attack from without and divided within. The rifts were between left and right, but also to some degree between officials and activist on the one hand, and a significant section of the membership on the other. Many miners seemed apathetic, fearful or cynical about action against closures. Right-wing officials at least spoke the language of resistance to closures; their critics would say that their rhetoric was never followed by action to create a more self-confident membership. But through all the stereotypes of NUM power, one hard fact is clear. There was nothing in the Union's history to suggest it could launch a united, lengthy and effective response to a closure programme.

The negative assessment is not the result of hindsight. Several NUM officials articulated the problems during 1983, most prominently at the Union's Annual Conference. From that autumn, it is possible to infuse the evidence with some sense of the battle that was to come. Yet in no sense does there seem any expectation of an aggressive bid to topple or discredit the Government; rather, any struggle was envisaged as clearly defensive. The avoidability of a clash in the spring of 1984 can be debated. In retrospect, it may be argued that a sagacious leadership would have deflected the Cortonwood challenge and husbanded the Union's resources. But for what purpose? An Area Director had declared his preference for the salami principle when implementing closures – and in the end the salami gets eaten.

Any explanation of the confusions and divisions of the strike's early weeks should not be content with allegations of abrasive picketing and dogmatic manipulation leadership. The splits in the National Union can be understood only through the diverse industrial and political traditions of the Areas with their attendant factional loyalties. These proved the spectacles through which many NUM members assessed the choices that they had to make.

Similarly, the lack of a national strike ballot should be seen in the context of the issue's divisiveness. It cannot be construed as a simple matter of procedural malpractice; rather, the controversy raised complex questions about democratic procedures in a situation where losses would be sustained by a broadly identifiable minority. This is not to deny that the method of spreading the dispute was costless. Throughout the dispute, picketing tactics and the lack of a ballot proved easy ammunition for opponents of the NUM and abundant fig leaves for those who wished to cross the picket lines. Yet any conceivable strategy entailed costs.

The division in Lancashire has to be understood in the context of the Area's politics. Yet the Area never became another Nottingham-shire. Eventually the bulk of the membership stopped work as several Branch officials backed the strike and local activists and fliers attempted to blockade the pits. The spread of the Lancashire strike was facilitated by a widely-felt loyalty to the Union. The coalfield's history of contraction and the depressed state of the local economy meant that optimism about the incidence and consequence of closures was difficult. The strike had an early legitimacy in Lancashire with two pits stopped from an early date and significant numbers on strike at some other pits. Arguably this local support limited the choice of police tactics. The treatment of locals may differ from that meted out to so-called invaders. Perhaps for the police and the Board, Nottinghamshire was the priority. Whilst Lancashire marked up clear successes for massed picketing, these have to be understood in the local context. There was no simple panacea for spreading the strike which was exportable to largely working coalfields.

The spreading of the Lancashire strike depended on, and in turn strengthened, the influence of a vigorous rank-and-file movement. Here was a driving force behind the strike – innovative, iconoclastic, dismissive of compromise, thoroughly suspicious of Area and Branch Officials. For the time of the strike this alternative to the Area's routines flowered, a robust statement of working-class creativity and a continuing challenge to staid trade union routines. Pre-strike officials had to accommodate to this activist radicalism.

For the committed strikers there could be no compromise short of a thorough but ill-defined victory. In Lancashire, that meant enduring until the issue was settled elsewhere. But from early on the evidence suggested that a favourable settlement was unlikely. The

NUM was split, other unions were often unwilling to take sympathetic action, policing was heavy and often effective, the Board and the Government showed a clear resolve to see the matter through. From the settling of the NACODS grievance, the priority was not to win, but the preserve and extricate the NUM. It is too easy to explain the failure to settle through a tactical retreat on the inflexibility of the National Officials. There is ambiguity over whether the Government would have permitted such an outcome or whether they had decided that the overt defeat of the NUM was desirable. Moreover, opposition to a formal settlement that would still permit closures was not the monopoly of the NUM Left. It was shared by pro-strike right-wing officials. The ground rules for negotiation had changed: the issue was intractable. Once the dispute had taken root, there was nowhere else to go.

No end to the strike could be easy. The return to work without any agreement perhaps saved the Union from further disintegration, but every issue remained unresolved. They have been settled conclusively to the employer's advantage. In the absence of a negotiated agreement, closures, wage levels, new conciliation procedures and the rationalisation of production have been imposed. With the continuing existence of the UDM, no collective action holds much promise of effectiveness. The continuing managerial aggression and the threatened mass closures resulting from the privatisation of the electricity supply industry leave the NUM with fundamental and unresolved problems.

An unsentimental demythologised reading of the history shows that the NUM has never been the solid militant politically radical union of legend. The Union has always embraced conflicts of economic interest and diverse political views. Its industrial strength has often been limited and its ability to protect its members has fluctuated with market shifts and political changes. The traditional stereotype never existed, so could never collapse as a consequence of 1984. It is not, and never has been, sufficient as a model for a miners' union.

Rejection of this influential stereotype should be accompanied by an insistence that the miners' recent experiences are central to the British crisis. It is one thing to be thoroughly realistic about the weaknesses of the NUM but quite another to launder the past in the service of such realism. The travails of the miners reveal much about the harsh inhumanities of Thatcher's Britain. This should be a necessary recognition in any history and in any project for the future.

In November 1984, with several Lancashire miners abandoning the strike, a Branch official contemplated the prospects. In no sense a radical, but a firm supporter of the strike, he talked of the problems at his pit and the pressures on the Union. 'This is what capitalism does to people.'

He was right. He still is.

Notes

1 British Coal – Western Area Colliery Review, 18 January 1988.

2 *Ibid.*

3 NWA Conference, 21 March 1987.

4 NWA Annual Conference, 7/8 May 1987.

5 NWA Executive, 17 April 1986. The original field was five candidates. After eliminations and redistribution of preferences Roy Jackson defeated Geoff Clarke of the Ashton and Haydock Craftsmen by 1,204 votes to 1,113. 527 votes were non-transferable. See also NWA pamphlet with candidates' Election Addresses.

6 NWA Annual Conference, 7 May 1987.

7 NWA Conference, 17 January 1987.

8 See, for example, *South Wales Miner*, October 1987; the front page, 'Care Needed on the Code' by Des Dutfield and Scargill's 'New Realism, The Politics of Fear' – the S. O. Davies Memorial Lecture given at Merthyr, 30 October 1987. In particular this attacked an article by Kim Howells, the South Wales NUM Research Officer, in the October *South Wales Miner*.

9 See, for example, NWA Conference, 20 December 1986 – a proposition was passed expressing concern at the proposed reorganisation and expressing Lancashire's desire to remain separate. For the state of play in the summer of 1987 see NUM Annual Report 1987, pp. 85–7.

10 The pro-Scargill Branches were Golborne, Parkside, Plank Lane and Sutton Manor; the pro-Walsh ones Billinge, Clifton and Pendlebury Craftsmen, Parsonage, Pendlebury, St Helens Craftsmen and Winders. The St Helens Craftsmen was the only Branch that breached the pro-strike/anti-strike division. The Ashton and Haydock Craftsmen favoured no nomination and abstained.

11 *Miner*, October 1987, for a breakdown of the vote by Area.

12 NWA Circular 186/87, Delegate's Report of NEC Meeting, 6 September 1987.

13 NWA Circular 190/87, report by Delegate of meetings between NEC, British Coal and ACAS, 14/15 September 1987, with accompanying documentation.

14 NWA Circular 191/87, report by Delegate of NEC Meeting of 17 September 1987, with texts of South Wales and Yorkshire proposals.

15 NWA Conference, 19 September 1987.

16   NWA Circular 206/87, report by Delegate of NEC Meeting of 8 October 1987.

17   British Coal – Western Area Minutes of Colliery Review Meeting Lancashire and North Wales Collieries, 12 October 1987.

18   British Coal – Western Area Colliery Review, 18 January 1988.

19   NWA Circulars 229/87 and 256/87, Delegate's report of NEC Meetings of 12 November and 10 December 1987.

20   *Times*, 3 February 1988.

Bibliography

A note on unpublished sources

These are the main basis for the manuscript. One indispensable source is provided by the records of the National Union of Mineworkers (North Western Area) supplemented by those of the National Union. In both cases the records incorporate two principal elements – the Minutes of the Area or National Executive and of Area or National Conferences. The former typically offer little more than a record of decisions but the Conference minutes attempt to provide a verbatim record. All contributions at Lancashire Conferences are taped and then written up by Area office staff. There is some slippage between the content of the tapes and the subsequent record but the discrepancies appear to be trivial.

A second vital contribution has been provided by my discussions with Union members during and after the dispute. Often these took place in relatively public places – Union cabins, canteens, clubs and pubs. Sometimes discussions involved several people. Notes were rarely taken at the time but instead were written up immediately afterwards. Significant issues were checked out in later discussions and by circulation of a draft manuscript. Since in many cases it would be impossible to connect claims to individuals I have adopted the practice of indicating the source by Branch only.

More formal interviews were carried out with two Area and one Branch Official – Sid Vincent, Bernard Donaghy and Jim Lord. Where information resulting from these discussions is used, specific citation is provided. I have also incorporated some material that emerged in discussion with Les Kelly, Branch Secretary, Point of Ayr NUM in North Wales.

I am also indebted to Steve Vickers for lending me his diary of the strike and the South Wales Miners' Library for a copy of a taped interview with Sid Vincent.

Newspapers

Bolton Evening News
Financial Times
Leigh, Tyldesley and Atherton Journal

Manchester Evening News
The Miner
Morning Star
Newton and Golborne News
Observer
St Helens Reporter
South Wales Miner
Sunday Telegraph
Wrexham Evening Leader

Books and articles

Martin Adeney and John Lloyd, *The Miners' Strike of 1984–85: Loss Without Limit* (Routledge, London, 1986)

Vic Allen, *The Militancy of British Miners* (The Moor Press, Shipley, 1981)

William Ashworth, *The History of the British Coal Industry Volume 5, 1946–82, The Nationalised Industry* (Clarendon Press, Oxford, 1986)

Huw Beynon (ed.), *Digging Deeper: Issues in the Miners Strike* (Verso, London, 1985)

Alex Callinicos and Mike Simons, *The Great Strike – The Miners Strike of 1984–5 and Its Lessons* (Socialist Worker, London, 1985)

Adrian Campbell and Malcolm Warner, 'Changes in the Balance of Power in the British Mineworkers Union: An Analysis of National Top-Office Elections 1974–84', *British Journal of Industrial Relations*, 1985, pp. 1–24.

Beatrix Campbell, *Wigan Pier Revisited: Poverty and Politics in the 80s* (Virago, London, 1984)

R. Challinor, *The Lancashire and Cheshire Miners* (Frank Graham, London, 1972)

Michael Crick, *Scargill and the Miners* (Penguin, Harmondsworth, 1985)

Norma Dolby, *Norma Dolby's Diary: An Account of the Great Miners' Strike*, (London, Verso, 1987)

Bob Fine and Robert Millar (eds.) *Policing the Miners' Strike* (Lawrence and Wishart, London, 1985)

Hywel Francis and David Smith, *The Fed: A History of the South Wales Miners in the Twentieth Century* (Lawrence and Wishart, London, 1980)

Geoffrey Goodman, *The Miners' Strike* (Pluto, London, 1985)

Joe Gormley, *Battered Cherub* (Hamish Hamilton, London, 1982)

Martin Harrison, *Trade Unions and the Labour Party since 1945* (Allen and Unwin, London, 1960)

Mark Hollingsworth, 'Using Miners to Bust the Union', *New Statesman*, 14 December 1984

Arthur Horner, *Incorrigible Rebel* (MacGibbon and Kee, London, 1961)

David Howell, ' "Goodbye To All That?" A Review of Literature on the 1984–85 Miners' Strike', *Work, Employment and Society*, September 1987, pp. 388–404

Richard Hyman, 'Reflections on the Mining Strike' in *The Socialist Register* 1985–86 (Merlin, London, 1986, pp. 336–54)

Ian MacGregor, *The Enemies Within* (Collins, London, 1986)

Lewis Minkin, *The Labour Party Conference* (Allen Lane, London, 1978)

Roy Ottey, *The Strike: An Insider's Story* (Sidgwick and Jackson, London, 1985)

R. Page Arnot, *The Miners: Years of Struggle* (Allen and Unwin, London, 1953)

R. Page Arnot, *The Miners in Crisis and War* (Allen and Unwin, London, 1961)

Tony Parker, *Red Hill: A Mining Community* (Heinemann, London, 1986)

Will Paynter, *My Generation* (Allen and Unwin, London, 1972)

Lord Robens, *Ten Year Stint* (Cassell, London, 1972)

Raphael Samuel, Barbara Bloomfield and Guy Boanas (eds), *The Enemy Within: Pit Villages and the Miners' Strike of 1984–85* (Routledge, London, 1986)

John Saville, 'An Open Conspiracy – Conservative Politics and the Miners' Strike 1984–86', *The Socialist Register* 1985–86 (Merlin, London, 1986), pp. 295–329.

Arthur Scargill, 'The New Unionism', *New Left Review* (90), 1975

Vicky Seddon (ed.), *The Cutting Edge: Women and the Pit Strike* (Lawrence and Wishart, London, 1986)

Marge Short, 'One Woman's Story' in *Bulletin of North-West Society for the Study of Labour History*, No.11, 1985–86

Andrew Taylor, *The Politics of the Yorkshire Miners* (Croom Helm, London, 1984)

E. P. Thompson, 'A Special Case' in his *Writing By Candlelight* (Merlin, London, 1980), pp. 65–76

William Thompson, 'The New Left in Scotland' in Ian MacDougall (ed.), *Essays in Scottish Labour History* (John Donald, Edinburgh, n.d.) pp. 207–24.

The People of Thurcroft, *Thurcroft: A Village and the Miners Strike, An Oral History* (Spokesman, Nottingham, 1986)

Peter Wilsher et al., *Strike – Thatcher, Scargill and the Miners* (Coronet, London, 1985)

Jonathan Winterton and Ruth Winterton, *Coal, crisis and conflict: the 1984–85 miners' strike in Yorkshire* (University Press, Manchester, 1989)

Index